Governance, Society, and Geopolitics in Times of Transformation

George M. Korres
https://orcid.org/0000-0002-4073-977X
University of Aegean, Greece

Maria Michailidis
https://orcid.org/0000-0003-1315-225X
University of Nicosia, Cyprus

Anastasios K. Sepetis
University of West Attica, Greece

Spyros Anagnostou
University of the Aegean, Greece

IGI Global
Scientific Publishing
Publishing Tomorrow's Research Today

Vice President of Editorial Melissa Wagner
Director of Acquisitions Mikaela Felty
Director of Book Development Jocelynn Hessler
Production Manager Mike Brehm
Cover Design Jose Rosado

Published in the United States of America by
IGI Global Scientific Publishing
701 East Chocolate Avenue
Hershey, PA, 17033, USA
Tel: 717-533-8845 | Fax: 717-533-7115
Website: https://www.igi-global.com E-mail: cust@igi-global.com

Library of Congress Cataloging-in-Publication Data

CIP Data Pending
ISBN13: 9798337387901
Isbn13Softcover: 9798337387918
EISBN13: 9798337387925
British Cataloguing in Publication Data
A Cataloguing in Publication record for this book is available from the British Library.

Table of Contents

Detailed Table of Contents

This paper investigates the decisive role that social capital can play in positively regulating the educational environment and influencing some of the internal dynamics. To this end, the dimensions of trust, reciprocity and altruism, which come into play in the relational dynamics of the school community, were analysed as proxies for students' social capital. The study of these dimensions took place through the administration of a self-assessment questionnaire to pupils in two schools, located in two different socio-economic and cultural contexts, one urban and one suburban. The objective was to test the questionnaire proposed as a tool to measure certain value dimensions connected to the feeling of living in environments characterised by trust (TR), support and sustainment (HE), protection and safety (SA), autonomy and responsibility (RE), and the frequency of pro-social attitudes characterised by altruism towards others (AL), also taking into account the subjects' different living contexts.

This paper produces an added value for the fiscal policy literature during the COVID-19 pandemic, analyzing the way Western Balkan countries responded adopting fiscal policy expansion or restriction measures, in order to manage the pandemic crisis. This research examines the national governments' fiscal policies established to manage the COVID-19 pandemic within economical context, focusing on the six Western Balkan countries, that are keen on entering European Union, but still remain in negotiations. In order to compare the size of differentiation in fiscal policy of Western Balkans, we compare it to the fiscal policy response of Eurozone countries, during the outbreak of COVID-19. The analysis is being demonstrated in three dimensions of fiscal policy responses to COVID-19 (the size of fiscal spending,

According to Anglo-Saxon geopolitical theory, Turkey is a key part of Rimland. Its geographical position gives it the privilege of becoming a crossroads of Western markets, but also of many unstable, geostrategically and economically important regions, such as the Middle East, Russia and the Caspian Sea region. This paper analyses Turkey's energy needs and argues that in order to meet its growing energy demand, Turkey is trying to transform its energy mix by reaching out to global and regional actors in order to become a focal point for energy trade in the region and a natural gas hub, taking advantage of its geographical position and access to energy-rich neighbors, without having hydrocarbon resources of its own. This energy dependence has an impact on its internal and foreign policy, as reforms will have to be designed and implemented to meet both its internal challenges and its geopolitical ambitions.

Social enterprises are established upon the deliberative will of groups of citizens and through the use of entrepreneurial models they provide general interest services aiming at addressing social needs. Like any other civil society organization and in order to succeed in their social missions, they engage in establishing networks of people and organizations and in this respect, they generate social capital and collective action, what Field calls the "nursery of a democratic society" (Field, 2003:30). By engaging in social innovation, they develop new working models and ethics and work opportunity for under-represented groups of people with a disadvantaged background (unemployed, Neets, disabled, immigrants, ex-convicts etc). This chapter is focusing on the Euro-Mediterranean countries of Italy and Spain, where the deliberative manifestations of civil society through social entrepreneurship endeavors has developed a stronghold for people belonging in disadvantaged groups, by deliberating and democratizing opportunity, promoting inclusive development and active citizenship

Preface

INTRODUCTION

In recent decades, societies around the world have faced intersecting pressures—from economic crises and public health emergencies to geopolitical tensions and environmental challenges. These overlapping transformations have reshaped institutions, disrupted traditional structures, and demanded new approaches to governance and social resilience. Understanding these shifts requires interdisciplinary perspectives that transcend geographic, political, and disciplinary boundaries.

This volume emerges from a recognition that contemporary transformations cannot be studied in isolation. Social cohesion is directly linked to economic stability; geopolitical dynamics are intertwined with technological, demographic, and ecological change; and governance systems must evolve to address emerging needs while preserving democratic values. By examining these dimensions together, this book seeks to illuminate the underlying forces that are shaping societies today and to provide analytical tools that can guide more sustainable and equitable futures.

The chapters assembled here bring together diverse methodological frameworks—from qualitative political and historical analysis, to empirical social research, to comparative policy assessment. Together, they offer a panoramic view of how governance, society, and geopolitics are evolving during this period of global transition. The goal is not only to document these changes, but also to highlight potential pathways for reform, cooperation, and resilience.

CHAPTER OVERVIEW

Chapter 1 investigates territorial variations in students' social capital within urban and suburban school environments. By analyzing dimensions such as trust, safety, altruism, and responsibility, the chapter highlights how relational dynamics shape educational experiences and community well-being.

Chapter 2 examines fiscal policy responses to the COVID-19 pandemic, comparing Western Balkan countries to Eurozone member states. The analysis provides insight into spending magnitudes, policy instruments, and national strategies during an unprecedented economic challenge.

Chapter 3 explores the impact of two major crises—the Eurozone financial crisis and the COVID-19 pandemic—on labor markets, workers' rights, precarity, and welfare state retrenchment. It offers a critical assessment of how austerity and emergency measures have reshaped work and social protections.

Chapter 4 analyzes socio-political leadership during emergencies by revisiting interwar Greece and the institutional contributions of Alexander Papanastasiou. It reflects on how historical lessons may inform contemporary governance challenges, particularly in times of crisis.

Chapter 5 discusses Greece's evolving maritime strategy in the Eastern Mediterranean, emphasizing geopolitical shifts, economic interests, and naval capabilities. It underscores the role of strategic partnerships and the blue economy in shaping national policy.

Chapter 6 assesses Turkey's pursuit of geopolitical autonomy across historical phases, examining its regional ambitions, security priorities, changing alliances, and independent defense development. It contextualizes Turkey's current posture within broader global power transitions.

Chapter 7 focuses on Turkey's energy needs and the geopolitical implications of its pursuit of diversified energy partnerships. By analyzing Turkey's strategy to become an energy hub, the chapter connects domestic policy with regional and international dynamics.

Chapter 8 highlights the transformative potential of social entrepreneurship in Italy and Spain, particularly for disadvantaged groups. It underscores how civil society initiatives cultivate social capital, inclusive development, and democratic participation.

Chapter 9 examines the role of coaching in supporting individuals with special needs, particularly regarding labor market inclusion. The chapter evaluates coaching as a tool for empowerment, skill development, and sustainable professional integration.

Chapter 10 analyzes sustainable food consumption in Greece, assessing consumer behaviors, ethical concerns, and socio-demographic influences. The study contributes to broader debates on sustainability, climate awareness, and responsible consumption.

Chapter 11 investigates Turkey's foreign policy evolution from the "Strategic Depth" to the "Blue Homeland" doctrine. It evaluates how maritime strategy, regional disputes, and energy considerations have shaped Turkey's increasingly assertive geopolitical posture.

CONCLUSION

The chapters in this volume collectively underscore the complexity of governance and societal transformation in a rapidly changing world. Whether examining fiscal policy, labor markets, social innovation, or maritime strategy, each contribution reveals how deeply interconnected domestic and global processes have become. No single institution, discipline, or nation can address contemporary challenges alone; rather, multidisciplinary collaboration and cross-regional perspectives are essential.

A recurring theme across the research presented here is the need for adaptive, forward-looking governance that responds not only to immediate crises but also to long-term structural change. From education and social inclusion to geopolitical strategy and energy security, the findings point toward the value of resilience-building, institutional innovation, and participatory approaches. These lessons are particularly relevant at a time when political uncertainty, environmental pressures, and technological disruptions continue to redefine the limits of traditional policymaking.

Ultimately, this book aims to contribute to a growing body of knowledge that supports more informed decision-making and fosters dialogue among scholars, practitioners, and policymakers. By situating local case studies within broader global transformations, we hope to provide analytical depth and comparative insights that will inspire further research. The transformations of our time demand reflection, cooperation, and imagination—and it is our hope that this volume will serve as a meaningful resource for those engaged in shaping the governance and geopolitics of the future.

Chapter 1
Exploring Social Capital in Urban and Suburban School Contexts:
A Look at Territorial Differences

Stefania Badiglio
National Research Council, Italy

Giuseppe Chiazzese
https://orcid.org/0000-0002-0228-6204
National Research Council, Italy

Luciano Seta
https://orcid.org/0000-0003-3223-0997
National Research Council, Italy

ABSTRACT

This paper investigates the decisive role that social capital can play in positively regulating the educational environment and influencing some of the internal dynamics. To this end, the dimensions of trust, reciprocity and altruism, which come into play in the relational dynamics of the school community, were analysed as proxies for students' social capital.

DOI: 10.4018/979-8-3373-8790-1.ch001

The study of these dimensions took place through the administration of a self-assessment questionnaire to pupils in two schools, located in two different socio-economic and cultural contexts, one urban and one suburban. The objective was to test the questionnaire proposed as a tool to measure certain value dimensions connected to the feeling of living in environments characterised by trust (TR), support and sustainment (HE), protection and safety (SA), autonomy and responsibility (RE), and the frequency of pro-social attitudes characterised by altruism towards others (AL), also taking into account the subjects' different living contexts.

INTRODUCTION

The concept of social capital can be fundamentally divided into three dimensions: the structural one, which refers to social relations and the role it plays within the various networks; the normative one, i.e. the set of rules, norms and obligations external to the subject that influence and determine his or her behaviour; and finally, the cognitive dimension, which includes all the mental processes internal to the subject that determine how he or she perceives and interprets external norms and values (Uphoff, 1999).

The structural dimension of social capital focuses on networks of relationships between actors in a community, which act as channels for the dissemination of information and knowledge (Nahapiet, 1998). These networks are significant resources that facilitate both individual and collective action, reducing uncertainty and establishing lasting relationships.

The normative dimension of social capital focuses on values such as trust, reciprocity and solidarity, which promote cooperation (Nahapiet, 1998). Trust, for example, reduces the uncertainty in social interactions and serves as a coordinating mechanism, both through interpersonal and competence-based trust (Luhmann, 2022; Barber, 1983). Mutual trust, associated with consistency and reciprocity, becomes a key resource for cooperation (Pellagra, 2002).

The cognitive dimension, on the other hand, concerns the sharing of a common vision and the adoption of prosocial values, such as truthfulness and justice, facilitating cooperation (Fukuyama, 2002; Dasgupta, 1999).

The three dimensions are closely interconnected and together contribute to the development of a community, and trust and shared vision emerge from close and frequent social interactions (Tsai & Ghoshal, 1998). The concept of social capital, although complex and multifaceted, represents a crucial resource in economic and social dynamics. However, transforming it into an operational tool requires effective measurement (Putnam, 2000; Fukuyama, 1995).

This study focuses on measuring social capital within educational institutions, examining as proxies trust, reciprocity and altruism, considering that within schools, social capital manifests itself in relational networks that foster a positive educational climate, characterised by mutual trust and cooperation (Coleman, 1988).

Social networks, both between teachers and between students, act as channels for the dissemination of knowledge and resources, while trust and reciprocity create an environment of cooperation and support. Altruism, in this context, is expressed in students' involvement in community service activities, reinforcing a sense of social responsibility (Putnam, 2000). In order to develop social capital in the school context, it is necessary to act on three dimensions: the structural one, related to the quality of interpersonal relationships; the normative one, linked to organisational dynamics; and the cognitive one, which includes the quality of teaching and the development of transversal skills (Bourdieu, 1986).

The theoretical approaches of scholars such as Putnam, Coleman, Bourdieu and Fukuyama have been essential in analysing social capital in schools. Through a questionnaire, it was possible to measure trust, altruism and reciprocity, highlighting cooperative practices and the importance of a school climate conducive to collective well-being (Putnam, 2000; Coleman, 1988).

METHODS

In order to assess the individual level of social capital of students aged between 9 and 12, a self-assessment questionnaire was developed and administered in two schools from different socio-economic and geographical backgrounds: l'Istituto Comprensivo Statale "*Silvio Boccone*", located in the municipality of Palermo (Sicily, Italy) and the Istituto Comprensivo Statale "*Altofonte-Armaforte*" of Altofonte (Sicily, Italy).

In particular, the tool was to reflect the multidimensional character of social capital, i.e. to measure both the endowment, in terms of values and norms to which the individual assigns particular importance, and the mechanisms of distribution and reproduction of social capital itself, in terms of the social networks to which they belong. This means that the survey instrument also had to provide a measure of the importance the individual attaches to these values in the various spheres of social life, such as family, school, friendship networks.

The main objective of this investigation was certainly not a rigorous validation of the instrument, but rather a preliminary verification of the factorial structure and internal consistency of the proposed scale, as well as establishing its discriminating capacity regarding the results obtained in the two different school contexts.

Urban and Suburban Geographical Contexts

The school "*Silvio Boccone*" is an educational institution with a long tradition, located in a central area of the city of Palermo. The district has a fairly atypical housing morphology, with an obsolete building stock, where more recent social housing constructions stand alongside rather run-down historical buildings. Demographic data indicate that the district is the fourth largest in terms of total population (about 6% of the 653715 inhabitants surveyed as of 31/12/2022 reside there). It is the first district by foreign population (with 4487 residents) in the municipality of Palermo. Compared to the total resident population, foreigners make up about 11.5%, an incidence rate that places it third among the city's districts. The main areas of origin were West Africa (1688) and Central South Asia (1222). These data help us to delineate a school characterised by a very varied student population, with pupils from different socio-economic backgrounds and a strong presence of students of non-Italian nationality, mainly belonging to families from non-EU countries.

The Institute, distributed over two buildings not too far apart, has an educational offer that ranges from pre-school to secondary school. For the school year 2022/23, there were 174 pupils enrolled in the primary school, divided into 10 classes, and approximately 450 students in the secondary school, divided into 29 classes. In total, there were 709 students, including those enrolled in kindergarten. For the school year 2022/23, 96 special need students (13.5%) were identified. The Institute had in a. s. 2017/18 an incidence of foreign students in line with the density of the district. Available data indicated a value of 10% for primary, 9% for secondary, and 17% for preschool. The predominant nationalities of origin were Ghana, Bangladesh, and Morocco.

The second school, the "*Altofonte-Armaforte*" institute of Altofonte, is a school that belongs to a social context characterised by a good level of basic social capital, belonging to a rather homogeneous community, and at the same time is not too isolated from the urban context. The municipality of Altofonte is located 12 km from the centre of Palermo, is well connected to the city, and commuting characterises the daily life of its inhabitants. As of 2021, the resident population was approximately 9900. Mostly employed in the tertiary sector in the city, although agricultural activity maintains a certain liveliness. Foreigners make up no more than 1% of the resident population, with a predominance from the EU area (especially Romania).

The school "*Altofonte-Armaforte*" is the only educational institution in the municipality, and its offer ranges from pre-school to secondary school. The total number of pupils enrolled in the 2022/23 school year was 924, of which 210 in kindergarten, 414 in primary school (divided into 26 classes), and 300 in secondary school (divided into 18 classes). The incidence of foreign pupils is between 1 and 2 per cent, with a total number of around 15 enrolled in the three levels.

Overall, the territory presents a reality with both some of the characteristics of a rural centre and those of a suburb, the relationship with the city centre being close and constant.

Participants

A group of 126 students (49.2% male) from the two schools (N=72 Armaforte, N=54 Boccone) engaged in primary school (classes 4 and 5 grade, N=64) and secondary school (classes 6 and 7 grade, N=62) participated in a between-groups comparison. The group of school students belonging to the urban (Boccone school) and suburban (Armaforte school) context (independent variable) were submitted to a questionnaire to measure the individual endowment of social capital (dependent variable). The age of the participants ranged from 9 to 12 years (M=10.7, SD=0.9).

Materials

The questionnaire used to measure social capital (see Annex) consists of 23 items, structured with the aim of investigating five main constructs describing the subject's value dimension: trust (TR), support and assistance (HE), protection and safety (SA), autonomy and responsibility (RE), and altruism (AL). To consider the subject's different spheres of life, each value dimension was assessed by considering social distance, declined in the sense of emotional-psychological closeness, involving four main spheres of life: Family (FA), School (SC), Friends (FR), Others (OT). To facilitate the quantification of respondents' perceptions, a five-level likert scale was chosen, known for its effectiveness in providing systematic quantitative data and for its ability to measure attitudes and perceptions.

The administration of the questionnaire was conducted in compliance with ethical regulations, ensuring the anonymity of participants and collecting informed consent from parents or legal guardians. The data collection, approved by the Palermo 1 Ethics Committee of the 'Paolo Giaccone' University Hospital, involved students in educational contexts with the aim of measuring variables such as trust, reciprocity and altruism, key elements of social capital in educational institutions.

The questionnaire is divided into three parts: the first one collects socio-demographic information (e.g. age, gender, family status), the second one is inspired by the structure of the *International Survey of Children's Well-Being* (ISCWeB) and investigates satisfaction and well-being in key life contexts (family, friends, school, neighbourhood), through 17 statements assessed on a likert scale. The third part is devoted to assessing the frequency of prosocial and altruistic behaviours. Key constructs of the questionnaire include:

- **Trust (TR)**: the propensity to believe that others will act fairly and honestly (e.g. 'I trust my family members/schoolmates/neighbours/ school staff/friends').
- **Support and Sustainment (HE)**: the perceived support from one's social contexts (e.g. 'If I have a problem, a friend/family will help me').
- **Safety (SA)**: the perceived sense of safety in various contexts (e.g. 'I feel safe at home/school').
- **Responsibility (RE)**: the perceived sense of responsibility and autonomy (e.g. 'My teachers listen to me and take what I say into account').
- **Altruism (AL)**: the frequency of prosocial actions (e.g. 'I try to help others / I share things I like with friends').

The chosen methodological approach aimed to obtain an accurate assessment of social capital within educational institutions, placing particular emphasis on how relational dynamics contribute to the well-being of students.

RESULTS

The analysis of the results grouped the 23 items of the questionnaire according to two categories: the **value** dimension and the **social distance**. The items were associated with each value and social dimension as shown in Tables 1 and 2.

The Value Dimension and Social Distance

The items were grouped according to the relevant value dimension (Table 4.1) and social distance (Table 4.2).

Table 1. **Grouping of items according to values**

Value	Item
Trust (TR)	IT1 - IT6 - IT13 - IT15
Help (HE)	IT2 - IT12 - IT14
Safety (SA)	IT3 - IT4 - IT7 - IT8 - IT16
Responsability (RE)	IT5 - IT10
Altruism (AL)	IT18 - IT19 - IT20 - IT21 - IT23

Table 2. **Grouping of Items by Social Distance**

Social Distance	Item
Family (FA)	IT1 - IT4 - IT7 - IT8 - IT10 - IT14
School (SC)	IT3 - IT5 - IT6 - IT13 - IT16 - IT17
Friend (FR)	IT2 - IT12 - IT15 - IT19
Other (OT)	IT18 - IT20 - IT21 - IT23

Three items were excluded from the analysis:

- **IT9** (*'I trust my neighbours'*) for several missing answers (NA=7).
- L'**IT24** (*'I am kind to others'*) because it is not very discriminating (85% of respondents scored between 3 and 4).
- L'**IT11** (*'I worry about how much money my family has'*) failed the KMO test with a value below the minimum threshold of 0.50.

The remaining items passed Bartlett's sphericity test ($\chi^2(19) = 80.71$, $p < .001$). The exploratory factor analysis, conducted with an oblique rotation (promax), revealed a latent structure with 5 factors, as suggested by the *parallel analysis*.

Table 3. Descriptive statistics and coefficients of factor analysis

	Statistics				Factors					
Item	Mean	SD	Skew	Kurtosis	School	Family	Help	Friends	Trust	h^2
IT1	3.49	0.85	-1.57	1.41	0.19	**0.48**				0.36
IT2	2.81	0.98	-0.46	-0.36	-0.28	0.15		**0.70**	0.22	0.49
IT3	2.60	0.91	-0.30	-0.15	**0.57**		-0.11			0.42
IT4	2.48	1.22	-0.48	-0.74	0.28	**0.33**		-0.11		0.23
IT5	2.29	1.15	-0.19	-0.73	**0.54**			-0.12	0.12	0.31
IT6	2.48	1.00	-0.12	-0.72	0.45				**0.48**	0.44
IT7	3.00	1.14	-1.03	0.26	0.21	**0.47**		0.11		0.41
IT8	3.62	0.77	-2.28	5.28	-0.11	**0.72**	0.37	-0.14		0.63
IT10	2.40	1.27	-0.44	-0.76	0.29	0.15	**0.36**		-0.12	0.29
IT12	2.54	0.96	-0.17	-0.28	0.19			**0.55**	0.15	0.51
IT13	2.65	1.09	-0.55	-0.41	**0.60**		0.11			0.40
IT14	3.55	0.84	-2.13	4.60		**0.70**		0.35	-0.23	0.73
IT15	3.00	0.91	-0.44	-0.84				0.24	**0.65**	0.49
IT16	2.65	1.04	-0.30	-0.58	**0.61**			0.16		0.49
IT17	2-97	0.99	-0.76	0.13	**0.47**	0.11	-0.20	0.35	-0.28	0.63
IT18	2.94	0.98	-0.94	0.77		-0.11		**0.55**		0.36
IT19	2.68	1.12	-0.65	-0.24			0.15	**0.60**		0.50
IT20	2-97	1.05	-0.95	0.33	0.23	-0.28	**0.60**	0.26		0.58
IT21	3.18	0.98	-1.26	1.22			0.34	**0.52**		0.49
IT23	3.28	0.85	-1.32	2.08	-0.18	0.21	**0.52**	0.17		0.38

From the data analysis, the factors that emerged do not reflect the value structure initially hypothesised. Instead, the items tend to cluster according to social distance, with factors representing School (**SC**), Family (**FA**) and Friends (**FR**) respectively. Two other factors are cross-cutting with respect to social distance and can be classified as related to prosocial behaviour of 'help' and 'trust'.

In conclusion, the factorial analysis seems to support the hypothesis that in the investigated subjects' value assessment, social distance has a prevailing importance over value per se. For the students of the sample, the answers aggregate more in relation to their spheres of life than in relation to the type of value involved. This result, which certainly deserves to be further investigated, may have many causes, some of which are related to the context and others to the subjects' specific stage of psychological development. A more in-depth analysis of the results may help us to understand whether and how these results vary with context and age.

The Armaforte school of Altofonte

At the '*E. Armaforte*' school in Altofonte, the survey involved six classes: two fourth grade (4C and 4D, N=13) and two fifth grade (5C and 5D, N=31) primary school classes, and two secondary school classes (1B and 2B, N=28). A total of 72 subjects participated, 62.2% of whom were male. The analysis of the overall scores of the questionnaire administered did not reveal any significant differences between the sexes, as confirmed by the non-parametric *Kolmogorov-Smirnov* test ($D = 0.19$, $p = 0.39$), showing an absence of significant differences in male and female responses.

Figure 1. Gender comparison in terms of total score

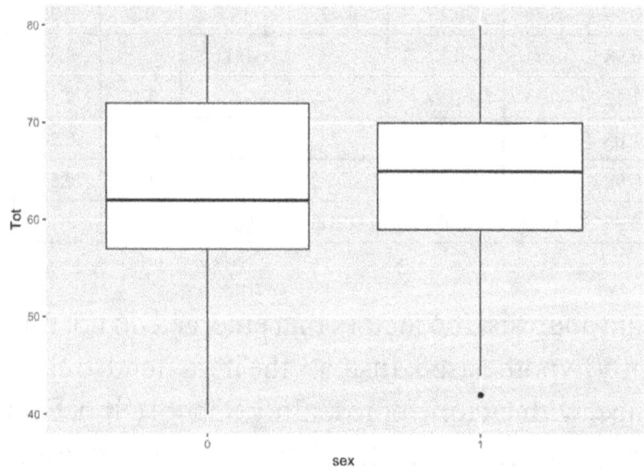

Even when analysing the different value categories, the differences between the mean scores of males and females were non-significant, except for the items relating to responsibility and autonomy (RE). In this category, in fact, a significant difference between the sexes emerged, with a higher mean score for females ($M = 7.21$) than for males ($M = 5.85$), as evidenced by the Wilcoxon test ($W = 400.5$, $p < .01$). Grouping the items according to social distance, no significant differences emerged in the mean scores between males and females, apart from the items related to the greatest social distance (OT). In this dimension, the mean scores of females (M=16.5) were significantly higher than those of males (M=14.5), with a significant difference (W =426, $p < .01$).

Next, the differences in the scores between the different classes of the Armaforte school were examined. In this case, the analysis of variance (*ANOVA*) revealed some significant differences in the overall scores between classes 4D and 5C of the primary school compared to class 1B of the secondary school, taken as a reference (Table 4.4). In particular, classrooms 4D ($\beta = 13.52$, $SE = 3.846$, $t = 3.515$, $p = .001$) and 5C ($\beta = 7.978$, $SE = 2.821$, $t = 2.828$, $p = .006$) reported significantly higher scores than classroom 1B, while no significant differences were found for the other classrooms.

Table 4. Anova of average scores between classrooms (reference class IB)

	Estimate	SE	t value	Pr(>|t|)
(Intercept)	59.647	1.964	30.366	0.000
Class 2B	-3.647	3.134	-1.164	0.249
Class 4C	3.924	3.637	1.079	0.285
Class 4D	13.520	3.846	3.515	0.001
Class 5C	7.978	2.821	2.828	0.006
Class 5D	3.620	2.869	1.262	0.212

Contrast analysis (Table 4.5) showed that the scores of the primary school classrooms were significantly higher than those of the secondary school classrooms (Contrast C1). Furthermore, the fourth classrooms (Contrast C2) and the fifth classrooms (Contrast C3) scored significantly higher than the secondary classrooms. However, there were no significant differences between the fourth and fifth classrooms between them (Contrast C4).

Table 5. Contrasts between primary and secondary classrooms

Contrast	Diff est.	SE	df	t ratio	p value
C1: (prim. vs sec.)	9.084	2.062	66	4.404	0.000
C2: (4 vs sec.)	10.546	2.744	66	3.843	0.000
C3: (5 vs sec.)	7.622	2.139	66	3.564	0.001
C4: (4 vs 5)	2.923	2.682	66	1.090	0.280

When analysing the differences between classrooms in relation to the scores of the *items* grouped according to values, similar results are obtained, where the difference between the four primary school classrooms and the two secondary school classrooms appears significant only when considering the items concerning safety (SA) (*Estimated difference* = 3.11, $t(63)=4.87$, $p < .01$) and trust (TR) (*Estimated difference* = 2.61, $df(64)=5.10$, $p<0.01$).

When the items are grouped according to social distance, the differences remain significant in relation to the items concerning family (FA) (*Estimated difference* = 2.12, $t(65) = 2.69$, $p = .01$) and school (SC) (*Estimated difference* = 4.66, $t(61) = 5.80$, $p<.01$), i.e. the two dimensions least socially distant from the subject.

These results seem to say that, in the case of the Armaforte school, an age-related maturation process can be recorded: where younger subjects, in classes 4 and 5, appear to give more weight to the value dimension, especially in relation to more socially proximal spheres of life, such as family (FA) and school (SC). With the transition to the higher school level, perhaps due to a broadening of the child's emotional world, there is a decline in the overall value dimension, especially with respect to values such as security (SA) and trust (TR), in which emotional-psychological proximity plays an important role.

The Boccone School of Palermo

For the '*S. Boccone*' school in Palermo, 4 classrooms participated in the questionnaire (4A and 5A of the primary, N=20, 1F and 1E of the secondary, N=34).

The analysis of the differences in the scores between the two sexes did not give any significant differences ($D = 0.1931$, $p = 0.54$) (Figure 4.2).

Figure 2. Gender comparison in terms of total score

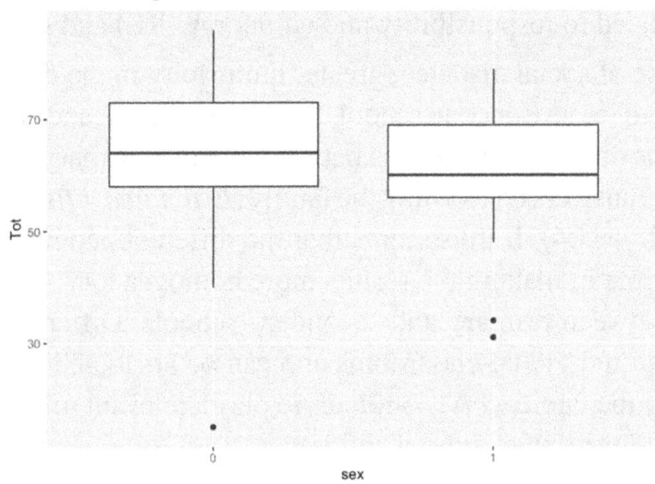

Even when aggregating the items by value categories, no significant differences emerge.

In the case of aggregation by social distance, although males' scores are generally slightly higher than those of females, no difference emerges as significant.

The analysis of the differences in the scores between the classrooms shows a slightly different pattern from that revealed by the data collected in the Armaforte school. Some classrooms are characterised by higher average scores, but the difference between primary and secondary school classrooms disappears (*Estimated difference* = 1.123, $t(50) = 0.306$, $p = 0.76$). Two classrooms (4A and 1F) emerge from the data as characterised by higher scores (Table 4.6).

Table 6. Difference between primary and secondary school classrooms

Class	Mean	SE	df	min	max
1E	57.60	3.31	50	50.95	64.25
1F	65.74	2.94	50	59.83	71.64
4A	68.75	4.53	50	59.65	77.85
5A	56.83	3.70	50	49.40	64.27

If we look at the areas corresponding to the different values, we find that classroom 4A has on average higher scores, especially when considering the items related to responsibility and autonomy (RE) and support (HE).

In the case of social distance, greater uniformity in the distribution of scores is noted in the Boccone school. Below the significance threshold of .05% remains only the differences between the two primary classerooms regarding the answers concerning the family (*Estimated difference* = 3.35, $t(49) = 2.22$, p=.04). It thus seems that the different geographical location plays a role in making the results more homogeneous, flattening the difference between primary and secondary schools. Differences remain at the level of individual classrooms and can be attributed to contingent factors. Only the family (FA) continues to play a relevant role as the value environment for primary school children.

In essence, it seems that the urban environment leads to children's early value involvement even in areas that are more emotionally and psychologically distant from the subject's life.

The social capital of urban students seems to be distributed over wider and more varied social networks, whereas students in suburban schools have a distribution of their social capital over networks characterised by strong ties, where family and school are prevalent, at least up to primary school. Primary school seems to offer a more protective and secure environment than secondary school, and trust at school also appears to be higher. Furthermore, there is also a difference in scores in favour of the primary when family-related items are considered.

In contrast, the Boccone school shows fewer clear-cut results, two classrooms stand out, but the difference observed between primary and secondary classrooms is not reproduced.

DISCUSSION AND CONCLUSION

This paper is a preliminary proposal for the definition of a tool for measuring some dimensions of social capital to be used with students in the 9-12 age group. The instrument was developed with the aim of achieving an assessment both value dimension linked to the individual capital endowment of students, and of the importance that these values assume in the various spheres of the subjects' lives, i.e. the relevance of the extent of the social networks to which the student belongs. Indeed, research on social capital has long highlighted the dual nature of this construct, on the one hand a factor through which values of trust and reliability circulate and are reinforced in society (*social capital bridging*), on the other hand, social capital also plays a cohesive role in relation to *ingruop* members, helping them to achieve shared goals, with reduced benefits, if not costs, for the rest of society (social capital bonding) (Tajfel et al. 1971; Putnam, 2000; Nowak, 2006; Degli Antoni & Grimalda, 2024). Therefore, it is not only important to assess how much importance students give to values such as trust, mutual aid, support, security, responsibility, but also whether the sharing of these values goes beyond the circle of closest affection.

On the other hand, the literature, since Putnam's early research (2000), has also highlighted how social capital is a construct strongly dependent on the social, economic and cultural context. We therefore wished to evaluate our instrument using two schools located in two different territorial contexts: an urban reality, strongly influenced by phenomena of rapid transformation, such as immigration, changes in the social economic structure, demographic and urban variations, and an apparently less turbulent territory, i.e. a school in a suburban reality, which appears to be subject to less rapid and turbulent rhythms of change.

The results seem to point to a different conformation of social capital in the two contexts. While the social capital in urban school students seems to have more bridging characteristics, being similarly oriented towards both intimates and strangers, the social capital of the suburban school appears to be characterised as being more connected to bonds of closeness and intimacy, typical of a bonding social capital.

The present study has several limitations, starting with the non-representativeness of the sample chosen, the need to improve the psychometric characteristics of the instrument proposed, and the need to verify the results using other measuring tools, with a view to improving the convergent validity of the scale. In any case, the results obtained suggest that it is possible to measure social capital even in young subjects and that this measure can provide interesting information on how the surrounding social and demographic reality influences the development and growth in values of young people. These results deserve further and more in-depth research.

REFERENCES

Barber, B. (1983). *The Logic and Limits of Trust*. New Rutgers University Press.

Bourdieu, P. (1986). The forms of capital. In Richardson, J. G. (Ed.), *Handbook of theory and research for the sociology of education* (pp. 241–258). Greenwood Press.

Coleman, J. (1988). Social Capital in the Creation of Human Capital. *American Journal of Sociology, 94*, S95–S120. DOI: 10.1086/228943

Dasgupta, P. (1999). Economic progress and the idea of social capital. In *S. I. in Dasgupta. P., Social Capital. A Multifaceted Perspective*. The World Bank. DOI: 10.1596/0-8213-4562-1

Degli Antoni, G., & Grimalda, G. (2024). Is social capital bridging or bonding? Evidence from a field experiment with association members. *Theory and Decision, 97*(1), 167–190. DOI: 10.1007/s11238-023-09971-7

Fukuyama, F. (1995). *Trust. The Social Virtues and the Creation of Prosperity*. Free Press.

Fukuyama, F. (2002). Social Capital and Development: The Coming Agenda. *SAIS Review (Paul H. Nitze School of Advanced International Studies), XXII*(1), 23–37. DOI: 10.1353/sais.2002.0009

Luhmann, N. (2002). *La Fiducia*. Il Mulino.

Nahapiet, J. G. (1998). "Social Capital, intellectual capital and the creation of value in firms". *Accademy of Management Best Paper Proceedings*, 242.

Nowak, M. A. (2006). Five rules for the evolution of cooperation. *Science, 314*(5805), 1560–1563. DOI: 10.1126/science.1133755 PMID: 17158317

Pellagra, V. (2002). "Rispondenza fiduciaria: principi e implicazioni per la progettazione istituzionale". *in Stato e Mercato, n. 65*, 335-357.

Putnam, R. D. (2000). *Bowling Alone: The Collapse and Revival of American Community*. Touchstone Books.

Tajfel, H., Billig, M. G., Bundy, R. P., & Flament, C. (1971). Social categorization and intergroup behaviour. *European Journal of Social Psychology, 1*(2), 149–178. DOI: 10.1002/ejsp.2420010202

Tsai, W., & Ghoshal, S. (1998). Social Capital and value creation: The role of intrafirm networks. *Academy of Management Journal, 41*(4), 464–476. DOI: 10.2307/257085

Uphoff, N. (1999). Understanding Social Capital: Learning from the Analysis and Experience of Participation. In *P. Dasgupta, & I. Serageldin, (a cura di), Social Capital. A Multifaceted Perspective*. The World Bank.

APPENDIX

CODICE ETA' ____Sesso

Hai fratelli e/0 sorelle Se si quanti? ____

Che lavoro fanno i tuoi genitori: ________________________________

____

Table 7. Mi puoi dire quanto sei d'accordo con le seguenti affermazioni?

		Per niente	**Poco**	**Abbastanza**	**Molto**	**Moltissimo**
1	Mi fido dei miei familiari					
2	Se ho un problema, ho un amico che mi supporterà					
3	Mi sento al sicuro a scuola					
4	Sono soddisfatto del mio aspetto					
5	A scuola ho l'opportunità di prendere decisioni su cose che sono importanti per me					
6	Mi fido dei compagni di scuola					
7	I miei genitori mi ascoltano e prendono in considerazione quello che dico					
8	Mi sento al sicuro a casa					
9	Mi fido dei miei vicini di casa					
10	Mi piace aiutare in casa nelle faccende domestiche					
11	Mi preoccupo di quanti soldi ha la mia famiglia					
12	Se ho un problema a scuola altri bambini mi aiuteranno					
13	Mi fido del personale scolastico					
14	Se ho un problema, le persone della mia famiglia mi aiuteranno					
15	Mi fidodei miei amici					
16	I miei insegnanti mi ascoltano e tengono conto di ciò che dico					
17	Se ho un problema a scuola, i miei insegnanti mi aiuteranno					

Table 8. Mi dici quanto spesso ti capita di compiere una delle seguenti azioni?

		Quasi mai	**Poche volte**	**Qualche volta**	**Tante volte**	**Quasi sempre**
18	Cerco di aiutare gli altri					
19	Divido con gli amici le cose che mi piacciono					
20	Mi preoccupo per gli altri					
21	Cerco di consolare chi è triste					
22	Sono gentile con gli altri					
23	Faccio volentieri compagnia agli amici che si sentono soli					

Chapter 2
Fiscal Policy Response in the COVID-19 Crisis:
A Cross-Country Comparison Between Eurozone and Western Balkans

Maria Karamanoli
https://orcid.org/0000-0001-8319-9358
University of the Aegean, Greece

ABSTRACT

This paper produces an added value for the fiscal policy literature during the COVID-19 pandemic, analyzing the way Western Balkan countries responded adopting fiscal policy expansion or restriction measures, in order to manage the pandemic crisis. This research examines the national governments' fiscal policies established to manage the COVID-19 pandemic within economical context, focusing on the six Western Balkan countries, that are keen on entering European Union, but still remain in negotiations. In order to compare the size of differentiation in fiscal policy of Western Balkans, we compare it to the fiscal policy response of Eurozone countries, during the outbreak of COVID-19. The analysis is being demonstrated in three dimensions of fiscal policy responses to COVID-19 (the size of fiscal spending, the type and targets of fiscal policy

DOI: 10.4018/979-8-3373-8790-1.ch002

responses) across 6 Western Balkan countries and 19 Eurozone countries (before the participation of Croatia). The time period of analysis starts the pandemic outbreak, in December 2019, and ends in January 2022.

INTRODUCTION

Political Economy of Health Systems in Western Balkans

The Treaty on the Function of the European Union has given health policy a prominent role as it provides that "a high level of human health protection shall be ensured in the definition and implementation of all Union policies and activities" (Article 168(7) TFEU). Health care systems and the protection of public health are the responsibility of the State. EU continues to play an important role in improving public health, preventing and managing disease, mitigating threats to human health and harmonizing Member States' health strategies. Similarly, the acceding Member States have the same obligations.

The recent pandemic has highlighted the importance of the EU being able to reinforce itself immediately and respond rapidly and in a coordinated manner to serious health threats, especially in a globalised era where rapid transport facilitates the spread of diseases. Accordingly, the Commission has created a new dedicated European Health Emergency Preparedness and Response Authority (HERA) in response to the health crisis in September 2021, directly after the outbreak of the health crisis.

More generally, the question of "health as a public or private good" has been the subject of big debate. On the market side, it is argued that market forces can achieve a more efficient allocation of health resources, while on the opposite side it is argued that market forces do not provide an efficient and socially equitable allocation of health services. For this reason, three health systems have been developed: public, private and mixed. The public system is financed by the state and aims to provide equal services free of charge to the whole population. The mixed system combines public and private and is considered more flexible in addressing serious health problems, especially in times of economic crisis (Mazaraki H., 2012).

Figure 1. Eurozone Fiscal Spending in the Pandemic (% of GDP) Notes: The figure report estimates of additional discretionary fiscal spending and foregone revenue during 2020 as a share of GDP. These numbers are calculated as the sum of "health", "non-health" and "accelerated spending" above the line categories.

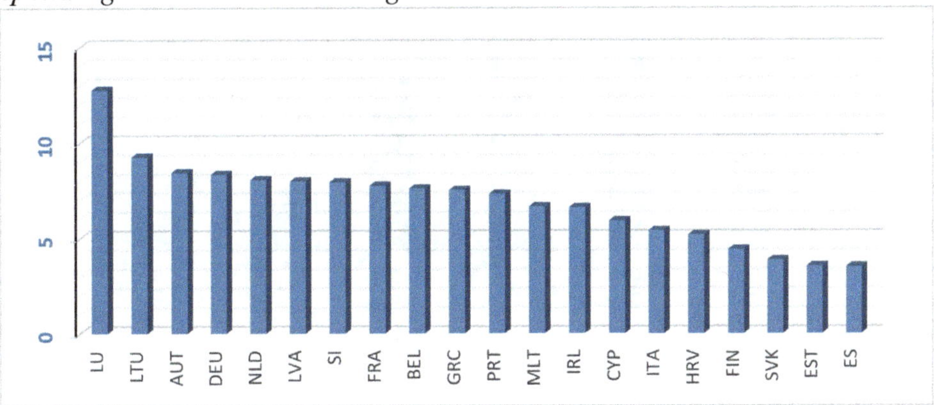

Source: Karamanoli M., (2024)

Figure 2. Western Balkans Fiscal Spending in the Pandemic (% of GDP)
Notes: The figure report estimates of additional discretionary fiscal spending and foregone revenue during 2020 as a share of GDP. These numbers are calculated as the sum of "health", "non-health" and "accelerated spending" above the line categories.

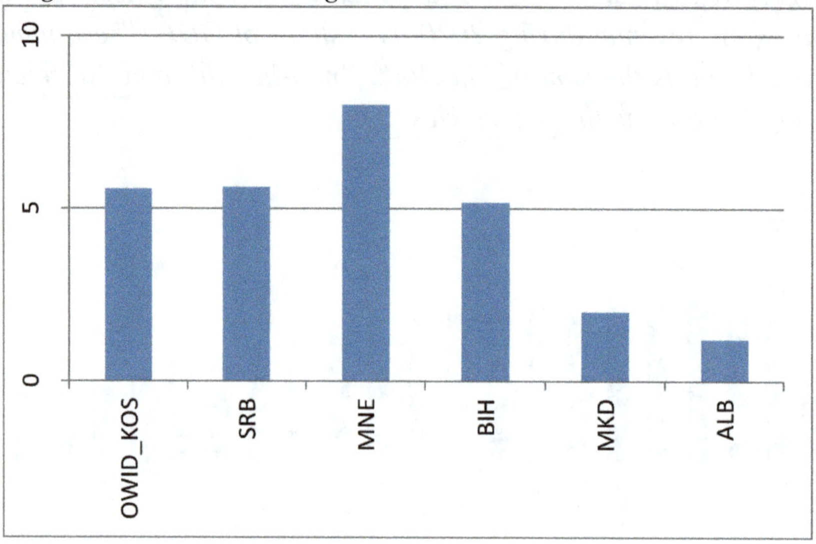

Source: IMF Fiscal Policy Database.

From "public" to "private" health systems

Society is complex and structured according to the intentions and behaviour of man, the citizen. For this reason, the priorities and the results of this behaviour must be consciously considered. It is quite important to understand that even in the modern century health is a political-economic problem. The majority of health experts refuse to see this relationship and deal with the impact that modern capitalism brings to the issue of health, as a result it remains as one of the biggest obstacles to its betterment even today. As Gutenschwager G., (1984) states, the socio-economic approach to health is still necessary today. But in order for experts to turn their attention in this direction, he commented that only a global change in the socio-economic system would allow this problem to be understood and solved in ways commensurate with its extent and causes. In this direction, we come with this paper to transform the problem of the health crisis that has erupted worldwide and threatened millions of human lives into a socio-economic problem by analyzing it quantitatively with the corresponding variables, counting the behavior of state officials, i.e. governments, and contrasting on the one hand the death rates and on the other hand the liquidity of money that the institutions engaged in to ensure the health of both citizens and the economy.

Medical care is supposed to be one of the basic state benefits to citizens, especially to working citizens who contribute with their work and their taxable income to the state coffers. Therefore, they expect to receive from the state, as they themselves provide liquidity to the state, benefits, social welfare, measures to ensure their health. Consequently, when the global health crisis erupted in December 2019 and was followed by an upward infectious trend in both the periphery of the Eurozone and the Balkans, taxpaying citizens expected their elected governments to act promptly and effectively to protect them from the infectious and deadly virus. Governments at this point were confronted with two viruses, one for the health of citizens and the other for the health of public finances.

Considering that public health should be protected and provided by the state, it is concluded that it is a public, free good. Despite the enormous efforts of states across geographical areas to protect their citizens, inequalities based on income criteria and the state failed to protect everyone, if one looks at the upward trend of both the graph showing deaths from Covid-19 and infections, for 2020 and 2021. The fact that health is ultimately not a public free good, beyond the case of the health crisis, is also demonstrated by the phenomena of corruption and black money that are circulating in this sector.

Given that such financial transactions belong to the underground economy and black money trafficking, since doctors working in public institutions are paid by the state, it is worth exploring the extent of corruption recorded at EU and Balkan level. In contrast to the recent health crisis and the fact that governments have had to increase public spending in all sectors, especially in health, it is interesting to explore the shift in public spending and the preference of governments as to where to turn first to manage the new extraordinary form of crisis.

Health Crisis and Fiscal Response

The Covid-19 pandemic has provoked a variety of responses from governments around the world. In this paper we explore the fiscal policies of national governments in managing the pandemic at the economic, political and institutional levels, comparing what happened at the Eurozone and Western Balkan levels. We are able to show similarities and heterogeneities in three dimensions of policy response to the pandemic (size of fiscal expenditure, type and targeting of fiscal policy), looking at the period from the start of the health crisis to 2022. The inspiration for this research was drawn from a similarly published cross-country comparative analysis study by Chen et al. (2021).

The new form of crisis, which most governments had to deal with in the most effective way in order not to hit the well-being of societies hard, the pandemic, created a new burden for many countries around the world, especially in European and Western Balkan countries, which do not have access to European EU funding due to incomplete integration. This crisis has created a new challenge to political, economic and institutional systems. All forms of crises in recent decades have highlighted the importance of national fiscal policies to stimulate employment levels, raise people's living standards and maintain social equality and economic growth (Cottarelli et al., 2014).As is particularly evident, each country, whether European or Western Balkan, must be able to adopt fiscal policies that are appropriate according to the circumstances.

In this paper, the primary objective is to make a timely and timely comparison between the Eurozone and Western Balkans' countries, on their fiscal responses to the health crisis.

The main research questions are the following:

1) What kind of fiscal policies have Eurozone and Western Balkans', countries introduced in response to the health crisis?
2) How have governments' fiscal policy responses varied between two different country – groups of Eurozone and Western Balkans?

In order to answer these specific research questions, we used a comparative approach for the selected countries of the two different geographical and economic zones to analyze their fiscal policies throughout the outbreak of the health crisis in order to capture the different fiscal policies, different approaches and different stages of crisis management. In addition, we wanted to check whether the fiscal response of the selected countries in our sample followed the path of the countries in Chen C. Et al. (2021).

RESEARCH CONTRIBUTION

This paper contributes in two ways to the academic contribution to the literature on fiscal policy during a health pandemic. A main contribution of this research is that it is one of the first studies on comparative analysis that focuses on comparing European territory with that of the Western Balkans regarding the fiscal policies adopted during the pandemic. Existing studies on the response of fiscal policies to the health crisis have mainly focused on prevention and public health protection measures (Ferguson et al., 2020; Flaxman et al., 2020; Chen et al., 2021). However, little research has been conducted using cross-country comparative methods of national fiscal policies during the Covid-19 pandemic, including the article on which we based this study. In addition, this study proposes a three-dimensional theoretical framework based on the first pillar, the size of fiscal policy expenditures, the second on fiscal policy objectives, and the third on the fiscal policy instruments used to implement new fiscal policy measures and such as the current health crisis under consideration.

COMPARATIVE ANALYSIS METHOD

In order to perform a comparative analysis of the fiscal response to the health crisis of the eligible countries in our sample, we used an ad hoc multivariate framework, as in Chen et al., (2021), which is presented in the table below:

Table 1. Scheme of comparative policy analysis of fiscal policy responses to COVID-19, Source: Chen et al., 2021

Dimensions	The policy focus of each dimension	Key indicators/sectors/tools
The first dimension	The size of fiscal policy spending	Total COVID19 related fiscal policy spending (2019 US dollars)
		Total COVID19 related fiscal policy spending as share of GDP (%)
The second dimension	Fiscal policy targets	Health sector
		Business sector
The third dimension	Fiscal policy tools	Direct govt spending[1]
		Direct govt cash transfers[2]
		Debt contract and relief[3]
		Tax benefits, cuts & exemption[4]
		Tax deferral & social security contribution delay[5]
		Govt credit assistance (loans & loan guarantee)[6]
		Govt subsidies to business[7]

The economies of all countries have been affected by the spread of the coronavirus due to globalisation and therefore their interconnectedness. The Fiscal Response in Covid-19 Crisis tool, by the DNT, demonstrates that some Eurozone countries have taken unprecedented fiscal actions by implementing expansionary fiscal policies (such as Germany and France) in response to the pandemic and an ensuing future economic downturn, while other Eurozone countries with lower economic capacity (such as Bulgaria) have implemented conservative fiscal policies with very little opening of their respective public spending in response to the crisis. The general assumption adopted is that countries spend more money in response to a sudden crisis and in this case such a crisis is the health crisis.

Analyzing the contents of the three dimensions we used in our analysis, the first dimension relates to the magnitude of fiscal expenditure associated with the health crisis, while the second and third dimensions describe the adoption of fiscal policy and its corresponding instruments.

Figure 3. Fiscal Spending in Health Sector in Eurozone Source: Karamanoli M., (2024) Note: The figure report estimates of total direct government spending in USD billion during 2020 & 2021. These numbers are calculated as the sum of "health" above the line categories.

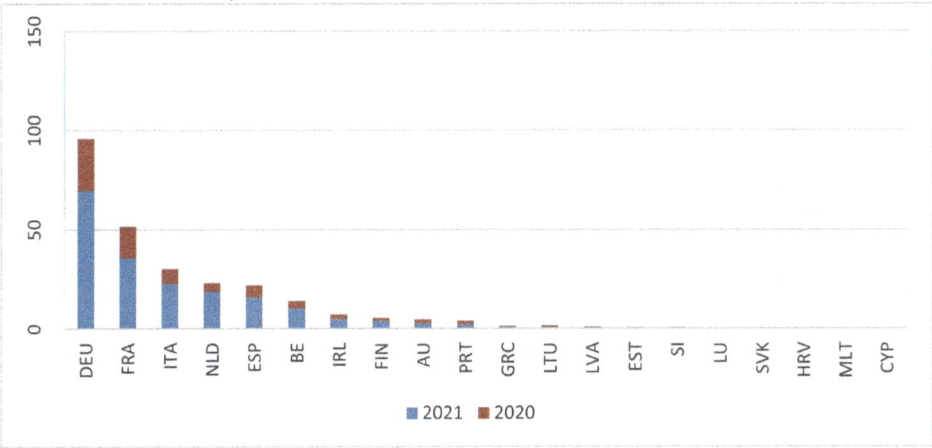

Figure 4. Fiscal Spending in Health Sector in Western Balkans Note: The figure report estimates of total direct government spending in USD billion during 2020 & 2021. These numbers are calculated as the sum of "health" above the line categories.

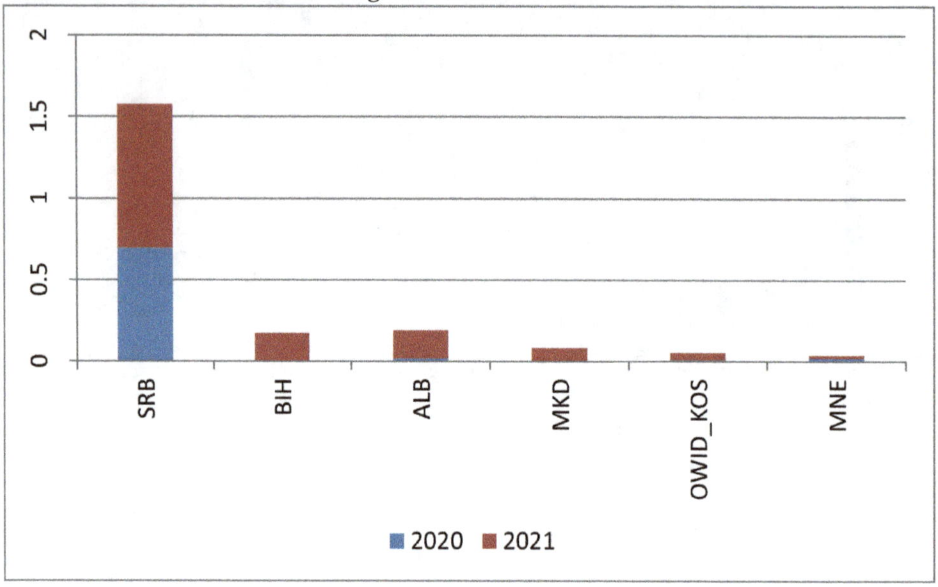

Source: IMF Fiscal Policy Database.

The second dimension shows what the targeting of the fiscal policy adopted is. In general, fiscal policies are designed to help different sectors among countries (OECD, 2020). In the initial stage, Covid-10 is a health crisis but then the problem spreads to all forms of life and affects the whole economic and social world. This is because financial assistance is required for the economically affected private businesses, households, individuals and all parties involved in economic life to survive due to forced incarceration, restriction of economic life and reduction of liquidity because of them.

Figure 5. Fiscal Spending in Non- Health Sector in Eurozone Source: Karamanoli M., (2024) Note: The figure report estimates of total direct government spending in USD billion during 2020 & 2021. These numbers are calculated as the sum of "non-health" above the line categories.

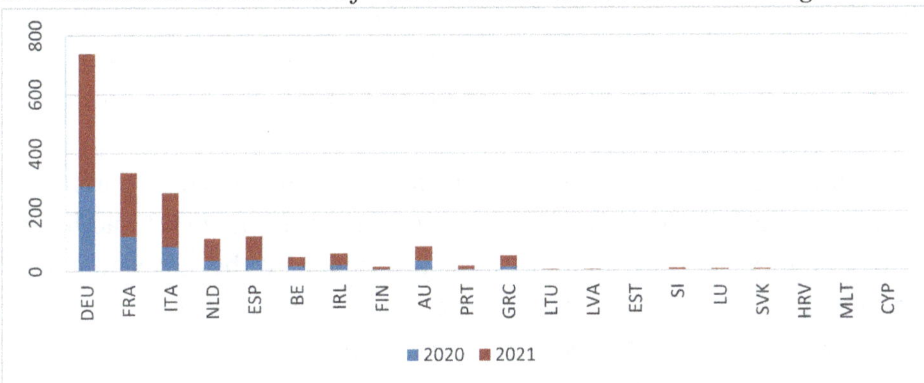

Figure 6. Fiscal Spending in Non Health Sector in Western Balkans Note: The figure report estimates of total direct government spending in USD billion during 2020 & 2021. These numbers are calculated as the sum of "non-health" above the line categories.

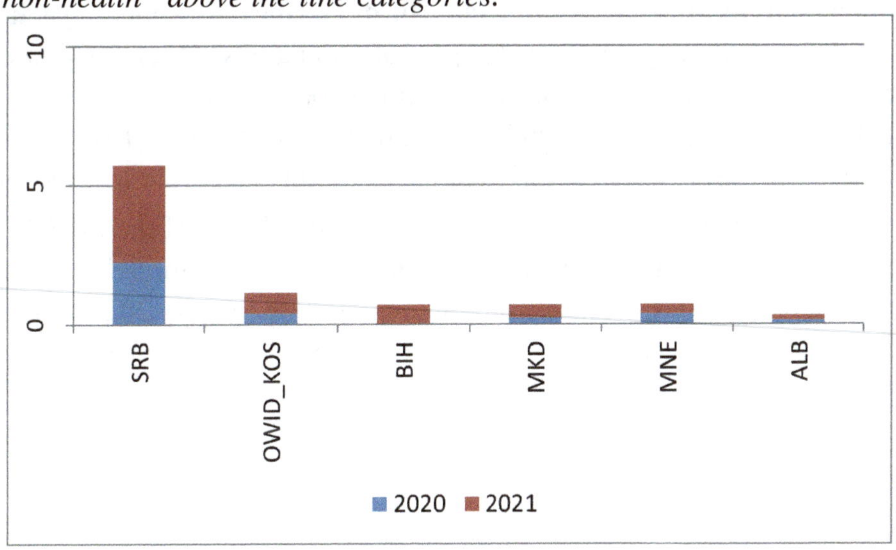

Source: IMF Fiscal Policy Database

The third dimension of the framework on which we based our methodological analysis refers to the fiscal policy instruments adopted by each country. We show that governments have responded to the pandemic using a plethora of workable fiscal policy instruments (Cavallo and Cai, 2020). The role of fiscal policies is mainly focused on implementing tax cuts and expanding public spending. The tools adopted in all three dimensions are proposed by the OECD (2020) and the IMF (2020). Analysing more specifically the fiscal instruments of the third dimension: direct government expenditure refers to direct spending on goods and services purchased by governments (such as medical supplies and equipment). In addition, direct liquidity support refers to cash payments by the government as benefits to poor families as well as unemployment benefits. In the cases of the instruments mentioned, governments do not actually spend. Furthermore, consolidation and debt relief means that the government freezes the financial obligations of taxpayers during the pandemic by freezing loan repayments, enforced tax and social security collection measures, and freezing utility cuts such as water or electricity cuts in case of debt. In turn, tax benefits, exemptions and reductions indicate the offer of tax benefits and cuts to alleviate the financial obligations of already affected individuals or legal entities. The tax benefits also include the extension of the deadlines for filing and paying tax returns and the corresponding delay of social security payments on the part of companies. The provision of credit by the government includes government loans and loan guarantees in order to support businesses, while government subsidies refer to financial assistance to the business sector to enhance liquidity and prolong turnover.

The data analysed were collected from the databases of the IMF, Eurostat, the World Bank, John Hopkins University and Oxford University. The time period considered is from January 2020 to January 2022 and the sample covers the 19 Eurozone countries and 6 Western Balkan countries.

RESEARCH RESULTS

Regarding the data collected by the IMF, some Balkan countries seem to have expanded their public spending considerably, such as Greece, in order to cope with the pandemic and a possible economic downturn, while other Balkan countries with less economic capacity, such as Kosovo, have implemented very limited fiscal policies and correspondingly tight public spending, which contradicts the general assumption we adopted in this paper that countries are expected to spend more money than in the past.

If one compares the number of deaths caused by the pandemic per year, the amount of infections with the amount of corresponding public expenditure, in the Balkans there is a greater discrepancy per country in 2021, even though the health crisis continued to grow.

To be able to correlate the rate of deaths from Covid-19, the rate of pandemic infections and the size of public expenditure, we conducted a correlation test (0.637) at the 1 percent level of significance

Fiscal Policy Objectives and Tools to Tackle the Pandemic

Western Balkans' economies, focused on increasing public spending to safeguard their economies, just as the Eurozone countries did, from the health crisis. It appears that the measures taken by their governments were more intensive in the business sector first. Secondly, measures were taken in the Health Sector and were mainly measures crisis management. This shift of public spending towards the business world is related to the fact that a coming recession had to be avoided at all costs. The same pattern was followed by the Eurozone countries according to our analysis, of course the numbers recorded are smaller, presumably due to the smaller size of the economy. Moreover, turning our attention to the fiscal policy instruments used, we find that government credit provision through loans, liquidity support and government subsidies were the main forms of provision to the affected persons, while tax incentives show a significantly low average.

According to Alberola et al., (2020), the greater expansion of the pandemic is expected to have a greater adverse impact on the economy and thus trigger stronger fiscal spending to deal with it. We can conclude that in both Eurozone and Balkan economies, the fiscal response has been towards securing the economies from the crisis rather than addressing the crisis as a threat to the health of citizens.

Table 2. Fiscal Policy targets and tools Eurozone vs Western Balkans Note: The data are accumulative value at the end of July (N=105 Observations).

Percentage distributions of fiscal policy targets and fiscal policy tools	*Eurozone Mean [bilion USD]*	*Western Balkans Mean [billion USD]*
Fiscal Policy targets		
Health Sector	5.74	0.64
Business Sector	43.34	3.96
Fiscal policy tools		
Direct Government Spending	49.08	4.45
Direct Government cash payment	103.66	8.95
Tax deferral and social security contribution delay	12.7	1.84
Debt contract and relief	103.5	1.11
Govt credit assistance [loans & loan guarantee]	5.61	7.84
Goverment subsidies to business	37.75	4.26

Source: Karamanoli M., (2024) & Author's calculations based on University of Oxford's COVID-19 Government Response Tracker data

CONCLUDING REMARKS

As argued by Alberola et al., (2020), the high incidence of the disease through high death and infection rates adversely affects the economy and consequently draws strong fiscal responses from states. In this paper we have shown that Balkan countries that had the financial capacity to immediately expand public spending and increase benefits to citizens did so, while low GDP countries acted a little more conservatively. It is noteworthy that public spending was expanded first to provide and support the business sector during the health crisis and secondly to manage the health crisis at the sectoral level.

The health sector seems to be operating at a mixed level taking into account the percentages of GDP in the Balkans and the corruption perception index which for all Balkan countries is around 50 with no signs of improvement for the period under review. The European Union has taken measures to address the health crisis but much remains to be done even at the cross-border level. As has been demonstrated by all forms of crises in recent decades, the EU has been very slow to act in terms of preventing emergency crises, but its contribution in terms of designing new response and management policies and in terms of financial provision has been remarkable. Accordingly, Western Balkans, seem to fiscally expand very slowly, in order to cope with the pandemic. As their economic capacity is small, and the negative characteristic of being out of a Eurozone system or European Union, as well, they do not have the means to spend more to manage the crisis.

REFERENCES

Alberola, E., Arslan, Y., Cheng, G., & Moessner, R. 2020, The fiscal response to the COVID-19 crisis in advanced and emerging market economies. Available at https://www.bis.org/publ/bisbull23.htm (accessed 20 January 2022).

Cavallo, A. F., & Cai, T. 2020, HBS COVID-19 global policy tracker. Available at https://www.hbs.edu/covid-19-business-impact/Insights/Economic-and-Financial-Impacts/Global-Policy-Tracker (accessed 20 January 2022).

Chen, C., Shi, Y., Zhang, P., & Ding, C. (2021). A Cross-Country Comparison of Fiscal Policy Responses to the COVID-19 Global Pandemic. *Journal of Comparative Policy Analysis, 23*(2), 262–273. Retrieved January 20, 2022, from. DOI: 10.1080/13876988.2021.1878885

Cottarelli, C., Gerson, P., & Senhadji, A. (Eds.). 2014, Post-Crisis Fiscal Policy (Cambridge, MA: MIT pressF)

Ferguson, N., Laydon, D., Nedjati-Gilani, G., Imai, N., Ainslie, K., Baguelin, M., ... (2020). Impact of non-pharmaceutical interventions [NPIs] to reduce COVID-19 mortality and healthcare demand. https://doi.org/ DOI: 10.25561/77482

Flaxman, S., Mishra, S., Gandy, A., Unwin, H. J. T., Mellan, T. A., Coupland, H., Whittaker, C., Zhu, H., Berah, T., Eaton, J. W., Monod, M., Perez-Guzman, P. N., Schmit, N., Cilloni, L., Ainslie, K. E. C., Baguelin, M., Boonyasiri, A., Boyd, O., Cattarino, L., & Bhatt, S. (2020). Estimating the effects of non-pharmaceutical interventions on COVID-19 in Europe. *Nature, 584*(7820), 257–261. DOI: 10.1038/s41586-020-2405-7 PMID: 32512579

International Monetary Fund (IMF)'s Tracker of Policy Responses to COVID-19. (2020). Available at https://www.imf.org/en/Topics/imf-and-covid19/Policy-Responses-to-COVID-19 ((accessed 20 January 2022).

Karamanoli, M. (2024). Fiscal response in covid-19 crisis – The case of the Eurozone. *Acta Scientiarum Polonorum. Oeconomia, 23*(3), 5–18. DOI: 10.22630/ASPE.2024.23.3.9

Mazaraki, H. (2012). *Health: Public or Private Good? Achaiki Medicine, 31 (1).* Patra.

OECD. 2020, Tax and fiscal policy in response to the Coronavirus crisis: Strengthening confidence and resilience. Available at https://www.oecd.org/ctp/tax-policy/tax-and-fiscal-policy-in-response-to-thecoronavirus-crisis-strengthening-confidence-and-resilience.htm (accessed 20 January 2022).

ENDNOTES

1 Government direct spending refers to the direct spending on goods and services purchased by governments [such as medical supplies and equipment].

2 Direct government cash transfers mean government cash payments for poor families and unemployment insurance payments. In these cases, governments are not doing the actual spending.

3 Debt contract and relief means the government is freezing financial obligations during the COVID-19 pandemic, such as stopping loan repayments, preventing services like water from stopping supplies.

4 Tax benefits, cuts and exemptions indicate offering tax benefits and cuts for people or businesses and adding tax exemptions.

5 Tax deferral and social security contribution delay involves extending tax filing and payment deadlines and delaying business social security payments

6 Government credit assistance includes loan guarantees to support businesses.

7 Government subsidies to business refers to government cash subsidies to the business sector.

Chapter 3
Financial Crisis and Austerity, Pandemic Crisis, and Lockdown:
Their Effects on Labor

Maria Markantonatou
https://orcid.org/0000-0003-3722-1707
University of the Aegean, Greece

ABSTRACT

This chapter examines the effects of two major crises on labor: the Eurozone financial crisis of the 2010s and the COVID-19 pandemic crisis (2020-2022). First, it contextualizes the socio-economic transformations that contributed to the deregulation of the welfare state, the rise of neoliberalism, and the erosion of labor's bargaining power in the decades following the economic downturn of the 1970s. Second, it evaluates the impact of austerity measures implemented in several Eurozone countries during the financial crisis of 2010, focusing on their consequences for labor markets and workers' rights. Third, it explores labor-related developments during the COVID-19 pandemic, including new forms of precarity and insecurity, exacerbated work and gender inequalities, and the proliferation of teleworking. The chapter argues that despite the profound challenges posed by these consecutive crises – marked by declining

DOI: 10.4018/979-8-3373-8790-1.ch003

living standards, reduced incomes, and deteriorating working conditions – essential reforms to enhance social protection and strengthen welfare systems were largely eschewed.

INTRODUCTION

With the end of World War II, states initiated extensive nationalization programs in strategic sectors and implemented partial oversight of the industrial sector (Van Creveld 1999). Concurrently, they promoted the social regulation of market economies and capitalist growth through policies designed to ensure domestic demand and sustain mass consumption. Until the early 1970s, post-war industrial capitalism operated in tandem with the welfare state, which was financed primarily through taxation, and sought to mitigate the shortcomings of the market economy and address its adverse effects on key social strata integral to production. Consequently, income inequality diminished in the post-war years compared to the stark disparities of the early 20th century[2].

The weakening of the welfare state can be attributed to a confluence of heterogeneous factors, including persistent inflation, the oil crises of the 1970s, stagnation in international trade during the 1980s, a declining industrial profit rate in the US and Europe, and the gradual internationalization of transactions and capital flows. During this period, entrepreneurial classes increasingly advocated for labor regulations that favored their interests, while the financial sector steadily eclipsed the industrial sector in economic prominence (Calhoun 2011: 25–26). Additionally, the relocation of capital investments to countries with lower labor costs and more flexible regulatory frameworks exacerbated state revenue shortfalls and public deficits. These fiscal pressures, in turn, prompted significant reductions in public expenditure, fueling social crises and further undermining the welfare state.

Governments in Europe and the US retreated from the commitment to try to secure full employment. Gradually, what dominated in the next decades was similar in most countries, despite the different national contexts: neoliberalization, the deregulation of the welfare state and the institutions of social protection, the diffusion of forms of unstable, flexible and part-time employment, the weakening of trade unions and their role in collective bargaining processes, the reduction of trade union density, the decrease of expectations related to one's work, and the weakening of the social acceptance of strikes and their effectiveness in achieving labor goals. Unemployment in OECD countries for the period from 1960 to 1973 was at 2.2%; it increased to 7.1% from 1990 to 2001; it rose to 5.8% from 2002 to 2008 and reached 6.6% in the period from 2009 to 2012 (Streeck 2014).

Neoliberalization, implemented as a response to the economic crises of the 1970s, exacerbated social inequality. By the 1980s, the wages of the poorest 10% of industrial workers had fallen to half their levels from the 1960s, a decline attributed to various factors including the adoption of new production technologies, the internationalization of capital, an influx of inexpensive labor through immigration, the erosion of union power, and state policies favoring entrepreneurial interests (Cohen 2014). The transition to debt-driven economies in the 1990s further deepened income disparities. While the workers experienced stagnation or decline in earnings, high-ranking managers and consultants in the financial sector witnessed increases in income – rising up to nine times in some cases between 1996 and 2006 (ibid). Rosanvallon (2014) shows this trend with data from France: by 2010, the top 10% of earners accounted for 50% of total income, compared to 35% in 1982. Similarly, between 1998 and 2006, the average income of the top 1% rose by 14%, the income of the top 0.01% nearly doubled, while the incomes of the bottom 90% increased by a mere 4%.

The 1970s crisis was followed by the gradual transformation of the welfare state to a "Schumpeterian workfare post-national regime" (Jessop 2002), which promoted competitiveness, entrepreneurial values, managerialism, and labor flexibility, both at the level of the nation-state and at the level of the European Union after the 1992 Maastricht Treaty. Since the 1980s, as shown in a study by Höpner et al (2014), liberalization policies have been a general trend across policy fields and different groups of countries. According to the authors (ibid.), liberalization was manifested in various forms, reshaping economies and societies over the past decades. Key features include privatization, transformation of public services, employment protection being reduced for both permanent and temporary contracts, capital-based pensions becoming increasingly important, public health expenditures declining, and corporate governance reforms becoming shareholder-oriented. During the 1990s and 2000s, under varying national circumstances, at different speeds, and through various economic shocks (for instance the stock market shocks in 1990 and 1998, and the dot com stock market panic of 2000), states implemented liberalization policies and promoted competition. The 2008 financial crisis, which originated in the US and spread to the Eurozone after 2010, served as a catalyst for intensified attacks on labor and the working classes, particularly in the countries of the European South, with Greece experiencing these effects most acutely.

The following subchapter examines key aspects of labor deregulation during the Eurozone crisis. Subsequently, the discussion turns to the consequences of the COVID-19 pandemic for labor, highlighting its impact on working conditions, inequalities, and employment security.

CRISIS AND AUSTERITY AFTER 2010

In many countries, more than a decade after the outbreak of the Eurozone crisis, neoliberal reforms have significantly weakened the economic position of the working classes, lower social strata, and those reliant on welfare provisions. The narrative employed during the crisis played a pivotal role in facilitating the implementation of these reforms. As de Matos and Pusceddu (2021) observe in the cases of Italy and Portugal, the ethos of "sacrifice" was central to the ideological legitimization of austerity measures. The crises were framed as "dramatic" and "urgent," necessitating swift action to safeguard "national stability". Labor forces were positioned as the primary bearers of the crisis's burden, justified by two main arguments: the need to align with the priorities of economic "modernization" and adherence to the rules set by the Eurozone and the IMF. These institutions frequently emphasized issues such as an excess of civil servants, insufficient competitiveness, and overly permissive labor regulations, particularly in the public sector compared to the private sector. De Matos and Pusceddu (2021) argue that the ideology of "sacrifice" was adapted to diverse national contexts, often infused with cultural or even religious undertones. Similar narratives emerged across many countries, emphasizing a moral obligation to the "homeland" and casting blame on select social groups. This rhetoric perpetuated a "divide and conquer" strategy, making individuals not only comply with austerity measures but also internalize and reproduce them. This internalization reshaped people's attitudes, values, and everyday practices, altering their expectations of work, the state, and their future prospects.

Labor was worst attacked in Greece after 2010, when austerity was implemented in the framework of the "Memoranda of Understanding". They were a series of complex loan agreements concluded between the so called "Troika" (European Commission, European Central Bank, International Monetary Fund) and several Greek governments, which were formed in a series of turbulent national elections. To get the loans, Greek governments of various ideological guises (center-right, social democratic, leftist, and their various coalitions) had to implement sound budgets, privatizations, liberalization of domestic markets, public administration reforms, restructuring of the tax, wage, pension, and social benefits system, as well as the deregulation of welfare services. Cuts in public expenditure, reduction of personnel in the public sector, slashing social incomes, and the dismantling of the pre-crisis institutions of labor protection have been the fundamental aims underlying a barrage of measures and legislation after 2010 (Markantonatou 2013). As a result of these policies, unemployment rose from 7.8% in 2008 to 27.5% in 2013 and fell to 20.2% in 2017 (Greek Institute of Labour 2018). Millions of jobs were lost, employment protection legislation deteriorated, and collective bargaining was severely undermined, causing increased fragmentation of wage setting practices and a divergence of firm-level agreements from sectoral standards. The average wage for the period 2010-2013 fell by 21% compared to 2009 and the minimum wage by about 26%, and by 35.4% for people under 25 years old (ibid.). Involuntary part-time employment increased from 49.7% of part-time employment in 2009 to 71.1% in 2017 (OECD 2018).

In Spain, which for the period before the Eurozone crisis had been praised as a country that had "at least tried to achieve some restraint through the instruments of macroeconomic policy that were still available nationally" (Scharpf 2011), austerity policies were followed initially by the social democratic government of J. L. Zapatero (*Partido Socialista*

Obrero Español) in 2008. Austerity intensified with the outbreak of the crisis, and from 2011 the conservative government of M. Rajoy (*Partido Popular*) imposed much sharper reforms and reductions in public spending (e.g. shrinking of the public sector, and cuts in public sector wages) with the argument of calming down investors and coping with an escalating crisis. The crisis hit the booming real estate market, led to the downgrading of the economy by international rating agencies, then to a series of bank bailouts, to a recession, a new increase in public debt, and a further worsening both of labor market conditions and unemployment. According to Alonso and Rodríguez (2020), the aftermath of the crisis and its management left behind a more fractured and unequal society, a weakened welfare regime, stagnant wages, rising social discontent, increased child poverty, and numerous challenges for the future.

Before the crisis, Portugal faced high levels of atypical employment, low productivity and wages, and the politicization of collective bargaining processes, characteristics that were further exacerbated by the economic downturn (Estanque, Costa, Fonseca, Santos 2019). From 2011 to 2014, under the government of P. P. Coelho, austerity measures, public spending cuts, and legislation aimed at promoting labor flexibilization and facilitating layoffs were imposed at the behest of Eurozone creditors. These policies had a profound impact on the country's labor market and social structure. As noted by Estanque (2020), the Troika intervention "resulted in a huge social setback, particularly for the most vulnerable segments of the working and middle classes." However, Troika's intervention also played a role in the political shifts that followed, contributing to the overthrow of the right-wing government in 2015. The result was the formation of a coalition government between the Social Democratic Party (*Partido Social Democrata*), the Democratic and Social Center (*Centro Democrático e Social*), and the Left Block (*Bloco de Esquerda*). Despite widespread social unrest, strikes, and numerous anti-austerity protests during the years of Troika supervision, measures that deepened labor precariousness persisted. These measures continued after the Troika's departure in 2014, and under the leftist coalition government (ibid.: 97).

As regards Italy, the crisis found the economy in the conditions, which Cangiani (2020) describes as follows: decline during the last decades of the Italian industry due to low investment in innovation and acquisitions by foreign investors, capital flight, relocation of companies (some of which held a leading position internationally), privatization of state-owned industries, clientelism, chronic tax evasion. The high public debt of the country (nearly 120% of the GDP in 2010 and more than 150% in 2021) and the efforts to avoid "moral panic" were presented as the reasons for the policies followed in the period 2011-2013 by the unelected, "technocratic" government of M. Monti who replaced that of S. Berlusconi, after pressure was exercised by Eurozone elites. In addition to increasing household and property taxes, the government also raised the retirement age and implemented labor law reforms aimed at liberalizing the labor market. These reforms included opening up previously closed occupations, raising the limit on layoffs within companies, and expanding the use of short-term contracts, all with the goal of fostering greater competition and flexibility within the economy (ibid.).

In France, the neoliberal policies of recent decades have led to the fragmentation of the labor market and collective bargaining, the expansion of part-time and temporary employment, and a sharp decline in union membership. The proportion of unionized workers in France fell from approximately 25% in the 1970s to around 10% by the 1980s, where it has remained more or less ever since (Yon 2019: 74). To cope with the Eurozone crisis, a pension reform, and regulations to remove labor protection in the framework of the "National Pact for Growth, Competitiveness and Employment" were imposed. Although both the center-right Republican party (*Les Républicains* and former *Union pour un Mouvement Populaire*) and the Socialist Party (*Parti socialiste*) followed policies of neoliberalization which affected labor, the government of E. Macron (*La République En Marche!*) intensified them. The new labor code promoted by the Macron-government was a decisive step towards flexicurity (Vranken 2018). An additional step in the same direction was the "*ordonnances*", the legally mandated "executive orders" that strengthen company-level agreements over the national collective ones, facilitate layoffs, and reduce the number, financial resources, and legal means of the representative institutions of workers (Yon 2019: 79-80).

As for Germany, the Eurozone's largest economy, it was not hit by the crisis of 2010 as were other countries, and there were huge capital inflows and low interest rates on its sovereign bonds (Schmalz and Schneidemesser

2019). Unemployment was not high during the crisis (from 7.7% in 2008, it fell to 5% in 2013 and 3% in 2019 [OECD 2020]) as it was in countries of Southern Europe. However, precariousness is increasing for low-paid, flexible jobs, and in sectors where unions are absent or weak (Dörre 2015). In Germany's postwar "social market economy", the term "social" means less and less, as those who do not benefit from the export industry, the precariously working people, the poor, and those dependent on social help find themselves exposed to an increasingly aggressive market competition (ibid.). This process started after Germany's reunification with the liberalization policies of G. Schröder's government (1998-2005). The so called Hartz IV labor market laws promoted the liberalization of temporary agency work and the "mini-jobs" (tax free jobs paid less than 450 euros per month). Consequently, as Schmalz and Schneidemesser (2019) note, "employer associations have a number of possibilities to avoid standard employment relationships and to push for lower payment". Moreover, the same authors (ibid) characterize Germany as a "precarious full employment society", where collective bargaining agreements are partial, as they cover only 41.7% of all employees, and note that fear and increasing insecurity have increased in the lives of low-wage workers.

THE PANDEMIC CRISIS AND LOCKDOWNS

The outbreak of the COVID-19 pandemic found labor in an already weakened position, largely as a result of the economic crisis of 2008 and the neoliberal policies that followed, as discussed earlier. Around the world, lockdowns were implemented starting in March 2020, encompassing a wide range of restrictive measures. These included the closure of businesses, schools, universities, cinemas, theaters, archaeological sites, playgrounds, parks etc. Movement restrictions and travel bans were imposed, and international visitors were required to undergo quarantine. As part of the efforts to curb the spread of the virus, many schools and universities transitioned to online teaching, and thousands of public and private sector employees shifted to teleworking. Various protocols were introduced, specifying limitations on social and public gatherings, while strict checks at tollgates and border controls prevented transportation between municipalities. Additionally, there was a noticeable increase in police surveillance on the streets, including more frequent stop-and-search incidents. New forms of social control emerged through the implementation of technologies, such as smartphone applications for tracking movements and contact tracing, further embedding digital surveillance into everyday life.

Lockdowns had some dramatic effects. Children poverty skyrocketed; millions of children faced conditions of absolute poverty in 2020 due to the loss of family income; 1.5 billion children interrupted schooling; faced the risk of never returning to school; millions lost access to school meals (United Nations 2020). Overall, lockdowns led national economies around the world into recession (a 4.4% drop in global GDP in 2020 [Fuchs 2021). The cessation of many economic activities led to huge losses of income and payments, and tax collection by the state. Job insecurity, especially among the low-paid, vulnerable workers and those involved in the informal economy, took new forms under the threat of COVID-19. Fundamental labor rights such as freedom of association and collective bargaining, and the principle of non-forced labor were shaken by the lockdowns, the recession, and the shutdown of the economy (ILO 1998).

Regarding freedom of association, the pandemic introduced exemption regimes in collective bargaining and contracts, further undermining workers' rights. More than 60% of the global workforce, who were employed in the informal economy, were unable to collectively express their interests or demands. As precarity deepened, an increasing number of workers were pushed to operate outside the framework of collective agreements, further eroding their bargaining power and job security. This trend highlights the growing vulnerability of workers, especially those in informal sectors, who had limited access to protections and solidarity mechanisms (ILO 2021). During the pandemic there have been numerous reports of restrictions on freedom of association due to the state of emergency, and despite opposition from trade unions, according to the European Trade Union Confederation (ETUC 2021). As regards forced labor, the pandemic exacerbated socio-economic vulnerability, as workers in the informal economy lost income and their safety net, even if it was weak in the pre-pandemic era. Workers unable to solve COVID-caused problems (unemployment, loans that could not be repaid due to job losses, unexpected costs of health care etc.) were forced into new forms of precarious labor, and sometimes at any kind of work in order to provide basic care for their family (ILO 2021).

A new form of labor that intensified in the pandemic was teleworking[3]. Before the outbreak of the pandemic, various forms of teleworking were practiced in Europe and the US (e.g. homebased teleworking, telework centers, telecottages, digital nomadic work etc.). They provided an opportunity for employers in the information and service sector to take advantage of innovative and relatively cheap computer and internet technologies and reduce functional costs of the enterprise. In many countries, it was not widespread before the pandemic, or it remained largely unreported. The lockdowns, however, have been a catalyst for the expansion of teleworking, with a large number of public and private sector workers being required to work remotely.

The pandemic and the teleworking brought sudden rearrangements in the organization of work, work performance, the blurring between free time and working time, the lengthening of the working hours, many changes (or even confusion) regarding work responsibilities, and the burdening of the home environment. Homes became offices, which, however, more often than not, lacked a suitable workplace (e.g. appropriate internet access and speed, office equipment etc.). Although teleworking was presented as an emergency measure, it is likely that it has come to stay even after the pandemic ends. Thus, worries are justified that the contractual relationship between employer and employee may be challenged in the future, and that self-employment or even self-insurance and non-protection by the employer are widened. These issues threaten the social state, its funding, and its survival.

On the other hand, despite the new problems they had to face, workers obliged to work from home were less exposed to the virus than those workers who had to leave the house, use public transportation, and contact people during the workday. Such workers were characterized during the pandemic as "essential workers" and their work as "socially necessary" (carers, medical staff, factory and agricultural workers, workers in catering, supermarkets, street cleaners, distributors, transporters, etc.). They were the ones to carry out the material tasks of everyday life. They were at a higher risk of being exposed to the virus, especially in the first phase of the pandemic, when community testing was not widespread. Staying home was not at all an option for some workers; doing so would deprive them their daily wage. Before the pandemic, this "essential" labor was characterized by low wages and a low social status. Politicians highlighted the usefulness of the "essential workers" in the context of the pandemic, but this did not ultimately lead to an improvement in their wages or working conditions. There was a moral recognition of their personal efforts (especially in the field of hospital and medical care), but not a substantial change and strengthening of the public healthcare system, which was weak due to cuts in infrastructure and personnel in the past decades.

Another population group affected by the pandemic was women, although they do not constitute a homogeneous group and their situation varied according to their class position, age, and profession. Being at risk of poverty, job loss and social exclusion was the reality for most women of working and lower middle classes long before the pandemic. Women perform more than three times the amount of unpaid care work compared to men, which has severe consequences for their economic and career prospects, as well as their mental health and well-being (Ryan and Ayadi 2020). The pandemic increased care emergencies, disaffecting women and escalating gender disparities. As explained by Bijl (2020), "70% of the global health and social workforce (...) are women. Cashiers and cleaners are largely female as well. They are (...) at a higher risk of being exposed to the virus". Because of the pandemic unpaid work for women, the pressure on them and their insecurity increased. As Bijl (2020) observed during the lockdown, this caused "additional mental and physical strain, in particular for single parents, 85% of whom are women. Women were economically disadvantaged before the crisis, they are risking poverty, unemployment, social exclusion and homelessness now".

During the pandemic, women were again threatened by unemployment, as in the economic crisis in 2010. The pandemic delayed entrance to the labor market for women who were planning to look for work after their children reached school age, but also for young females (ages 15-24). Informally or precariously working women were often expelled from the labor market during the pandemic. Others experienced new forms of precariousness, unregulated working hours, increased demands from employers, work overload, or even burn out. As Burawoy notes (2021) about the US: "At home women are more likely to take up the slack, home-schooling their children, reorganizing family life, giving up their jobs and careers. For others, the second shift becomes a third and a fourth shift – working multiple jobs to keep family alive". Moreover, gender-based and domestic violence increased during the lockdowns, as reported by shelters for abused women, for instance in Greece (Dionellis 2020).

Conditions were equally problematic for refugees and displaced people living in an emergency inside the wider pandemic-emergency. They experienced higher health risks because of the bad living conditions in the overcrowded camps of Europe. Undocumented refugees faced higher health risks, as they avoided visits to medical centers and hospitals because of the fear of getting arrested or deported. Those working informally lost their income sources, and others trying to get a job confronted new hardships. Instead of a public discussion about the bad conditions in which they lived, refugees were often presented as possible "threats" for public health.

FINAL REMARKS

Both the financial crisis of the 2010s and the pandemic crisis of 2020–2022 exposed and deepened long-standing weaknesses in welfare systems, shaped by decades of neoliberal policies. During the financial crisis, policies centered on stabilizing markets and rescuing financial institutions, while austerity measures severely cut public spending, undermining essential social services and labor protections. These measures disproportionately affected vulnerable populations, exacerbating inequality and fueling social discontent. The pandemic highlighted the consequences of underinvestment in public healthcare and the expansion of private markets. Public healthcare systems, weakened by neoliberal reforms, were unprepared for the crisis. COVID-19 revealed the urgent need to strengthen healthcare systems and reverse privatization to ensure equitable access. However, many governments continued to favor market-driven solutions over significant public investment, despite growing demands for a robust welfare state.

Both crises led to substantial economic interventions – during the Eurozone crisis, these focused on financial stabilization, while in the pandemic, they sought to mitigate the effects of lockdowns and economic disruptions. Together, these crises transformed work and society, posing challenges for labor and social movements. While governments remain resistant to reversing privatization, enhancing the welfare system, prioritizing public investments, and strengthening labor protections, societies and social movements struggle to address the long-term effects on incomes, working conditions, and public services.

REFERENCES

Alonso, L. E., & Rodríguez, C. J. (2020). Crisis and sacrifice in Spain, International Karl Polanyi Society, Debate: Crisis in Southern Europe, Available at: https://www.karlpolanyisociety.com/2020/06/29/crisis-and-sacrifice-in-spain/

Bijl, M. (2020). The Covid-19 crisis is exacerbating gender inequalities—But who cares? *Social Europe*, •••, 5.

Burawoy, M. (2021). Letter from Oakland, 15th International Karl Polanyi Conference: The Role of the State in the post-COVID 21st Century, Concordia University, Montreal

Calhoun, C. (2011). From the Current Crisis to Possible Futures. In Calhoun, C., & Derluguian, G. (Eds.), *Business as Usual: The Roots of the Global Financial Meltdown*. New York University Press.

Cangiani, M. (2020). Italy: New Problems are not New, International Karl Polanyi Society, Debate: Crisis in Southern Europe. Available at: https://www.karlpolanyisociety.com/2020/06/29/new-problems-are-not-new-i/

Cohen, D., & Economicus, H. (2014). *The (Lost) Prophet of Modern Times*. Polity Press.

De Matos, A. P., & Pusceddu, A. M. (2021). Austerity, the state and common sense in Europe: A comparative perspective on Italy and Portugal. *Anthropological Theory*, *21*(4), 21. DOI: 10.1177/1463499621991326

Dionellis, M. Not everyone is safe at home. Efsyn Newspaper, 22.11.2020 (In Greek). Available at: https://www.efsyn.gr/efkriti/koinonia/269727_den-menoyn-oles-asfaleis-otan-menoyn-sto-spiti

Dörre, K. (2015). Social Capitalism and Crisis: from the internal to the external Landnahme. 2015). Sociology-Capitalism-Critique, 247-277.

ECB (European Central Bank). (2012). Speech by M. Draghi, President of the ECB at the Global Investment Conference in London. Available at: https://www.ecb.europa.eu/press/key/date/2012/html/sp120726.en.html

Estanque, E. (2020). Commodification and Countermovements: Portugal against the Trend, International Karl Polanyi Society, Debate: Crisis in Southern Europe, Available at: https://www.karlpolanyisociety.com/2020/06/21/commodification-and-countermovements-portugal-against-the-trend/

Estanque, E., Costa, H. A., Fonseca, D., & Santos, A. (2019). Are Trade Unions Trapped? Precarious Movements and Labour Struggles at the Left Turn in Portugal. In Schmalz, S., & Sommer, B. (Eds.), *Confronting Crisis and Precariousness*. Organized Labour and Social Unrest in the European Union, Rowman and Littlefield.

ETUC. (2021). Anticipating and managing the COVID-19 crisis impact on jobs and workplaces: Swift action needed to enforce rights to worker involvement. Available at: https://www.etuc.org/sites/default/files/page/file/2020-06/ETUFs%20ETUC%20letter%20to%20Mr%20Schmit_Enforcement%20of%20ICP%20rights_20%20May%202020.pdf

Fuchs, C. (2021). *Communicating COVID-19: Everyday Life, Digital Capitalism, and Conspiracy Theories in Pandemic Times*. Emerald Publishing Limited. DOI: 10.1108/9781801177207

Greek Institute of Labour (INE/GSEE). (2018). Greek Economy and Employment: Annual Report. Athens [In Greek]. Available at: https://www.inegsee.gr/ekdosi/etisia-ekthesi-2018-ine-gsee-i-elliniki-ikonomia-ke-i-apascholisi/

Höpner, M., Petring, A., Seikel, D., & Werner, B. (2014). Liberalization policy: An empirical analysis of economic and social interventions in western democracies.

ILO (International Labour Organization). (1998). Declaration on Fundamental Principles and Rights at Work and its Follow-up. Available at: https://www.ilo.org/wcmsp5/groups/public/---ed_norm/---declaration/documents/normativeinstrument/wcms_716594.pdf

ILO (International Labour Organization). (2021). Issue paper on COVID-19and fundamental principles and rights at work, Available at: https://www.ilo.org/wcmsp5/groups/public/@ed_norm/@ipec/documents/publication/wcms_757247.pdf

Jessop, B. (2002). *The Future of the Capitalist State*. Polity Press.

Markantonatou, M. (2013). *Diagnosis, Treatment, and Effects of the Crisis in Greece: A" Special Case" or a*. Test Case.

Messenger, J. (2019). Introduction: Telework in the 21st century – an evolutionary perspective. In Messenger, J. C. (Ed.), *Telework in the 21st Century, The ILO Future of Work series*. DOI: 10.4337/9781789903751.00005

. OECD (2020), Unemployment rate, Germany (indicator). DOI: 10.1787/997c8750-en

. OECD. (2018). Incidence of FTPT Employment; Incidence of Involuntary Part-Time Workers. Available at: http://dx.doi.org/DOI: 10.1787/lfs-data-en

Rosanvallon, P. (2013). *The society of equals*. Harvard University Press. DOI: 10.4159/harvard.9780674726444

Ryan, N. E., & El Ayadi, A. M. (2020). A call for a gender-responsive, intersectional approach to address COVID-19. *Global Public Health: An International Journal for Research, Policy and Practice*, *15*(9), 1404–1412.

Scharpf, F. W. (2011). Monetary Union, Fiscal Crisis and the Pre-Emption of Democracy, Zeitschrift Für Staats- und Europawissenschaften (ZSE). *Journal for Comparative Government and European Policy*, *9*(2).

Schmalz, S., & Schneidemesser, L. (2019). The End of the German Model? The Transformations of German Capitalism and fragmented Labour Relations. In Schmalz, S., & Sommer, B. (Eds.), *Confronting Crisis and Precariousness*. Organized Labour and Social Unrest in the European Union, Rowman and Littlefield.

Streeck, W. (2014). The politics of public debt: Neoliberalism, capitalist development and the restructuring of the state. *German Economic Review*, *15*(1), 143–165.

United Nations. Policy Brief: The impact of COVID-19 on children, 2020, Available at: https://unsdg.un.org/sites/default/files/2020-04/160420_Covid_Children_Policy_Brief.pdf

Van Creveld, M. (1999). *The Rise and the Decline of the State*. Cambridge University Press. DOI: 10.1017/CBO9780511497599

Vranken, M. (2018). *Labour Law Reform in France: The Macron Effect* (Vol. 24). Comparative Law Journal of the Pacific.

Yon, K. (2019). Holding its Own: Labour among Social Movements in France. In Schmalz, S., & Sommer, B. (Eds.), *Confronting Crisis and Precariousness*. Organized Labour and Social Unrest in the European Union, Rowman and Littlefield.

ENDNOTES

1 Associate Professor, Department of Sociology, University of the Aegean, Lesvos, Greece. Email: mmarkant@soc.aegean.gr

2 Rosanvallon (2014: 3–4) observes: "In France, the wealthiest 1% owned 53% of the national wealth in 1913 but only 20% in 1984. In the United States, the top 10% of earners shared nearly 50% of total income on the eve of the Great Depression but less than 35% from 1950 until the mid- 1980s. In Sweden, a shining example of inequality reduction, the top 1% of earners claimed only 23% of all income in 1980, compared with 46% at the turn of the twentieth century. These spectacular reductions were achieved by a rapid increase in low incomes, slower growth of high incomes, social transfer payments, and a highly progressive tax system, the upper brackets of which paid steeply increasing rates".

3 Teleworking with the use of computer technology appeared in the US in the 1970s and was implemented in the 1980s by American companies such as Yahoo (Messenger 2019: 1).

Chapter 4
Governing the Commons in Emergencies:
The Dynamics of Socio-Political Leadership in Interwar Greece – Lessons for the Present?

George Odysseas Tsobanoglou
https://orcid.org/0000-0003-3006-2758
Hellenic Open University, Greece

Charalambos Nicou Louca
https://orcid.org/0009-0003-1160-1821
American College, Cyprus

ABSTRACT

Greece considers the 100th anniversary of the events which led to removal and catastrophe of three millennium old Ionian Communities (Asia Minor). 1,5 million refugees of Hellenic heritage to Greece gives birth to the registry of Modern Greece. The protagonist to these socio-political institutions, is the Political Sociologist Alexander Papanastasiou. His leadership skills allowed him to institutionalize an organizational regime which developed cooperation for development combining, a crisis, the settlement of refugees,

DOI: 10.4018/979-8-3373-8790-1.ch004

with community development solutions in the manner of cooperatives, founding the Agricultural Bank and setting in place agricultural research and development to develop new seeds, while establishing a unique Import Substitution mechanism to finance all these, as credit was not available (The Papanastasiou-Koryzis Model). The paper focuses on this unique and key moment of Greek socio-political history to illustrate that the present Greek crisis may need such leadership skills and intervention to get the country out of the acute social crisis it is found in at present.

1. SUSTAINABLE DEVELOPMENT: LOOKING AT THE CULTURE AND COMMUNICATION OF THE PAST TO THE FUTURE OF SUSTAINABILITY IN GREECE

The year 2022 was the 100th anniversary of the Asia Minor Disaster of the almost 4000 years old Greek communities of Ionia. This year (2024) is the 100th anniversary of the Balkan Exchange of Minorities, a unique event of global significance which brought to a war-torn Greece (10 years of wars) of 5 million over 1,5 million impoverished Christian Greeks from areas of the newly established Turkish Republic (1923).

Through a historical review of the interwar period (1922-1940), we find that when politics, administration, science, and innovation coexist harmoniously and interdependently, high quality work is produced with the goal of social benefit. Two important personalities of the time, Alexandros Papanastasiou and Ioannis Papadakis would engage us in research into their work and the decisive role they had in resolving the dramatic social changes required of that period.

Alexandros Papanastasiou (1876 -1936) studied Law and Sociology in Heidelberg, Berlin, Paris and London, and founded the Popular Party of Greece usually referred as the Sociological Party in 1910. The main philosophy was that of evolutionary socialism aiming to develop social integration political problems in very difficult period which can only be described as of a perfect storm. The Refugee problem was a top problem so was the high number of wounded veterans returned from the wars in the Balkans, the First World War, the Asia Minor and Crimea Military

Campaigns who resulted to some 14,000 wounded and 75,000 relatives if killed in action (Makris, 2023). They all wanted support and solutions.

In this period Papanastasiou emerged as the visionary and architect of Greek social democracy through his actions, speeches, and writings, including the famous "Democratic Manifesto". The establishment of the University of Thessaloniki and the Agricultural Bank, projects of his own, were foundations in the fields of education and economy respectively. A leader whose position in the historical assessment of the people did not and has not taken the dimension it should. (Anastasiadis, 2003).

Alexandros Papanastasiou, as the Minister of Communications in the Venizelos government, had to form the urban plan of Thessaloniki, which was devastated by the Big Fire of 1917. It was a major problem as it was necessary to precede the cadastral survey, the preparation of which was considered impossible due to the large area of the fire-burning zone, the alteration of its surface and the property to many owners. The cadastral survey was completed in nine (9) months and the next stage was to deal with the exercise of speculation on the plots to proceed quickly with the reconstruction. To achieve that, Papanastasiou introduced the system of "demand" cooperation of owners (forming agricultural coops), thus not burdening the State financially but rather maintaining the value of the land at normal levels so that an urban plan that block the uncontrolled land speculation could be implemented. That was a basic act to protect the value of housing, a first social housing policy, aiming to reconstruct a disaster area (Papadakis, 1987, Anastasiadis, 2003).

Papanastasiou himself set up the "Committee for the elaboration of a new street plan for the city of Thessaloniki", where he appointed as its members: Thomas Mawson, and English architect; Jean Pleyber, a French civil engineer, Ernest Hebrard, an architect-urban planner, Angelos Ginis, a Professor at the Technical University of Athens, Aristotelis Zachos and Konstantinos Katsikis, architects and the then Mayor of Thessaloniki Konstantinos Aggelakis.

This new plan would ensure for many decades the full functionality of the city and the quality of life of the inhabitants as it was drafted based on the orientation of the city to the sea, its climate, the seven hills of its territory, the restoration of its monuments and the prospect of integrating into the city the hitherto surrounding desert areas (eastern part swamps) which were later settled with the Greek refugees who entered the country in 1922 and 1923, as a result of the destruction of Smyrna (Izmir) and Pontus (Black Sea) during Asia Minor Disaster (1022) and, later, during the Exchange of Minorities involving the population of the Greek Communities of Ionia. The central sector of the city, although with several interventions in the visions of Papanastasiou and the committee, acquired a street plan and a modern look, thus vindicating Papanastasiou and the committee and proving the urban planning messages of the future that they had conceived.

As Prime Minister in 1924, Alexandros Papanastasiou announced the proclamation of the Republic, pointing out the democratic character of Greek education and introducing new measures to elevate education. That resulted in the announcement of establishing the Aristotelian University of Thessaloniki (or University in Thessaloniki) and its completion (1928-1929); he also envisioned the establishment of chairs of Slavic and Balkan historical and philological studies as well he proposed the establishment of a Balkan Institute (Anastasiadis, 2003,).

Alexandros Papanastasiou's contribution to the 1917 agrarian reform of Greece was significant, which remained however on paper until 1923, the year Greece had to accommodate the 1,3 million of Greek refugees. The main pillars of that agrarian reform were the abolition of large properties and the division of usable lands into small productive units of family character, which responded better to the new productive and social conditions. That was a radical measure that was implemented in Greece at the time, since it radically changed the relations of land ownership by generalizing the system of small family farming under a system of co-operatives (Mariadis, 1992, 2003: Mavrogordatos, 2003, Papagaroufali, 1985-86, Pelagidis, 2009).

Within that historical and political context, the aim of the Venizelos Government (with Papanastasiou as the Minister of Communications), was, first, to support and multiply Greek land holdings in the newly acquired areas after they had been liberated from the Ottoman Empire in 1912 (e.g. the city of Thessaloniki, and the islands of Lesvos and Chios); second, to rehabilitate Greek Refugees from Anatolia, and to prevent social tensions in the rural area. Developments in the agricultural sector were accompanied by an increase in investment in agricultural production in the form of credits and a rapid development of the cooperative movement. Undoubtedly, the success of the 1917 agrarian reform was contributed by the establishment of cooperatives, which aimed to protect small producers and to increase the security of investments in the rural economy (Zoiopoulos, 2003, 2024, Karamanos, 2020).

On the initiative of Alexandros Papanastasiou, the first Agricultural Research Institute was founded in Larissa as well as the Plant Cultivation Station, which by Ioannis Papadakis, in 1925.

In 1924, Alexandros Papanastasiou, as the Prime Minister of Greece, supported local empowerment and participation of the refugees, who arrived in the city of Thessaloniki with the Exchange of Minorities in 1923 (Mazower, 2002, 2014, Maurogordatos, 1992, Pelagidis, 2009, Chatziiosif, 2002).

Papanastasiou's support to Greek refugees was initially underlined through his collaboration with the agronomist Ioannis Karamanos (1891-1966), carrying out the rehabilitation of Greek refugees by distributing land in Macedonia and Thrace, with the main goal of ensuring their survival and their smooth social and economic integration in a short period of time. The Committee for the Rehabilitation of Refugees (Ε.Α.Π.) paid particular attention to the establishment of agricultural cooperatives from the very first year of its operation (1924), while the Greek refugee agricultural cooperatives of Macedonia, with 44,815 members showed (Mavrogordatos 1992) an impressively increased financial movement for the data of that time.

Apart from his collaboration with the agronomist Ioannis Karamanos, Papanastasiou with Ioannis Papadakis (1903-1997) was catalytic. The world-renowned agronomist Ioannis Papadakis was appointed to the Ministry of Agriculture in 1923, on the initiative of Alexandros Papanastasiou, and a few years later the first Agricultural Research Institute was a fact (1925). The improvement and creation of new seed varieties, more resistant to diseases and with higher yields per hectare, was an innovation. Few years later, Papadakis collaborated with Karamanos for the Greek refugee settlement in Macedonia and Thrace. The increase in wheat production, farmers' incomes, and the establishment of the Special Station for the

Improvement of Plants, which evolved into the Grain Institute of Thermi (a region of the wider area of Thessaloniki), Thessaloniki, contributed to feeding the population of Greece in hazardous times.

The aim was to underline both the role of the Greek State in the organization of the Greek refugees' Cooperative Rural and Residential Rehabilitation, as well as the important role of the sociological practice of Alexandros Papanastasiou in organizing this complex solution for the rehabilitation of Greek refugee flows.

2. THE GREEK MODEL OF PAPANASTASIOU-KORYZIS FOR RURAL DEVELOPMENT

Before 1923 Greek farmers as in an underdeveloped country practiced subsistence farming thus not buying anything from the national market as that market was not developed; the merchants act as mediators to the market in every way. They bought agricultural produce and sold everything to farmers. Thus, farmers were deeply indebted to those merchants. At harvest time farmers sold their production at low prices and they paid at much higher prices. There was an unequal exchange between farmers and merchants which led to the inability of farmers to engage in transactions with the national market and contribute to its development. Thus, there were many small local markets whereby local producers were indebted to the credit holders and unable to escape debt and subsistence farming. There was no possibility to increase production applying new agro-farming crop-science technics at all. At the same time, they had difficulty buying what they needed for production to increase yields. The lack of a national policy in food production was a challenge for the development of the country involved. The attempt of certain governments to fix minimum prices at which governments buy certain agricultural products is usually opposed by the mediator-merchants who control credit and demand payment of all debts sometimes at usury rates. What is needed is cooperative promotion whereby the value chain form farm to fork is fully developed (cropping, processing, marketing) and thus the mediators are not in the market as is the situation in most of the European Union and OECD areas and unlike present Greece. In the beginning of the 20th century Greek farmers were producing cereals in Thessaly, Peloponnese, Macedonia and Thrace under previously described conditions. Only those producing tobacco and raisins were producing for the large export market. Cereal producers were not proprietors of the land and the wheat they were cultivating was being imported at high prices. The prices paid to sharecroppers by merchants were less than half that of foreign what going out to the custom house; cereal producers were not paying their debts, so that it could not continue; yields were at very low, 600 kg/ha, and the country was importing 2/3 of what it was consuming (Papadakis, 1987). At that time one million and a half Greek refugees (from Anatolia) arrived suddenly at the end of 1922 (Chatziiosif, 2002).

To face that situation all properties exceeding 30 hectares, in the cereal producing zones, had been expeditiously expropriated and given immediately to share-croppers or Greek refugees. In 1927 the government began to buy directly from the farmers all wheat production at the price of the foreign wheat going out of the custom house. That was the standard set by the pricing authority of the National Bank. Payment was made with a check by the Agricultural Bank. This institutional innovation (Agricultural Bank) was to take the place of the myriad of local merchants of credit in the rural areas. The packet of measures to buy wheat directly from the farmers was conceived by Al. Papanastasiou, Minister of Agriculture and Al. Kuryzis, sub-governor of the National Bank of Greece, applied immediately in the summer of 1927 (Papadakis, 1987). The Director of the Institute for Plant Breeding (established in 1925) introduced wheat varieties that were yielding 50% more than those previously grown; the Institute also organized seed production in Greece. The seed was sold at credit by the Agricultural Bank. Thus, there was an end to the black-market practices of local credit producers (usury) and seed distribution controllers in the highly survival practices in the rural economy. The situation was deemed as disaster relief measure to accommodate the low production of wheat and its highly subsistence character with a policy synthesis of Papanastasiou, the Sociologist Minister of Agriculture, who established land distribution for the settlers in an organized manner by introducing Banking intervention in seed and by distributing credit along with agro-ecological scientific application of global innovation (Papadakis was to develop the system of Agro-Ecology in 1938) in the manner of The Institute of Plant

Breeding (1925). That was a unique social organizational regime that with very limited international borrowing managed to set a full proof socio-technical system whose basic concern was the Protection of the Producers, the farmers, by credit and seed provision. The aim was the human survival of the country under long term emergency conditions that required import substitution, formation of the national food market and the emerging social protection system in the production level. Participation of farmers was enabled through cooperation at the level of governance [political power (Papanastasiou), economic power (Koryzis) Scientific innovation and application (Papadakis)] - which eliminated local poor subsistence farming and developed a national farm market that increased production from 300,000 tons of wheat that had been before (1923) before to 850,000 before the war (1940). The value of industrial production increased 128% between 1931 and 1937 like agricultural production (Papadakis, 1987). Wheat production increased from 850,000 before 1940 to 2,700,000 in 1983 at the point of entry to the European Union. The country became a net exporter of wheat, similarly, sugar beet production initiated in 1961 led to a volume of 270,000 tons in 1978. The number of people occupied in industry and manufacturing increased from 149,250 in 1940 to 671,496 in 1978 (Zoiopoulos, 2003).

This was the Greek Model (Papanastasiou-Koryzis) for rural development for the Greek self-sufficiency in wheat (sitarkia or wheat sufficiency).

Ioannis Papadakis was a key protagonist in that unique period of Greece's social history. He was born in 1903 in Naxos Island, Cyclades, Greece. After examinations of the Ministry of Agriculture, he received a state scholarship. He studied agriculture in Gembloux, Belgium, graduating first in 1922. He completed his studies in France specializing in plant breeding, and, when he returned to Greece in 1923, was appointed to the Ministry of Agriculture.

In 1925, based in Larissa, Thessaly the Plant Improvement Station, the first Agricultural Research Institute in the country, was founded under the direction of I. Papadakis 1925-1927. In 1927 the Station was moved to Thessaloniki and was renamed as the Institute of Plant Improvement (today Grain Institute) and was directed by I. Papadakis (1927-1946). Papadakis was awarded membership to the Academy of Athens in 1927 and taught as a lecturer the courses of plant improvement in the Postgraduate

School, Department of Agriculture at the newly established University of Thessaloniki.

Early on, even in the second decade of the 20th century, two of the greatest agronomists, Panagiotis Gennadius and Spyridon Chasiotis, touched on the major problem of wheat sufficiency in the country in their writings. After the Asia Minor Disaster occurred, voices about the possibility of effectively dealing with the dramatic food production (wheat and cereals) issue began to be heard more often. To understand the magnitude of the problem, one should know that eminent agronomists such as Nikos Anagnostopoulos had publicly stated that Greece, while it can improve wheat production with new cultivation techniques, for reasons of soil and climate will never be able to become self-sufficient.

In 1932-1933, a multitude of well-known agronomists, using the platform offered to them by the magazine "Ergasia", argued that increasing the yield of wheat would be both possible and advisable, since it was a species, whose disposal is certain. Moreover, the strategic importance of self-sufficiency in cereals for the existence of a nation was obvious as the pressure from the settled population and the lack of credit for imports was a reality.

Finally, a discussion between the two factions of distinguished agronomists of the time, led by Ioannis Papadakis and Georgios Kyriakos, who took a position "for" and "against" grain sufficiency respectively. Kyriakos opposed Papadakis on the issue as he simply believed that the monoculture of wheat would be at the expense of exportable tobacco products, raisins, and livestock farming, by limiting other cereals used as animal feed, such as maize, barley, etc., a fact that partially vindicated him with the observed lack of parallel development of Greek livestock farming.

While the choice of wheat as a target is a political act, achieving this objective is a mainly technical process, because in addition to yielding new areas for wheat cultivation, to the detriment of other crops, it required finding new, more efficient varieties of wheat. And in the technical, scientific side of the issue, the pioneer agronomist Ioannis Papadakis excelled.

When he returned in 1923 from his studies at the Agricultural School of Gembloux, near Liège, in French-speaking Belgium (Wallonia), where he graduated "Avec Grande Distinction", he was only 20 years old. Ioannis Papadakis carried on his shoulders the burden of solving the most difficult problem of our country at the time, that is, the Food Issue, and he successfully carried it out. Papadakis was appointed to the Ministry of Agriculture in 1923 where, with the support of Sp. Hassiotis began experiments in a network for the evaluation of foreign varieties for the production of seed for wheat cultivation. Those works by Papadakis marked the beginning of systematically executed, centrally organized, planned and supervised agricultural research in our country. Papadakis was then transferred to the newly founded Larissa Plant Improvement Station (1925), which, by decision of Alexandros Papanastasiou in 1927, was transferred to Thessaloniki, where he (Papadakis) had the support of the Greek Refugee Settlement in Northern Greece. Ioannis Karamanos, the Director of Settlements since 1923, became General Director of Agriculture in 1928, and constantly strengthened the Station, upgrading it to the Institute for Plant Improvement in 1931.

Of the foreign varieties, the best was the Italian "Mentana" and the Australian "Canberra", which, because of its precocity, avoided the destructive effects of heated winds. Those two varieties, together with the variety "Limnos", sharply increased wheat production. Papadakis then worked on the creation of new wheat varieties of high yield, adaptability, and quality. In 1934, his work led to the creation of the wheat variety C38290, which was a cross between Italian Rieti and Australian Quality. It should be emphasized that Papadakis' role was an engagement in a long -lasting process, since the lab fertilization of a new variety and its introduction into cultivation required 16-17 years. It should be noted that until 1941, the use of fertilizers and pesticides in wheat cultivation was insignificant, while at that time herbicides were unknown, (Kounias, S. (2016).

The creation of the variety C38290 (Eucarpia I), known in the agricultural world as the "numero", was a milestone in the development of Greek agricultural research. This variety after 1950, and for 20 years, was sown on 70% of the wheat area in Greece. Ioannis Papadakis, succeeded in increasing national grain production from 300,000 that had been before 1930 to 850,000 tons in 1940, almost three times.

After World War II, and especially after 1950, wheat production increased greatly, and Greece reached wheat sufficiency in 1957. That increase was due mainly to fertilizers and nitrogen. Papadakis also made an important contribution in this field since he was a strong supporter of the spread of nitrogen fertilizers and drafted a study by the Technical Chamber of Greece for this purpose in 1946.

At this point, the contribution of the 24-year-old Papadakis in 1927 to the adoption of a legislative framework under Minister of Agriculture Papanastasiou should be highlighted, where, together with Koryzis (National Bank of Greece), he proposed measures to protect wheat production, by introducing the state collection of wheat and the safeguarding the income of farmers, who until then had been exposed to private merchants who were also credit providers at high prices. In addition to the technical support the agronomists provided farmers, they were part of a value chain that also provided economic support in this production and distribution process. A harmonious cooperation of politicians and technicians that, as the lawyers, economists and politicians Babis Alivizatos and Andreas Lambropoulos emphasize in their writings, led to the agricultural miracle of the interwar period (1922-1949).

The success in policy development of Papadakis did not gain him values in the Agrarian University of Greece located in Athens as he was not successful in gaining a position despite three attempts. Moreover, in 1945 I. Papadakis, was accused of being “motivated by anti-national views”, and, as a result, was expelled from the Institute he founded and provided the technical support of the country’s unique success in gaining a praise by the International Community while enabling his war-torn country to recover (Zoiopoulos, 2014).

Some others, however, knew who Papadakis was. In 1946, Papadakis was invited to Argentina to draw up the country's ecological map. He responded positively and immigrated permanently to Argentina. In 1953, he was invited by the UN’s FAO (Food and Agricultural Organization of the United Nations) to contribute to the agricultural development of Peru and Bolivia (1954-57). The FA O also commissioned him to make ecological maps in the countries of West Africa, India, Chile, and invited him to Rome to contribute to the study of food production in developing countries (1964-1968).

He became world famous for his ecological maps. In 1972, he was elected professor at the University of Buenos Aires (1972-1978).

The Greek State took a long time to show its gratitude to Papadakis. He was firstly recognized academically and honored by his second homeland, Argentina.

The Academy of Athens elected him a full member of the Agriculture Chair at the age of 80, and Athens University of Agriculture made him an honorary professor at the age of 90, the highest honor.

He was the author of many books, monographs, and articles on ecological agriculture and, through his experiments, developed the method of improving errors, known as the Papadakis method.

Papadakis tripled his wheat production, but, unfortunately, in his own country he remains largely unknown.

3. CONCLUSIVE REMARKS AND THE ESSENCE OF SUSTAINABLE DEVELOPMENT (INCLUSIVE GROWTH AND THE PAPANASTASIOU-KORYZIS-PAPADAKIS MODEL)

The focus of our research on the application of the Sustainable Development Goals (SDG'S) led us to reveal that a century ago a sociologist politician (Papanastasiou) in Greece developed an organizational perspective to engage science as a practical way to solve basic developmental issues in the main issue of food production. Fighting hunger is an issue in today's world including Greece now. The ghosts of Papanastasiou - Koryzis and Papadakis are hanging over Greece who is fragmented between private and public market interests and unable to see the importance of general and social protection of farmers in our case. Petty commercial mediators controlled then (as now) the market for agricultural produce defining the price level and seeds and fertilizers. The national market is thus fragmented, and huge imports are at play. Nowadays, Greece imports 90% of its soft wheat needs from neighboring countries. Coops are standing at a mere 8% of agricultural production. The time we are referring to, Greece was a war-torn devastated country which received a million and a half Greek refugees from Anatolia and required to import wheat to fulfill the basic needs of the prewar population. The humanitarian catastrophe was averted by a unique sociotechnical organization by the Papanastasiou Government who understood that import substitution of wheat was possible by means of a Recombination of State Policy, whose primary aim was to build: (1) a national market for food based on social protection of farmers' income (*by building coops*); (2) the scientific growth in plant science and its applications, both at import and local science engineering, financed by the state Agricultural Bank (a new Institution); and (3) to credit farmers who supplied the production along with the collection in prices set by the cost of imported wheat. The act of this system drove out of the small and bid market the merchants who had been creating a national market eliminated the value appropriated by the mediators and gave it to the farmers who saw their gains increase. That led to an increased production market for the general population in other sectors of the economy. All those happened under extreme and unfavorable market conditions. Greece experienced political turbulence in the 1930s with regime changes events which have attracted the attention of students of Greek social and political history ever since. However, there was a paradox experienced and managed by a Greek politician (i.e. Papanastasiou) who was educated in most of Europe as a sociologist and lawyer and who managed a social development model, called the Papanastasiou-Koryzis Model, which was unique in solving the food crisis in Greece and avoiding a humanitarian catastrophe. The public sociology model of developing state regulation of financing and science development for the State population within the national territory has been a unique paradigm whose success has yet to be recognized by the social science community. What is important is that the success of this Model was its focus on safeguarding the farmers' incomes and protecting them from local loan usurers. The role of public credit and the value creating of local varieties of seeds, instead of only imported ones, was a basic element in the dramatic increase of wheat production. Greece went to defend the county from the Axis in World War II in 1940 with sufficient wheat production. Despite many sociopolitical challenges in post war Greece, the institutions set by the Papanastasiou team were in effect acting till Greece's access to the European Union. Unfortunately, political conflict was a reason to stigmatize Papadakis who became a global expert at FAO and a real power force to transform Argentina. There may be a reason that now Argentina exports lemons to Naxos (Papadakis birthplace) while Naxiot lemons remain outside the local market.

Acknowledgments: Thanks to Dr Aikaterini Nikolarea for reading the manuscript and commenting on it and to Christina Vraka for her research assistance.

REFERENCES

Anastasiadis, G. (2003). Alexandros Papanastasiou. His important contribution towards Democracy and the Constitution. In: Anastasiadis, G. (Edit.) *The Creative relationship of Alexandros Papanastasiou with Thessaloniki and her University.* Athens: Foundation of the Greek Parliament for Parliamentarism and Democracy. (In Greek).

Chatziiosif, Ch. (2002). History of Greece during the 20th Century. The Interwar period 1922-1940. In Chatziiosif, Ch. (Ed.), *The Refugee Problem, the constants and the Changes in the Greek Economy* (Vol. B1). Bibliorama. (In Greek)

Karamanos, A. (2020). Skirtings of Creativity in Late Greece. The Life and Work of Ioannis Karamanos. In Kontogiorgis, E. (Ed.), *Ioannis Karamanos and the agrarian settlement of the refugees*. Papazisi. (In Greek)

Kounias, S. (2016). Ioannis Papadakis (Jean Papadakis) (1903-1997). In: Proceedings 29th PanHellenic Conference of Statistical Analysis of Risk in the Environment and the Economy, Thessaloniki & Naousa: Greek Statistical Institute. (In Greek).

Mavrogordatos, G. (1992). The unrepeatable achievement. [Athens.]. *Bulletin of the Center Asia-Minor Studies*, *9*, 9–12.

Mazower, M. (2002). *Greece and the economic crisis of the interwar period.* MIET. (In Greek)

Mazower, M. (2014). *Power networks in modern Greece.* Alexandreia Publishing. (In Greek)

Papadakis, I. (1988). Ioannis Papadakis for Ioannis Karamanos. In Karamanos, A. (Ed.), *Enlightened Ideas in Modern Greece. The Life and Work of Ioannis Karamanos*. Papazisi. (In Greek)

Papadakis, J. (1987). The increase of the income of peasants as a basis of economic development: The Greek model of Papanastasiou-Koryzis. Proceedings Academy of Athens, vol. 62, series A, pg. 59-77. (In Greek).

Papagaroufali, E. (1985-1986). Greek Female Farmer and women's cooperatives. Athens: Research Centre for the Women of the Mediterranean. (In Greek).

Pelagidis, E. *The Refugees of Macedonia in the economic life of the country*, Thessaloniki: Society for Macedonia Studies. (In Greek).

Zoiopoulos, P. (2003), The Epos od Sitikon, in Historika Eleythrotypia Newspaper, Vol. 185, May 2003.

Zoiopoulos, P. (2014). *Two blades of grass. The agrarian miracle*. Armos. (In Greek)

Chapter 5

Thoughts on Maritime Power in the East Mediterranean and the Potential of Greece

Ioannis K. Voudouris
https://orcid.org/0000-0003-0928-3417
Frederick University, Cyprus

ABSTRACT

The study examines the evolving maritime strategic model of Greece within the Eastern Mediterranean. It assesses the transformation of Greece's traditional conservative maritime policy towards a more comprehensive strategy, as expedited by contemporary geopolitical dynamics and shifting regional alignments. Greece's strategic advantages include its privileged geographic position, distinguished merchant marine capabilities, and steadfast adherence to international law. It evaluates Greece's potential to enhance regional stability through the protection of critical sea lanes, safeguarding of energy infrastructure and development of strategic partnerships with Cyprus, Israel, Egypt, and Libya in conjunction with the EU and the NATO allies and affiliates. The research further illuminates the symbiotic relationship between naval capability and economic prosperity, emphasizing on the shipbuilding infrastructure and the blue economy

DOI: 10.4018/979-8-3373-8790-1.ch005

initiatives. The findings advocate for an integrated maritime strategy that harmonizes naval modernization, diplomatic engagement and economic development.

Greece's highly advantageous geostrategic position at the connection of three continents; secondly, the intrinsic symmetry between Alliance objectives and Greece's national defense imperatives, characterized also by an absence of conflicting or competing interests; and thirdly, the nation's substantial merchant and military maritime capabilities that represent a crucial strategic asset in maintaining regional stability, particularly in addressing provocative actions that contravene established principles of international law. Naturally, the topic of naval power is interdisciplinary bringing together geopolitical strategy, international law and each of the nations' legacy and aspirations.

The objectives of this present inquiry are three:

First, it reviews the theoretical framework that warrants effective implementation, alongside an analysis of the multifaceted benefits that would accrue therefrom. To this end, the study commences with a comprehensive review of the theoretical foundations of naval power -that are relevant to our case- in conjunction with the principles of the Law of the Sea.

Second, the analysis evaluates the relative merits of prioritizing presence in East Libya, Cyprus, or expanding operations to encompass the Red Sea and East African maritime domains.

Third, it elaborates on Greece's optimal strategy for expanding its naval presence in the EMed, setting tests for success while examining the socioeconomic advantages of such strategic investment.

1. ASPECTS OF NAVAL POLICY

In examining the geopolitics of the region, it is necessary to ground the analysis within the established theoretical framework of naval strategy doctrines. By controlling the sea, a country (or the alliance) can ensure that its own military and merchant ships can move around at will, while its rivals are forced either to stay in port or to try to evade it. It also enables free use of amphibious operations that can expand ground-based strategic options. This principle remains fundamental to naval discourse, whereas its interpretation and practical application have evolved considerably, generating substantial academic debate and strategic recalibration. This section mainly endeavors to review the evolution of relevant theories, offering a critical examination of conventional wisdom - while maintaining appropriate deference to established strategic principles - than exhausting the discourse. Moreover, it extends the proposition that contemporary understanding of naval power necessitates a sophisticated approach, one that shall recognize its inherently relative and contextual nature within modern geopolitical dynamics. Of paramount importance is the recognition that naval power serves as the primary mechanism through which nations project sovereignty beyond their territorial waters. This principle is particularly salient for Greece in asserting its sovereign rights within the EMed theatre. The region's strategic significance - characterized by its energy resources, critical trade routes, and multifaceted security considerations - necessitates the formulation and implementation of a comprehensive naval strategy. Consequently, Greece must prioritize the systematic development of its green and blue water naval capabilities across several critical domains.

The theories of naval dominance, primarily shaped by the seminal works of Alfred Thayer Mahan and Julian Corbett, continue to exert a profound influence on contemporary naval strategy and geopolitical thought. Central to Mahan' s thesis (1890) is the emphasis on controlling key maritime chokepoints, concentrating naval forces, and maintaining robust commercial shipping networks. (Mahan, 1918) The patriarch of naval strategy identified six fundamental elements contributing to sea power: geographic position, physical conformation,[2] (Author unknown, n.d.) extent of territory, (Author unknown, n.d.) population, national character, and the nature of government. We respectively examine them as follows:

Regarding the factor of "extend of territory", Greece also fulfils it as it mainly populated in the coastline than the *terra firma.* In accordance with the EU Statistics, some 44 of its 51 provinces of the country are coastal regions, while 98% of its population lives within 50 km from the sea. (Eurostat, 2013) Greece also fulfils the factor of "national character" (OECD, 2020) of its nearly with its deep maritime heritage and blue economy orientation. In particular, as per EU Commission data, Greece's Blue Economy sectors represent a significant component of the national economy, employing approximately 446,000 individuals and generating €6.5 billion in Gross Value Added (GVA). (European Commission, 2023)

The sector demonstrated remarkable resilience in 2021, with employment reaching 11.4% of the national workforce, marking a substantial recovery from 6.8% in 2020 and approaching pre-pandemic levels of 14.6% recorded in 2019. Moreover, the Blue Economy's contribution to national GVA reached 4.1% in 2021, showing notable improvement from 2.3% in 2020, though still shy of the 5.5% achieved in 2019. Particularly noteworthy is the *maritime transport*, which accounts for 14.1% of the Blue Economy's GVA. In addition, this disparity between fleet ownership and economic contribution suggests substantial untapped potential for growth in Greece's maritime sector (i.e. shipyards, green growth etc.).

With regard to the criterion of "population", "national character" and "governmental commitment" we observe a historical maritime nation endowed with modern maritime skills, and governmental commitment to essential maritime power (naval and merchant). The GVA figures mentioned above seem modest considering that Greece remains the top ship owning nation in the world, as Greek shipowners with 5,514 ships (in 2021) control approximately 21% of the global fleet, in terms of capacity (dwt). (Union of Greek Shipowners, 2023) Another detail that is worth noticing is the maritime culture and education (perhaps also paideia) of Greek population. Besides the history and tradition, Greece hosts two main universities that teach Maritime Transport Studies (Piraeus and Chios) plus they are numerous postgraduate university programs in maritime law and shipping business throughout the country; not mentioning the programs of study offered by the colleges. Moreover, it has 12 Merchant Marine Academies that provide a constant flow of officers, plus around 50 Maritime High Schools that prepare high school students for the profession. Compared to the rest of the Europe or even the US, Greece is one the leading global centres of maritime education. Another notable factor is that Greece is the only country in the EU and in the Western World that has an independent ministry of Shipping and Insular Policy.

As regards the criteria of "geographical position" and "physical conformation" Greece self-evidently fulfils them both; it is located at the heart of EMed, the only neighboring three continents and in proximity to the Black Sea and the Suez. In particular, the fundamental principles of geographical positioning, are all highly applicable to Greece's strategic considerations. According to Mahan's doctrine, maritime dominance is key to national power, and Greece, with its extensive coastline and strategic positioning, possesses the natural capacity required to leverage sea power effectively. This is particularly evident in Greece's responsibility to exert port state control over a vast sea area, encompassing hundreds of islands and vital ports such as Piraeus, Thessaloniki, Alexandroupolis, Patras, and Souda Bay. These ports, along with Limassol and Larnaca in Cyprus (which are also part of the greater Hellenic commonwealth), are crucial not only for the country's economic, political, and social stability but also serve as essential hubs for logistics and power projection. The strategic importance of these ports extends beyond national interests, enabling Greece to exert influence regionally and globally through its alliances with NATO and the European Union and ensure maritime security against non-traditional threats such as piracy and terrorism.

Julian Corbett's oeuvre on maritime strategy compliments Mahan and expands to the view that total naval dominance was necessary for achieving strategic objectives.[3] (Corbett, 2012) In particular, Corbett argued that control of the sea suggests the control of maritime communications - rather than outright control of the sea area - was the primary function of naval power. While both land and naval strategy involve communications, they serve different purposes. On land, communications mainly relate to supply lines and troop movements, while at sea, they encompass both military operations and commercial shipping routes. Unlike land warfare, which focuses on conquering territory, naval warfare's primary goal is to control sea-based communication channels. In practice, nowadays, command of the sea or command of communications is fundamentally about controlling maritime routes, passages, underwater cables and pipelines. Corbett also delves into the concept of constitution of fleets and the concentration – dispersal of force. In particular, ships in a fleet reflect the strategic and tactical thinking of their time. Their design and classification change based on both current military ideas and available technology. More broadly, ships evolve according to prevailing theories of warfare, even when those theories aren't formally stated. In naval operations, one must also carefully distinguish between concentration and mass, for this distinction yields profound strategic insights. The formation of mass, while powerful, sacrifices two crucial advantages: the element of surprise and tactical flexibility. Therefore, the true mastery of concentration lies in maintaining strategic ambiguity for as long as possible. This strategic patience and calculated ambiguity keep adversaries uncertain and enhances tactical advantage, making our eventual deployment all the more formidable. (Corbett, 2012, pp. 78–83; Mahan, 1905, p. 316) Concerning Greece, these two are particularly relevant given that it primarily needs a fleet - as it has not got any yet - and secondly needs to decide on the method of dispersion of that fleet.

Freedman (2013) unfolds a holistic overview about strategy analyzing history as well as the works of important thinkers. Overall, he argues that the control has always been more than a purely military tool. It is also a means for nations to exert influence and project power in a way that is less overtly aggressive than land-based military force. (Freedman, 2013, p. 33) Firstly he too endorses the view that once naval control is obtained, however, it is usually not maintained for a long time. (Freedman, 2013, p. 117) In essence, Freedman advocates for the integration of maritime power into a comprehensive strategic framework that encompasses diplomatic, (Freedman, 2013, p. 163; Schelling, 2020) economic, and military dimensions as well as cooperations and alliances. (Freedman, 2005, p. 604; Le Mière, 2014) Rather than considering naval capabilities in isolation, he proposes a synergistic approach that harmonizes maritime assets with other forms of state power, including air and land forces, as well as non-military instruments such as economic sanctions and diplomatic negotiations. This holistic strategy enables nations to leverage their maritime forces as a versatile instrument for achieving political objectives, transcending the limitations of purely military engagements at sea. Such an integrated approach aligns well with Greece's desired international image as a constructive and cooperative actor, rather than a revisionist or expansionist state with nouveau-colonial ambitions. By adopting this multifaceted strategic posture, Greece can project soft power and foster positive relations with both allies and third countries, reinforcing its position as a stabilizing force in the region while simultaneously advancing its national interests through a constructive, cooperative and sophisticated approach to international relations.

Building on the classical ideas of Mahan and Corbett, contemporary theorists such as Borgerson, Germond, Bueger & Edmunds, Till and Vego have adapted these to the modern context. We present their thoughts relevant to our case, as detailed below:

Borgerson's (2009) analysis posits that the control over maritime chokepoints and sea lines of communications (SLOCs) has emerged as a critical determinant of geopolitical power in the 21st century. (Borgerson, 2009, p. 14) He underscores the strategic significance of maritime routes, which facilitate the global flow of commodities, energy resources, and raw materials, rendering them indispensable to the global economy. Borgerson argues that a maritime state's capacity to secure and control these vital maritime corridors not only bolsters its economic security but also amplifies its geopolitical influence. The Mediterranean region, in particular, is profoundly affected by the strategic importance of regional maritime chokepoints such as the Gibraltar, Strait of Hormuz, the Bab el-Mandeb Strait, and the Suez Canal. These narrow and vulnerable stretches of sea serve as conduits for a substantial portion of trade and energy supplies, making them pivotal to regional and global economic stability. Borgerson stresses that the uninterrupted flow of maritime commerce is essential for maintaining global economic equilibrium, thus rendering control over these chokepoints a strategic imperative for powerful nations. For Greece, Borgerson's analysis holds particular significance, as it holds multiple choke points to the Black Sea and is strategically placed in proximity to Suez Canal. The nation's ability to secure the aforementioned SLOCs and project power in collaboration with regional allies such as Israel, Egypt and Cyprus would be crucial for ensuring both its economic prosperity and regional influence.

Germond (2015) posits the importance of developing a "maritime security governance" in order to contain the modern asymmetrical threats such as piracy, terrorism, human trafficking, and environmental challenges that all require comprehensive response. He also acknowledges that maritime power projection assumes paramount importance, though its utility extends well beyond conventional military operations. In particular, the pursuit of national security imperatives is connected with the advancement of the liberal international order. The prevailing security doctrine operates within a geopolitical framework predicated upon fundamental societal distinctions - namely, the dichotomy between stable, secure domestic entities and potentially volatile external actors. This paradigm legitimizes the assertion that domestic security necessitates proactive engagement beyond sovereign territories and territorial waters. Furthermore, this security doctrine maintains that the preservation of domestic interests requires the capacity to exercise meaningful influence over external entities, both through normative measures and, when necessary, direct intervention. Such projection of security encompasses multiple dimensions: the propagation of developmental initiatives, implementation of sound governance principles, dissemination of liberal democratic values, and establishment of security protocols. Additionally, it extends to preventive diplomacy, crisis management, and peace enforcement operations, necessitating the maintenance of conventional force projection capabilities. (Germond, 2015, p. 56) He moreover acknowledges the critical importance of multilateral cooperation in maritime security, emphasizing that it is a collective endeavor necessitating collaboration among states and international organizations. (Germond, 2015, pp. 85, 87, 89, 97, 127+) This perspective is particularly salient given the transnational nature of maritime threats, which frequently transcend jurisdictional boundaries and involve multiple stakeholders, such as port state control and coast guard. In this context, we would advocate for further cooperative frameworks such as the European Union's Common Security and Defense Policy (CSDP), as recently exemplified by the recent "Operation Aspides," and NATO's "Operation Sea Guardian." These initiatives align with Germond's proposed governance model, demonstrating the practical application of his theoretical framework. Furthermore, Germond argues for the efficacy of non-military strategies in maritime security. These include the development of robust legal frameworks, the enforcement of international sanctions, the implementation of disciplinary measures within international organizations such as the International Maritime Organization (IMO), and the pivotal role of port state control and coast guards in deterrence and low-level enforcement. This holistic approach facilitates a more flexible and dynamic response to maritime security challenges, enabling various actors to address a spectrum of evolving threats.

In practice, as a significant maritime nation, Greece must strike a delicate balance between enhancing its military capabilities and fostering broader governance initiatives. To achieve these objectives, Greece should prioritize regional cooperation with other Mediterranean states and international allies, while simultaneously strengthening its presence with supranational organizations such as the EU, NATO, and the IMO. Additionally, engaging private sector actors in maritime security initiatives can contribute to a more comprehensive and effective strategy. By adopting this multifaceted approach, Greece can play a pivotal role in fostering a more stable and secure maritime environment, aligning with Germond's vision of maritime security governance. For example, the recent Houthi attacks on Greek vessels serve as a pertinent example of how this approach can be operationalized. While Greece has demonstrated its commitment through military means, such as assuming command of Operation Aspides in the Red Sea, it can simultaneously pursue diplomatic and legal avenues. This may include leveraging its position within the IMO to address the issue on a global stage and exploring legal mechanisms to impose measures against state actors like Turkey, Yemen, and Iran, who may be directly or indirectly involved in these maritime security challenges.

Germond (2015) also highlights that key maritime chokepoints, like the Suez Canal, are critical, as they provide EU with routes for oil and liquefied natural gas (LNG) from the Middle East to Europe and North America. (Germond, 2015, pp. 20–21, 28+, 79, 85, 154) In light of the escalating global energy demand, scholars anticipate that any disturbance to critical maritime routes - whether stemming from political instability, piracy, or military confrontations - could precipitate far-reaching ramifications for international energy markets, potentially catalyzing price surges and supply shortages. This link between maritime security and energy geopolitics holds particular salience for Greece, especially in the context of recent natural gas discoveries in the Eastern Mediterranean. Also, as Greece and its sister state, Cyprus, aspire to establish themselves as regional energy hubs, mainly through electric connectivity the imperative to safeguard the maritime corridors connecting their gas and electricity commodities to European and global markets becomes increasingly pronounced. Consequently, Greece's naval strategy must necessarily prioritize the protection of these vital sea lanes, pipelines, and submarine power and telecommunication cables, thereby ensuring the uninterrupted flow of energy resources. This strategic imperative encompasses safeguarding against a diverse array of potential threats, including but not limited to piracy, regional conflicts, and geopolitical disputes with neighboring states.

Bueger & Edmunds (2017) argue that maritime security has evolved beyond traditional state-centric paradigms that primarily focused on inter-state conflicts and the control of territorial waters to include non-state actors and asymmetric threats. (Bueger & Edmunds, 2017) These non-traditional challenges, which eschew conventional state-to-state naval confrontations, manifest in various forms such as piracy, maritime terrorism, and cyberattacks targeting critical maritime infrastructure. The complexity of these threats necessitates a paradigm shift in maritime security governance, encompassing enhanced law enforcement capabilities at sea, sophisticated surveillance and intelligence-sharing mechanisms, and fostering closer collaboration between state and non-state actors, including non-governmental organizations (NGOs). This approach emphasizes on proactive measures and addressing issues at their source, reflecting a growing recognition that maritime security is a collective responsibility transcending state boundaries. For nations like Greece, whose economic and political stability is linked to maritime trade and energy resources, and it is relatively inexperienced and vulnerable to ballistic attacks and cyberwar, the imperative to address these non-traditional security challenges is particularly acute. The country faces additional pressures from asymmetric immigration flows via maritime routes, further underscoring the need for a comprehensive and adaptive security strategy. This entails not only modernizing naval capabilities but also investing in multi-stakeholder governance frameworks and strengthening regional and international cooperation. Recent events have underscored the urgency of this evolving security paradigm. The sophisticated and well-planned attacks by Houthi rebels on shipping routes in the Red Sea have inflicted significant economic damage on countries such as Egypt, Cyprus, Greece, and Israel, highlighting the far-reaching consequences of localized maritime threats. Similarly, the ongoing challenges posed by immigration flows from Libya and Turkey via maritime channels exemplify the complex, transnational nature of contemporary maritime security issues.

Likewise, Till (2018) emphasizes on the importance of sea control in the context of modern geopolitical challenges, including piracy, terrorism, with reference to the need to secure energy supplies. (Till, 2018, p. 318) Till examines the paramount importance of sea control in addressing contemporary geopolitical challenges within an increasingly interconnected global economy. He posits that the ability to exert influence over maritime domains has become crucial in safeguarding national interests and maintaining international stability. His perspective extends beyond the traditional military concept of sea control, presenting it as a multifaceted method that encompasses economic, political, and security dimensions. This comprehensive view is particularly salient in the context of combating transnational threats such as piracy and terrorism. This approach analysis also resonates with the work of Borgerson (2009), who emphasized the strategic significance of controlling maritime chokepoints. Furthermore, it aligns with the broader concept of "maritime security governance" as proposed by Germond (2015) and provides a holistic approach to understanding the complex interplay between various actors and factors in the maritime domain.

Vego (2019) acknowledges that although naval powers of lesser strength typically embrace defensive maritime strategies during peacetime, historical precedent shows notable exceptions to this pattern. In some instances, a numerically or technologically inferior naval force may pivot toward an expansive maritime strategy, often accompanied by ambitious fleet modernization and expansion programs. However, it is crucial to recognize that such peacetime offensive stance does not necessarily translate to wartime strategic execution. (Vego, 2019, p. 2) In parallel, Vego has recognized the importance of space and geography. The strategic positioning of nations relative to their maritime and terrestrial boundaries presents distinct implications for their naval capabilities and defensive stance. (Vego, 2005) For instance, nations possessing greater maritime frontiers than land borders exist in a peninsular configuration, offering inherent advantages for maritime supremacy. However, this geographic disposition often necessitates substantial resource allocation toward terrestrial defense, potentially constraining naval development. Insular nations, those situated entirely on single or multiple major landmasses surrounded by water, represent a unique strategic category. In particular, Crete and Cyprus and England demonstrate how resource-limited insular states naturally gravitate toward maritime endeavors for prosperity. Yet, this geographic advantage becomes truly potent only when coupled with effective control over adjacent waters. (Vego, 2005) For example, the struggle for Crete in May 1941 showed, among other things, that in the modern era, sea control could not be obtained without the control of the air. (Vego, 2019, p. 75; Gundelach, 1981, pp. 220, 447) Therefore, the strategic value of insularity maintains its potency even across multiple large islands, provided they maintain sufficient geographic cohesion. However, when a nation's territory disperses across numerous islands spanning vast maritime expanses, as exemplified by the Philippines or Indonesia, this fragmentation compromises the territorial concentration vital for robust maritime power projection and impedes the development of cohesive naval capabilities and maritime influence. However, the example of Greece may not apply here. Greece's geography is a combination of solid *terra firma* and archipelagic waters. Vego also advocates for a multidimensional, "jointness" approach. (Vego, 2005, 73+; Vego, 2019, 4, 94+; Vitale, 1995, p. 27) His thoughts are not delimited by the traditional segmentation about the components and understands air, land, and sea power employed in joint operations. This paradigm recognizes that the complexities of contemporary warfare necessitate naval forces to operate in close coordination and formation with air and land components to achieve strategic objectives, rather than in isolation. This integrated approach enhances the operational flexibility of military forces, enabling them to respond more effectively to a diverse array of threats, ranging from conventional state actors to asymmetric challenges such as terrorism, piracy, attack from proxies and cyber threats. For Greece, the adoption of Vego's framework would entail developing a naval strategy that extends beyond the mere control of ports and maritime spaces, instead integrating its naval capabilities with other branches of the military. Greece's unique geography, characterized by its numerous economically active islands, extensive coastline, and rich blue economy, coupled with its responsibility to protect distant Cyprus, necessitates an adaptive military force capable of operating across multiple domains. To counter potential adversaries, Greece could benefit from integrating superior naval operations, exemplified by the HN FDI frigates (Belharra class), with air force superiority, as demonstrated by the recently acquired Rafale, F16V and F-35 stealth jets. This integration, combined with active maritime patrols, surveillance drones, and air superiority missions, would provide Greece with enhanced situational awareness and the ability to project power well beyond its territorial waters. Furthermore, the synergy between naval and land forces, particularly in securing coastal areas and defending critical infrastructure such as ports and energy installations, would offer Greece a more comprehensive and robust defense posture. Vego's emphasis on joint operations suggests that Greece's naval forces should foster close collaboration with NATO allies and Israel, particularly in areas of intelligence sharing, joint exercises, and coordinated defense strategies. Greece's strategic position as a maritime hub in the Eastern Mediterranean underscores the importance of leveraging its alliances to counteract regional threats by revisionist countries, such as Turkey's increasingly assertive maritime claims, while ensuring the security of vital SLOCs and energy infrastructure in the region. In essence Greece can use its fleet and resources to better protect Israel and Egypt that are facing existential threats. In order to achieve this, Greece's strategy could be further enhanced by investments in cutting-edge technologies, including cyber defense systems, unmanned naval and aerial vehicles, and advanced surveillance equipment, which are critical components of modern joint operations. By cultivating a flexible and adaptive military force structure that seamlessly integrates naval, air, and land capabilities, Greece would be better positioned to address a wide spectrum of security challenges, thereby safeguarding the alliance's maritime interests and bolstering regional peace and stability.

2. PLAYING BY THE RULES COMES AT A PRICE

In formulating a maritime strategy and naval power projection, Greece fundamentally anchors its approach within the framework of the UNCLOS. As a signatory state to the treaty and with reference to the jurisprudence of the International Court of Justice (Hague), Greece maintains legitimate sovereign prerogatives over its continental shelf and Exclusive Economic Zone (EEZ), encompassing jurisdictional rights pertaining to resource exploration, exploitation, and management thereof. However, the Mediterranean Sea's complex geopolitical landscape presents diverse political challenges that interfere with legal solutions, notably due to the national strategies non-ratification and non-adherence of certain littoral states - most prominently Turkey - to the UNCLOS provisions. This legal divergence has precipitated persistent diplomatic tensions, hot incidents and disputes concerning sovereignty, the delimitation of EEZs and continental shelf boundaries, thereby creating an intricate impasse of competing (lawful or unfounded) legal rights. We shall proceed and analyze how these matters influence and shape the maritime strategic framework of Greece, with particular attention to their implications for national policy and regional naval operations.

Thus, Greece's maritime policy framework presents a seemingly balanced duality that merits careful examination, particularly within the context of law of the sea and regional geopolitics. The framework's foundational element rests upon Greece's unwavering commitment to the United Nations Convention on the Law of the Sea (UNCLOS), which serves two purposes: establishing a robust legal foundation for maritime interests while simultaneously positioning Greece as a principled actor within the international legal order. Recent diplomatic achievements exemplify this approach, notably through enhanced cooperation among Mediterranean stakeholders, including Greece, Egypt, Cyprus, and Israel. Moreover, the implementation of the "calm waters" policy vis-à-vis Turkey over the past two years has markedly reduced the risk of military escalation, fostering an environment conducive to diplomatic dialogue and mutual trust-building initiatives. Greece's interpretation and application of UNCLOS demonstrates an adherence to fundamental principles of equity and justice, suggesting a continued commitment to peaceful dispute resolution absent external intervention.

However, this measured diplomatic stance, while laudable for its contribution to regional stability and economic cooperation, leads to certain strategic limitations that warrant consideration. On the one hand, the country maintains a distinctly conservative and measured approach, fundamentally attached in the pursuit of equitable diplomatic solutions with its neighboring states; on the other, the same stance effectively circumscribing its naval operations within the confines of its territorial waters. Thus, the framework's conservative nature effectively constrains Greece's maritime operations within territorial waters, raising questions about its utility within broader alliance objectives. This self-imposed restraint is particularly evident in Greece's reluctance to unilaterally extend its territorial waters or establish a contiguous zone without securing prior diplomatic consensus has a deep effect on the "blue water" naval capability of the county. Such hesitation has generated two significant challenges: First, it has resulted in a persistent diplomatic stalemate with Turkey, effectively impeding Greece's ability to assert its continental shelf rights and establish its EEZ in relation to neighboring states. The consequent inability to exploit offshore hydrocarbon resources and other maritime assets represents a substantial opportunity cost in terms of unrealized economic potential. Second, the restricted scope of maritime control, particularly the reluctance to expand territorial waters and/or declare a contiguous zone, significantly limits the operational effectiveness of Greek enforcement authorities, such the port state control (PSC), the customs, tax, police etc. This limitation becomes particularly problematic in addressing contemporary challenges, such as the proliferation of Russian oil smuggling operations in the Aegean Sea, facilitated by the emergence of "dark" fleet activities, or even the sabotage to pipelines and cables.

3. THE TENETS OF GREEK MARITIME STRATEGY

Greece's strategic focus on safeguarding critical maritime interests goes hand in hand with enhancing its role within the broader Mediterranean and global geopolitical arena. Firstly, a proactive stance should constructively augment its role in concert with its allies. Conversely, a failure to project presence and/or implement any such efforts may precipitate a diminution of Greece's geopolitical sway, potentially leading to a decline in its strategic relevance, its diplomatic leverage and economic influence - a scenario that would also invariably impact the interests of its allied nations. In this milieu, we hold that a formulation and implementation of a robust maritime strategy is *sine qua non* for Greece. By adroitly leveraging its advantageous geographical position and cultivating strategic partnerships, Greece can position itself as an indispensable actor in securing vital maritime corridors. This multifaceted approach not only serves to safeguard Greece's national interests but also contributes significantly to regional stability and security of its allies. Furthermore, it elevates Greece's status as an important contributor in the intricate geopolitical tapestry of the Eastern Mediterranean, potentially enhancing on the global stage. The sensible execution of such a strategy could catalyze a transformation in Greece's geopolitical standing, enabling it to transcend its conservative role and emerge as an active member in regional security architecture; in particular:

Inevitably we revert to perennial question that confronts heads of state when presented with the option of spending billions for modern warships: "What am I supposed to do with them?"; "How can these assets be optimally utilized?" In other words, leaders grapple with the fundamental question of maritime power projection: whether to prioritize the control of strategic ports or to assert dominance over the maritime space; i.e. controlling only points A and B or the dominion over maritime spaces (the vector between A to B)? This dichotomy presents itself as a discourse on the nature of sea power, transcending mere tactical considerations to embrace broader geopolitical, economic, and diplomatic dimensions. The former approach necessitates a land presence, often manifesting as occupation, while the latter, though potentially less overtly aggressive, is constrained by temporal and logistical limitations. Both strategies offer distinct advantages and challenges, suggesting that an optimal approach likely involves a prudent combination of the two.

On the one hand, the control of strategic ports is of paramount importance for several reasons. Primarily, ports serve as essential logistical and resupply hubs for naval forces, enabling sustained operations and power projection. A good example is Greece's control of the naval port of Souda Bay, one of the most strategically significant naval bases in the Mediterranean. This asset allows Greece to exert influence throughout the Eastern Mediterranean while simultaneously functioning as a crucial logistical hub for NATO operations. Complementing this military advantage, the merchant port of Piraeus, one of Europe's largest, offers Greece a dual benefit of economic and strategic leverage. This transformation of Piraeus into a major commercial gateway underscores the importance of the blue economy as geo-economical factor. (Psaraftis & Pallis, 2012). Furthermore, port control extends beyond naval operations and commercial throughput: it provides a secure point of entry into the hinterland, enabling the reception, staging, and onward movement of expeditionary forces, critical supplies, strategic cargoes and, where appropriate, associated commercial activity. In fact, without secure port access, any military campaign or humanitarian mission venturing into the interior would swiftly encounter severe logistical challenges, potentially leading to operational nightmares. Especially, strategic ports serve as multifaceted force multipliers, exerting influence across the spectrum of international relations, from peacetime diplomacy to full-scale conflict. These we consider to be genuine maritime assets that enable nations to project soft power through humanitarian assistance and disaster relief operations, thereby enhancing their geopolitical standing and fostering goodwill among the international community. (Tangredi, 2013, 11+) Concurrently, strategic ports possess the latent capacity to function as critical chokepoints, offering the potential to constrain adversarial movements and influence the strategic calculus of rival powers during periods of heightened tension or outright hostilities.

On the other, patrolling maritime spaces, while potentially less provocative than maintaining a land-based military presence, is inherently limited by temporal constraints and resource scarcity. Vessels must contend with the need for regular resupply and maintenance, which can curtail their operational effectiveness over extended periods; and this represents a weakness of the system as the prolonged operations cause fatigue and dullness. (Speller, 2024, p. 28) Ultimately, our logic commands that the synthesis - consisting of both port control and maritime patrolling - emerges as the most efficacious model, adaptable to the unique geopolitical landscape of each region. This multifaceted strategy is further augmented by the advent of modern warships, which serve as formidable sea-based fortresses and quasi-ports in their own right. These vessels, with their extensive operational range and capacity for sustained deployment, effectively project power from the relative safety of outer anchorages and international waters. Their strategic positioning not only enhances their defensive posture against potential threats but also enables them to exert influence over vast maritime domains. The Eastern Mediterranean exemplifies this paradigm, where the discovery of substantial natural gas reserves coupled with the interconnections of pipelines and cables has significantly elevated the geopolitical importance of maritime domains, especially in the vicinity of Greece, Egypt, Cyprus and Israel. Greece's capacity to assert over some of these waters, safeguard its exclusive economic zone (EEZ), and secure vital SLOCs is paramount not only for protecting its economic interests but also for maintaining regional stability. In particular, for Greece, the most efficacious strategy likely entails a synergistic approach that combines port control with maritime dominance. By securing strategically the triangle of

Souda, Larnaca, and Derna, while simultaneously projecting naval power across the Eastern Mediterranean acting as the long arm of the alliance, Greece can ensure the unimpeded flow of commerce, protect its energy infrastructure, and maintain a credible deterrent posture against potential adversaries. This is particularly pertinent in light of Turkey's increasingly assertive challenges to Greek and Egyptian maritime spaces.

This evolution would not only redound to Greece's benefit but would also serve the collective interests of its allies and partners, fostering a more stable and secure Mediterranean region. Pursuant to contemporary strategic analysis, Greece's maritime framework, when systematically implemented, possesses the inherent potential to fundamentally recalibrate the nation's geopolitical positioning and establish its prominence as a pivotal sovereign actor within the modern international order. While Vego's theoretical framework (hereinafter the "Vego elements") delineates the essential components of peacetime maritime strategy, (Vego, 2019, p. 4) it is imperative to acknowledge that the efficacy of such strategic initiatives is intrinsically contingent upon the harmonious alignment of economic and diplomatic mechanisms. The successful execution of joint operations necessarily presupposes the optimal functionality of these underlying infrastructural elements. Therefore, any comprehensive maritime strategic framework must be anchored in sustainable principles and operate in accordance with the legitimate interests of the broader international community, while maintaining robust institutional coordination across all relevant operational domains. To this end, the following supplementary criteria must be incorporated into the core strategy:

- Economic Sustainability: Maritime ventures must demonstrate viable long-term financial sustainability and contribute to national economic growth;
- International Legal Compliance: All strategic initiatives shall strictly adhere to international law, law of the sea and established conventions;
- Cultural Diplomatic Leadership: Enhancement of Greece's position as a commonwealth leader through cultural diplomacy and soft power projection;

- Regional Cooperation: Development of collaborative frameworks with neighboring states through diplomatic persuasion rather than coercive measures and gunboat diplomacy, thereby fostering mutual longstanding trust and regional stability.

The following analysis embodies these elements in our reasoning in greater detail and specificity:

3.1 Maritime Security and Protection of Energy Interests

The EMed represents a significant repository of natural gas reserves, with substantial proven deposits within the EEZs of Israel, Cyprus, Egypt and Cyrenaica (east Libya). Preliminary assessments indicate that Greece's EEZ may also harbor considerable hydrocarbon resources of strategic importance, as recently evidenced by Chevron's interest in energy exploration. (Reuters, 2025) The protection and secure exploitation of these resources, along with the safeguarding of associated export infrastructure, constitute primary objectives for the Hellenic forces.

In pursuing its maritime energy interests, Greece must adopt a methodical, two-pronged approach: First, prioritizing the development and utilization of domestic energy resources to establish credibility and operational competence; second, engaging in multilateral partnerships based on mutual benefit and transparent cooperation. This sequential strategy serves to demonstrate Greece's commitment to responsible resource management and its rejection of unilateral or predatory practices. Furthermore, Greece's energy security framework should incorporate mechanisms for benefit-sharing and collaborative development with regional stakeholders. Such an approach would not only foster trust and diplomatic goodwill but also create a more stable and sustainable environment for resource exploitation. Unilateral actions, while potentially expedient, risk undermining long-term strategic interests and regional stability. Therefore, Greece's energy strategy must balance national interests with multilateral cooperation, ensuring both resource security and diplomatic legitimacy.

3.2 Deterrence and Defense

In light of the current landscape in the EMed and adjacent regions, Greece confronts multifaceted security challenges, primarily emanating from Turkey's assertive posture regarding maritime boundary delimitation and its revisionist territorial aspirations. (Daniel & Lindenstrauss, 2023; Yanarocak, 2021) The security environment is further complicated by Russian antagonism (hostility), (Russian Government, 2022) the Turkish-aligned Tripoli regime in western Libya, (Various international stakeholders, 2019) and Iran's proxy forces, notably the Houthi movement (Bockmann, 2024; Lloyd's List, 2024a, 2024b) and Hezbollah, (Ghaddar et al., 2024) whose activities pose significant threats to maritime commerce and navigation security.

To safeguard its strategic interests and uphold international maritime law, Greece must maintain a robust naval presence, particularly in the Red Sea and Eastern Mediterranean theatres. Such deployment serves multiple strategic objectives: it establishes credible deterrence against potential adversaries, ensures the protection of Greece's sovereign rights, and secures vital maritime trade routes critical to the Greek merchant fleet's operations. Furthermore, Greece's naval presence aligns with broader regional security interests, potentially extending protective capabilities to partner nations including Egypt, Jordan, Israel, and Cyprus. This strategic positioning not only serves to maintain open sea lines of communication but also reinforces Greece's role as a guarantor of maritime security and commercial stability in these strategically vital waterways, thereby promoting regional economic prosperity and security cooperation.

3.3. Projection and Influence

The fundamental doctrine of naval supremacy presents a complex interchange between force projection and sustained presence. While capital warships constitute the backbone of naval power, the mastery of maritime domains necessitates a sophisticated deployment of destroyer / frigate /

submarine formations capable of maintaining persistent surveillance and operational presence across vast maritime expanses.

Yet, building power necessitates substantial financial commitment from Greece. Nevertheless, the prospective advantages - encompassing both security and economic dimensions - markedly surpass the associated expenditures. The modernization of the Hellenic Navy, including the procurement of state-of-the-art frigates, submarines, and maritime patrol aircraft, is insofar projected to require an investment ranging from €6 to €8 billion over the coming decade. This comprehensive initiative would also entail the expansion of existing naval facilities, such as the strategically vital Souda Bay, as well as the establishment of new forward operating bases in Cyprus and potentially in East Libya and/or East Africa.

Paradoxically, in scenarios devoid of opposing capital vessels, these formations alone can effectively establish and maintain maritime control. This strategic dynamic illuminates a cardinal principle of naval doctrine: Formations serve as the executors of maritime control, while capital ships function as their supreme guarantors. This elegant symbiosis forms the cornerstone of advanced naval strategy, lending deeper significance to the time-honored maxim that maritime dominance ultimately resides with the battle fleet. The validity of this principle derives from its comprehensive embodiment of the underlying strategic framework. Consequently, the battle fleet's noble raison d'être emerges with clarity - to serve as the ultimate protector of cruiser and flotilla operations in their execution of vital maritime missions. The most decisive manifestation of this protective function lies in the pre-emptive neutralization of adversarial capabilities that might otherwise impede these essential operations.

As part of the deterrence, Greek policy should transcend -from barricading itself in the Aegean- to establish a robust network of diplomatic and military alliances, particularly with regional states such as Israel, Cyprus, and Egypt; it becomes paramount in fostering a unified bulwark against multifaceted security challenges in Africa, Asia and the Black Sea including but not limited to terrorism, maritime piracy, and regional destabilization. In the same context Greece should closely cooperate with France and Italy concerning affairs in Libya and with France respectively for Lebanon.

In furtherance of its regional influence, especially if it intends to use foreign ports and land bases, Greece ought to leverage its power from culture. However odd may be, Greece's cultural projection would be a suitable instrument, which should emanate not from assertive means but rather through the crystallization of its inherent credibility and demonstrated trustworthiness. Cultural diplomacy emerges as a sophisticated instrument of statecraft, transcending traditional diplomatic norms while serving as the foundational architecture for meaningful interstate engagement. Whereas conventional diplomacy often operates within the confined parameters of national interests, cultural diplomacy extends its reach to the very fabric of societies, fostering connections that supersede mere political and economic interests and considerations.

Through the deployment of its cultural assets within meticulously crafted diplomatic and cross-cultural frameworks, Greece possesses the capacity to cultivate profound bilateral and multilateral relationships, thereby enhancing its position within the global community. The scope of cultural influence extends far beyond the conventional domains of artistic expression, whether classical or contemporary. Nonetheless, at its fundamental core, it presupposes the existence of a well-governed Hellenic state - one that exemplifies the principles of justice, progress and societal well-being, thus serving as a paragon, a lighthouse of stability and prosperity throughout the Mediterranean basin and beyond. This manifestation of good governance constitutes, in essence, the most compelling credential of trust. The philosophical underpinning of this endeavor resides in the cultivation of an integrity-based culture - one characterized by unwavering commitment to contractual obligations, manifestation of solidarity, and steadfast adherence to human dignity, mutual respect, and collective welfare. Consequently, Greece must undertake initiatives only when prepared to uphold these fundamental principles both domestically and internationally; any deviation risks precipitating systemic failure with far-reaching implications.

Should - before embarking upon ambitious ventures - it be wiser to rekindle the philosophical foundations that historically distinguish the Hellenic civilization? The ultimate objective lies with a view to establish of a contemporary commonwealth - an evolved iteration of the Hellenic League - predicated upon intimate cooperation with regional partners.

While such a vision might appear idealistic (perhaps aspirational), we deem that it represents a more pragmatic and sustainable strategic framework for Greece's future trajectory than alternative approaches. On the other hand, pursuing an idealistic vision of a perfect society may be thus utopic; one must acknowledge that nations evolve through their encounters with challenges, problems and lived experiences. Hence, when nations intervene in foreign territories, even with noble intentions, their actions may reflect a lack of understanding of the localities and result in ineffective outcomes. Yet, Greece's path forward lies in steadfast commitment to cooperative frameworks and the proactive defense of Western democratic principles and international law, which have established time-tested procedures and best practices for addressing complex international matters. Strength lies not in isolation, but in the alignment with proven institutional mechanisms that have successfully navigated intricate global challenges.

3.4. International Cooperation and Alliances

The above bring us to Greece's naval power is not only about unilateral actions but also about participating in multilateral efforts to secure the Mediterranean. Greece's dense institutional embedment (EU/NATO/IMO and related regimes) is a strategic asset: it translates naval presence into legitimacy, interoperability, and enforcement leverage, particularly through maritime security operations, sanctions architectures, and port-state control. Its general policy and overall strategy should be aligned with these organizations' broader objectives of maintaining security, stability, and freedom of navigation in the Mediterranean. Also, in 2021 Greece has signed with France the Franco-Greek Defense Agreement, which includes a mutual defense clause (article 2) should either be attacked by a third country.

4. BENEFITS OF MARITIME PROJECTION

Investment in naval power has wide-reaching social and economic benefits for Greece, both directly and indirectly. The direct benefits include the creation of jobs in the defense industry, shipbuilding, and related sectors. Naval modernization programs require substantial investments in shipyards, technology, expertise and human capital, all of which contribute to economic growth. Additionally, naval power enhances Greece's ability to secure and exploit maritime resources, such as oil and gas, which can significantly boost national revenues. Indicatively, we present the following:

4.1 Blue Economy and Jobs

With reference to the EU goals on Blue Economy, naval expansion requires significant investment in infrastructure, including shipbuilding facilities, naval bases, and support systems. Greece has already revived its shipbuilding industry (Posidonia International Shipping Exhibition, 2024; Mitsopoulos, 2024) and is capable of supporting any kind of merchant and naval activities; either through newbuildings or ship repairs. Particularly, Greece's shipbuilding industry is experiencing a remarkable renaissance, marking a decisive turning point after decades of decline. The consolidation of major shipbuilding units in Syros and Elefsina, coupled with the revival of the Skaramangas shipyard, Salamis Shipyards and increased activities in Halkis, has breathed new life into the sector. Since 2019, when ONEX Shipyards and Technologies group assumed operations, the Neorion - Syros and Elefsis shipyards have successfully serviced over 500 vessels, both foreign and Greek-owned. This emergence has positioned Greece as a significant contributor to European shipyards' impressive annual production value of €43 billion, with a combined civil and naval orderbook that now surpasses Asian competitors. This revival is further exemplified by notable achievements such as the Salamis Shipyards' recent delivery of five pre-equipped blocks for the French Navy's frigates and the successful handling of American naval projects, including the upgrade of four Island-class coastal patrol boats. Through strategic partnerships and substantial investments, the Greek government and shipyard operators are demonstrating their unwavering commitment to the sector, which currently represents only 1% of the nation's GDP. The shipbuilding / shiprepair industry's resurgence not only strengthens Greece's economic position but also enhances its maritime security capabilities, while supporting the growth of Greek maritime equipment manufacturers and solidifying Europe's dominance in marine equipment production and supply. It is mostly believed that this trend shall continue and generate more direct employment opportunities in shipyards, engineering, logistics and maintenance sectors. Investing in modern naval capabilities often leads to technological innovation, as advanced ships, submarines, and weapons systems require cutting-edge technology. Greece's investment in naval modernization could foster growth in its technology and defense sectors, with potential spillover effects into civilian industries, such as telecommunications, aerospace, and robotics, as well as related industries such as metals and materials, electronics, commerce, logistics and innovation contributing to overall economic growth.

4.2 Resource Security and Economic Independence

From an economic perspective, the safeguarding of alliance's maritime interests - with the participation of Greece - has the potential to unlock immense value, yet to require vast ship finance resources. In practice, this can only be achieved by synergies between private and public sector and among governments. Besides the strategic considerations relating to naval power, Greece has an additional motive in view of the natural gas reserves that are estimated to be worth in excess of €700 billion. In this context, Greece has to carefully plan in order to derive significant benefits from its pivotal role as a transit hub for energy exports to Europe and take advantage of the necessary industrial and logistical investments in maritime infrastructure, with reference to the employment opportunities and the economic growth that will generate; hence a well-established navy ensures the security of Greece's maritime resources, including its significant natural gas reserves. These reserves represent a potential source of energy independence for Greece and the wider European market, reducing reliance on external suppliers like Russia. The secure extraction and transportation of these resources will have long-term economic benefits for Greece, positioning it as a key energy supplier in the region. For example, taking advantage the desert expanse of the Sahara, in conjunction with Egypt and East Libya (Cyrenaica) Greece may import solar thermal generated electricity and feed its power grid, with the realisation of the GRECY interconnection (between Greece and Egypt via Crete) and at the same time supply Cyprus and/or Israel with the excess via the Great

Sea Interconnector. These energy investments require protection against sabotage or hostile actions.

4.3 Routes and Trade

Naval power also plays a critical role in ensuring the stability of regional trade routes. The Mediterranean and the Red Sea are vital commercial arteries for global trade, and Greece, with its strategic position and fleet, can play a central role in securing these routes. Stable and secure maritime routes benefit not just Greece but also the entire region, attracting foreign investments and facilitating trade.

5. EPILOGUE. SAILING ALONG

5.1 To Help Israel and the Levant

The evolving relationship between Greece and Israel has witnessed significant development in recent years, underpinned by shared strategic interests in regional security, energy cooperation, and mutual concerns regarding Turkey's increasingly assertive and Islamist foreign policy. This burgeoning alliance has manifested in joint military exercises and a heightened Greek naval presence in the Eastern Mediterranean, which plays a crucial role in co-protecting Israel's offshore energy assets, particularly the Leviathan and Tamar gas fields.

Greece's potential to contribute to Israel's security can be articulated through several key strategic dimensions. Primarily, the Greek naval presence in the Eastern Mediterranean serves as a critical buffer against potential threats emanating from regional adversaries such as Iran, Hamas, Hezbollah and Turkey both of which harbor interests in destabilizing Israel's maritime space. Furthermore, Greece's participation in joint naval exercises with Israel enhances interoperability between the two nations' armed forces, thereby augmenting their collective capacity to respond effectively to regional crises.

Moreover, Greece's dual membership in NATO and the European Union confers additional diplomatic influence in garnering international support for Israel's security concerns. This is particularly outstanding in the context of ongoing disputes over maritime boundaries and energy resources in the region. By leveraging its position within these influential international organizations, Greece can amplify Israel's voice on the global stage and help to shape favorable policies and attitudes towards Israeli security interests. The evolving relation between Greece and Israel represents more than just a bilateral security arrangement; it embodies a natural symbiosis that serves both nations' strategic interests while fostering regional stability. Greece finds in Israel a dependable ally in the Levant and Middle East, while Israel gains a trustworthy Western neighbor. This reciprocal beneficial partnership not only strengthens both nations' positions but also contributes to a more balanced geopolitical landscape in this crucial Mediterranean crossroads.

5.2 To Cover and Protect Cyprus

Cyprus presents the most straightforward and advantageous area for Greek investment. As part of the greater Hellenic world, a fellow EU member and long-time ally, Cyprus shares many of Greece's security concerns in the Southeastern Mediterranean. Both Hellenic countries have overlapping interests in terms of EEZ delineation and resource exploration, particularly regarding natural gas reserves. Greece's naval synergy with Cyprus would not only strengthen bilateral ties but also ensure the protection of shared energy interests. Furthermore, Cyprus's geographical position makes it a key strategic point for controlling access to the Eastern Mediterranean and ensuring freedom of navigation. Naval collaboration between Greece and Cyprus could also serve as a deterrent to those who threat Israel. Moreover, as an active member state of the EU and other international organizations, Greece is uniquely qualified to contribute constructively to resolving the complex bicommunal situation in Cyprus, which has endured partition since the Turkish military intervention. Drawing from the European values of integration and mutual understanding, Greece advocates for a unified approach that transcends ethnic divisions. This stands in stark contrast to the fragmentary models witnessed in parts of Africa and the Middle East, where tribalism, religious segregation and isolated communities persist. Instead, Greece promotes the core European principles of tolerance, unity, inclusiveness, and solidarity, which are essential for fostering lasting peace and reconciliation on the island. This approach aligns with the broader European vision of harmonious coexistence and shared prosperity among diverse communities.

5.3 To stabilize East Libya (Cyrenaica)

East Libya, specifically the region of Cyrenaica, represents a more complex and uncertain investment option. This ancient land, once bound to Hellenic and Roman civilizations through profound cultural and commercial ties, now stands at a critical crossroads between instability and potential renaissance. The current political fragmentation and civil discord that plague Libya have transformed what could be a lighthouse of Mediterranean cooperation into a theater of uncertainty.

Nevertheless, this very challenge presents Greece with a unique opportunity to demonstrate wise leadership in the Mediterranean basin. By approaching Cyrenaica through the lens of constructive engagement, Greece could help forge a new model of Euro-African cooperation, one that transcends the traditional paradigms of mere resource exploitation or security concerns. The region's potential to serve as a transformative example for African development and European partnership remains largely untapped. From a geopolitical perspective, Greece's historical connection to Cyrenaica provides a legitimate foundation for deeper engagement. A carefully calibrated presence in this strategic corridor would not only enhance Greece's maritime influence across the Mediterranean but would also serve to secure its southern approaches. However, such an endeavor requires a sophisticated diplomatic architecture, one that harmonizes the interests of regional stakeholders while promoting stability and sustainable development. This long-term strategic vision must be predicated on patience and persistence, recognizing that the current instability, while significant, is not insurmountable.

5.4. To Assist in the Red Sea and East Africa

The Red Sea and East Africa present another option for Greek naval investment, particularly in the context of securing vital trade routes and countering piracy. The Red Sea is a critical chokepoint for global maritime trade, and instability in the region, including the threat of piracy, poses risks to Greece's shipping interests. A naval presence in the Red Sea (as it happens currently with the Operation Aspides) would allow the alliance to play a more active role in securing these trade routes and ensuring the safe passage of its commercial vessels.

However, the Red Sea is geographically distant from Greece's primary areas of interest in the Mediterranean, and investing in this region would require a significant expansion of Greece's naval capabilities. While securing the Red Sea is important, it should be considered a secondary priority after solidifying Greece's position in the Southeastern Mediterranean.

CONCLUSION

Greece's maritime engagement in the Eastern Mediterranean has evolved from a historical necessity into a strategic imperative, driven by an intricate interplay of geopolitical dynamics, security challenges, and economic opportunities. The nation's traditional defensive posture must now transform into a more comprehensive and proactive maritime strategy to safeguard its sovereign interests and strengthen the Western alliance framework. This evolution is particularly crucial as the region faces increasing competition from adversarial powers seeking to fill any strategic vacuum. Greece's unique geographic position, combined with its historical maritime legacy, positions it as a pivotal actor in maintaining regional stability and securing vital sea lanes from the Libyan Sea to the Levant.

To achieve these objectives, Greece must implement a sophisticated maritime strategy that encompasses naval modernization, economic development, and diplomatic initiatives. This includes strengthening partnerships within the tetralateral framework with Egypt, Cyprus, and Israel, while actively participating in NATO and EU maritime security initiatives. The strategy should prioritize the development of blue economy initiatives, enhancement of naval infrastructure, and establishment of a sustained presence across the region's critical maritime zones. Such comprehensive engagement will not only secure Greece's national interests but also contribute to regional stability, particularly in supporting Egypt's maritime security efforts in the Red Sea and Gulf of Aden. This multifaceted approach, balancing security imperatives with economic and diplomatic considerations, will ensure Greece's position as a key stabilizing force in the Eastern Mediterranean's evolving maritime landscape

REFERENCES

Bockmann, M. W. (2024, October 23). Greece-owned ships are top Houthi target. Lloyd's List. https://lloydslist.com/LL1151096/Greece-owned-ships-are-top-Houthi-target

Borgerson, S. G. (2009). The national interest and the law of the sea (Council Special Report No. 46). Council on Foreign Relations.

Bueger, C., & Edmunds, T. (2017). Beyond seablindness: A new agenda for maritime security studies. *International Affairs*, *93*(6), 1293–1311. DOI: 10.1093/ia/iix174

Cohen Yanarocak, H. E. (2021, November 8). Turkish irredentism and the Greater Middle East. Jerusalem Institute for Strategy and Security. https://jiss.org.il/en/yanarocak-turkish-irredentism-and-the-greater-middle-east/

Corbett, J. S. (2012). *Principles of maritime strategy*. Dover Publications. (Original work published 1911)

Daniel, R., & Lindenstrauss, G. (2023). Nationalism and Turkish foreign policy following the May 2023 elections. Strategic Assessment, 26(2), 117–124. https://inss.org.il/wp-content/uploads/2023/08/Daniel_Lindenstrauss.pdf

European Commission. (2023). EU Blue Economy Observatory: Country profiles. https://blue-economy-observatory.ec.europa.eu/country-profiles/greece_en

Eurostat, C. I., & Engelbert, A. (2013). Coastal regions: People living along the coastline, integration of NUTS 2010 and latest population grid (KS-SF-13-030-EN-N). https://ec.europa.eu/eurostat/statistics-explained/index.php?title=Archive:Coastal_regions_-_population_statistics

Freedman, L. (2005). The official history of the Falklands campaign: Vol. II. War and diplomacy. Routledge.

Freedman, L. (2013). *Strategy: A history*. Oxford University Press.

Germond, B. (2015). The maritime dimension of European security: Seapower and the European Union. Palgrave Macmillan.

Ghaddar, H., Nadimi, F., & Schenker, D. (2024, June 21). Hezbollah threatens Cyprus: Capabilities, intentions, and potential consequences. Washington Institute for Near East Policy. https://washingtoninstitute.org/policy-analysis/hezbollah-threatens-cyprus-capabilities-intentions-and-potential-consequences

Government of the Russian Federation. (2022). Directive No. 1998-r of 20 July 2022. https://publication.pravo.gov.ru/document/0001202409200036?index=2

Gundelach, K. (1981). *Die deutsche Luftwaffe im Mittelmeer 1940–1945* (Vol. 1). Lang.

Le Mière, C. (2014). *Maritime diplomacy*. Routledge. DOI: 10.4324/9780203555590

Lloyd's List. (2024, October 28). The week in charts: Container shipping rates show signs of life; Black Sea attacks threaten global food security; Greece-owned ships are top Houthi target. https://lloydslist.com/LL1151148/The-week-in-charts-Container-shipping-rates-show-signs-of-life--Black-Sea-attacks-threaten-global-food-security--Greece-owned-ships-are-top-Houthi-target

Mahan, A. T. (1905). *Sea power and its relations to the War of 1812* (Vol. 1). Sampson Low, Marston & Company.

Mahan, A. T. (1918). The influence of sea power upon history, 1660–1783 (12th ed.). Little, Brown & Co. (Project Gutenberg edition, updated 2007). https://classicsofstrategy.com/2022/02/09/alfred-thayer-mahan-the-influence-of-sea-power-upon-history-as-strategy-grand-strategy-and-polemic/

Mitsopoulos, D. (2024, July 29). Greek shipyard delivers blocks for France's second FDI. Naval News. https://navalnews.com/naval-news/2024/07/greek-shipyard-delivers-blocks-for-frances-second-fdi/

OECD. (2020). OECD territorial reviews: Regional policy for Greece post-2020. OECD Publishing. https://www.oecd.org/content/dam/oecd/en/publications/reports/2020/10/regional-policy-for-greece-post-2020_bb991164/cedf09a5-en.pdf

Posidonia International Shipping Exhibition. (2024, April 10). Posidonia 2024 marks the rebirth of the Greek shipbuilding industry [Press release]. https://posidonia-events.com/press-releases/posidonia/article/140/posidonia-2024-marks-the-rebirth-of-the-greek-shipbuilding-industry/

Psaraftis, H., & Pallis, A. A. (2012). Concession of the Piraeus container terminal: Turbulent times and the quest for competitiveness. *Maritime Policy & Management*, *39*(1), 27–43. DOI: 10.1080/03088839.2011.642316

Reuters. (2025, January 20). Chevron expresses interest in Greek energy exploration. https://reuters.com/business/energy/chevron-expresses-interest-hydorcarbons-exploration-greece-energy-ministry-says-2025-01-20/

Schelling, T. C. (2020). Arms and influence (A. M. Slaughter, Intro.; Original work published 1966). Yale University Press.

Speller, I. (2024). *Understanding naval warfare* (3rd ed.). Routledge.

Tangredi, S. (2013). *Anti-access warfare: Countering A2/AD strategies*. Naval Institute Press.

Till, G. (2018). *Seapower: A guide for the twenty-first century* (4th ed.). Routledge. DOI: 10.4324/9781315621210

Union of Greek Shipowners. (2023). Greek shipping: A strategic sector for the European economy. https://www.ugs.gr/en/greek-shipping-and-economy/greek-shipping-and-economy-2023/greek-shipping-a-strategic-sector-for-the-european-economy

United Nations Organization, NATO, WTO, OECD, Council of Europe, IMO, OSCE, BSEC, UNESCO, ICOMOS, UNT, IHRA, & Union for the Mediterranean. (n.d.). Membership list of international organizations. [Publisher unspecified].

Vego, M. (2005). *Naval strategy and operations in narrow seas* (2nd ed.). Frank Cass.

Vego, M. (2019). *Maritime strategy and sea denial: Theory and practice*. Routledge.

Vitale, M. C. (1995). Jointness by design, not accident. *Joint Force Quarterly*, (Autumn), 24–30.

ENDNOTES

1 This essay is dedicated to the memory of George X. Protopapas, whose friendship was a source of inspiration and encouragement throughout my life.

2 The principle of "physical conformation" examines the inherent geographical characteristics of a nation's permanent foundation. In particular, nations blessed with an abundance of deep, sheltered harbors possess distinct strategic and economic advantages over their counterparts who lack such natural maritime endowments. These geographical blessings have historically shaped the destiny of coastal nations, enabling them to flourish as maritime powers and trading hubs.

3 Julian Stafford Corbett, *Principles of Maritime Strategy* (1911, Annapolis MD, Dover Publications Mineola NY 2012 epub version) 67.

Chapter 6
Geopolitical Analysis of Greece and Turkey:
Autonomy Trends and Regional Sustainability

Konstantinos Bogiatzis
https://orcid.org/0009-0002-3136-4408
University of the Aegean, Greece

Spyros Anagnostou
University of the Aegean, Greece

ABSTRACT

This article examines Turkey's evolving geopolitical autonomy, highlighting its transition from dependence on foreign powers to a more autonomous strategic stance. It traces Turkey's efforts across different historical periods, from the Kemalist era to the present, emphasizing key geopolitical, economic, and military developments. Turkey's shift toward strategic autonomy is analyzed through various parameters, including the decline of U.S. hegemony, its balancing act between the West and emerging powers like Russia and China, and its aspirations for regional dominance. The study also examines the deterioration of EU-Turkey relations, the impact of demographic dynamics, and Turkey's proactive foreign policy in the Middle East, particularly in response to the Arab uprisings. Additionally,

DOI: 10.4018/979-8-3373-8790-1.ch006

the paper delves into Turkey's increasing role in the Eastern Mediterranean due to energy discoveries, its security concerns post-2016 coup attempt, and its growing defense industry. These factors collectively define Turkey's quest for a self-sufficient and autonomous geopolitical stance.

INTRODUCTION

Since its establishment as a modern state in 1923, Turkey has continuously strived for autonomy in political, cultural, economic, and geostrategic domains. Its trajectory has seen alternating phases of increased dependence on foreign powers and determined efforts toward self-sufficiency. Below is a chronological overview:

a) The Kemalist Era (1923-1938):

Mustafa Kemal Atatürk laid the groundwork for national autonomy by rejecting foreign interference and pursuing economic and military self-sufficiency. Turkey distanced itself from the Islamic world and aligned with the West through a series of modernization reforms. State intervention dominated the economy, leading to the creation of national industries. In foreign policy, Turkey sought diplomatic neutrality during the interwar period and World War II.

b) The Cold War Period (1945-1991):

Following World War II, Turkey aligned with the West due to the Soviet threat and joined NATO in 1952, which limited its autonomy. Economically, it became dependent on American aid through the Truman Doctrine and the Marshall Plan. In defense, its military relied on Western weapons and U.S. expertise. However, the 1970s saw an effort toward military self-sufficiency when an American arms embargo—imposed after Turkey's invasion of Cyprus—spurred the development of a domestic defense industry.

c) The Post-Cold War Period (1991-2002):

After the collapse of the Soviet bloc, Turkey sought a new role in the international system. It pursued geopolitical autonomy by asserting its influence in the Balkans, Central Asia, and the Middle East, while remaining a NATO member and aspiring to join the European Union.

d) The Erdoğan Era (2002–Present):

Under Recep Tayyip Erdoğan's leadership, Turkey has renewed its push for strategic autonomy, adopting a multidimensional foreign policy. It has strengthened ties with Russia and China. Although its purchase of Russian S-400 missile systems led to U.S. sanctions, strategic relations with the West were nevertheless maintained

ANALYSIS OF STRATEGIC AUTONOMY PARAMETERS

Turkey has embarked on a long and dynamic journey toward strategic autonomy, evolving from deep dependence during the Cold War to a more independent stance in recent years. It constantly balances between Westernization and reinforcing an independent, conservative identity, aiming to emerge as a global power with a strong domestic industry, energy self-sufficiency, and a multidimensional foreign policy. Turkey seeks to develop into a regional power that will project power on three continents (Asia, Africa, Europe). For this reason, the parameters of the last decades are analyzed below, describing the causes that led it to seek strategic autonomy in the international arena and enable it not only to maintain but also to strengthen its position in the global environment. Turkey's geopolitical claims are the product of many interrelated processes at the national, regional, global level, and are as follows:

Unstable Geopolitical Environment

In 1991, the Cold War ended with the US prevailing over the Soviet Union. The next decades were marked by US supremacy in political, economic and military power, without the existence of an equivalent competitor.

However, US hegemony began to decline as the system of interdependence of the internationalized economy it implemented - a main mechanism of US hegemony - entered into crisis and a group of new players emerged, especially China, which more effectively exploited the system that was set up by the US. It lost its superiority in agricultural and industrial production, over its potential competitors, thanks to the increasing liberalization of the financial sector, lower taxation of capital, but also the increase in its public borrowing. Thus, through successive miscalculations, they allowed Russia on the one hand - with energy mainly as a weapon - and China on the other - with the rapid economic boom and commercial penetration in the Western Hemisphere as a weapon - to overthrow the monopoly of the one and only superpower.

Within this framework, Turkey readjusted its stance, due to the power vacuums created by the decline of US hegemony, found an empty geostrategic space for maneuver and emerged as an important though highly controversial actor within this regional and international environment (Larabee & Lesser, 2003). More specifically, due to the questioning of the primacy of the USA, there is a redistribution of power, or rather, a concession of the imposition of power to regional actors, which act as proxies of the great powers in their geographical system of interest, in exchange for gaining relative autonomy of movements (Önis, & Kutlay, 2017), fully harmonizing with the historical, but also contemporary particularities of each geographical area.

Today's Turkey is trying to become such a regional power, which claims an important role in the emerging international system. It is fully aware of its significant geographical position, i.e. the fact that it functions as a geographical-geopolitical link between Europe, Eurasia and the Middle East, and for this reason it seeks to upgrade its projection of power (Huseynov, 2017), seeking to become a regional watchdog, yet with an international role, stronger, more active, but also more autonomous, without identifying itself with either of the two opposing poles - that is, neither the West nor Eurasia.

It is a fact that on the internal front, Ankara's pursuit of autonomy from the West in order to emerge as a regional power, has found great resonance, both in Turkish public opinion and in the opposition parties (Kınıklıoğlu, 2022). Government officials believe that the international system no longer has a "Western sign", but is in a post-Western transition, where would-be regional powers, such as Turkey, may have interests that may not be in harmony with those of the US and NATO, and they have to serve them by influencing different centers of power, such as: from Washington to Moscow and Beijing and from the World Bank and IMF to the BRICS (Dalay, 2021).

One of the decisive factors in Ankara's push for greater strategic autonomy was the global financial crisis of 2008, which contributed to the shift in power from the West to non-Western countries. Turkey, taking advantage of these structural changes in the global power landscape, felt that it had room to project its own interests, regardless of their alignment with the West. After the global financial crisis of 2008, Ankara implemented a multi-level foreign policy, strengthening its relations with China and Russia and at the same time made an unprecedented opening to countries in Africa, the Balkans, the Caucasus and Central Asia (Oğuzlu, 2020). On the other hand, it seized the opportunity of the expansion of global governance structures, such as the replacement of G8 with the G20, of which it has been a member since its foundation, something that makes it an active player, in contrast to its previous role as a passive observer.

Deterioration of Euro-Turkish Relations

The relations between the European Union and Turkey have a long history. In 1963, the Association Agreement of the then European Economic Community with Turkey was signed, which was considered as a preparatory act for its full integration. However, there followed a recession and tension in their relations, due to Turkey's invasion of northern Cyprus in 1974, the military coup of 1980, with harsh measures of repression and restriction of freedoms, and in 1997, due to Turkey's unilateral decision to end the dialogue with the European Union, because it was excluded from the status of a candidate country for accession.

A period of close cooperation followed. A crucial point was the Helsinki Agreement (1999), where Turkey received the status of a candidate country for EU membership and was forced to follow a "road map" with political and economic criteria for its accession course. The Turkish governments, including that of the Justice and Development Party, focused on the reforms required to comply with the criteria of the European Union, such as separation of powers in a more functional democratic governance, respect for human rights and minorities, functioning of the rule of law and harmonizing its economy with the dictates of the European Union. Initially, Ankara demonstrated a high pace of constitutional reforms that integrated it more and more into the European order, with the European Commission, in its October 2004 Progress Report, stating that Turkey met the political criteria for opening accession negotiations (Turan et al, 2019). In December of the same year, the European Council approved the European Commission's decision and negotiations began in 2005. It was a happy moment, especially for the modernizing wing of Turkey's political scene, but expectations were quickly dashed.

Then followed a period of stagnation in relations between the two sides. With the rise of conservative governments in Europe, in Germany (Merkel) and France (Sarkozy), which appeared to be more reluctant to accept full membership than the previous ones, but also Turkey's change in political priorities, caused aggravation in their association. On the one hand, a non-unified Cyprus fully joined the European Union, imposing its own conditions, and on the other hand, the Union began to face several internal problems in relation to its operation and development. The refusal of France and the Netherlands to accept the Euroconstitution in 2005 showed that the admission of Turkey was not a priority (Roubanis, 2019). For its part, Turkey rejected any form of relationship other than full integration. Since then, in 2006 the European Council blocked several chapters of the negotiations and froze the accession process. The rhetoric of rejection is based on Turkish inadequacy at the economic, political and cultural level, but also at the security level. The argument focuses on Turkey's economic weakness, political instability and potential difficulties arising from religious and cultural differences (Baç & Taşkın, 2007).

Therefore, the European Union decided that Turkey cannot be admitted as a full member, but must maintain its role in regional security and in the security of the eastern Mediterranean, continuing to be a model country for the Islamic world. Ankara, for its part, spoke of taunting and inconsistency of the Union in relation to the stated objectives of the accession agreement. The sweeping victory of the Justice and Development party in the 2007 national elections, combined with Turkey's discontent with the European Union, also contributed to the redefinition of the non-convergence with European directives reform process by the Turkish government (Danisi, 2017). In addition, the economic crisis in Europe and the Arab uprisings inspired the idea inside Turkey that the European Union needs Turkey more than Turkey needs the European Union.

The current situation is ambivalent, as the crisis in their relations began in 2013, due to the harsh suppression of the protests in Gezi Park. Although the accession process stopped, the European Union criticized Turkey in the areas of human rights, administration of justice, freedom of speech and civil liberties, but it was not able to prevent the Turkish government from implementing harsh and authoritarian repression measures (Erensü & Karaman, 2017). In addition, the executions, purges and many detentions of persons, after the coup attempt of 2016, but also the concentration of powers due to the super-presidential system in 2017, caused strong concerns in the European Union.

For Turkey, Europe has the ability to pile on crises while showing some resilience, without offering any solution. The 2015 migration crisis, where Ankara seized the opportunity to operate for its own benefit, was the generative cause of this adversarial relationship between them. The non-convergence and huge differences between the member states were interpreted by Turkey as a favorable moment to modify the terms in its favor, considering that the strengthened and expanded bilateral relations between them benefit it more than the integration policy. On the other hand, the currency crisis of Turkey in 2018, combined with the political choices in both its internal and foreign policy influenced the attitude of the European Union (Pierini, 2019). Turkey is seen as a partner that acts unpredictably and has low credibility. However, Europe also showed fatigue regarding its enlargement and put more emphasis on the policy of deepening. Western Balkan countries, such as North Macedonia, Montenegro,

Albania, Kosovo, Serbia and Bosnia-Herzegovina, while participating in the enlargement process since the beginning of 2000, until now there has been no substantial progress in this matter.

Today, Turkey's accession to the EU is not a vital interest of the country, but a geopolitical pursuit of prestige. Its goal is to emerge as a regional power and to achieve this it needs the economic strength, which the status of a permanent candidate for accession gives it, economic benefits, such as solvency in the international financial markets, which take into account the low labor cost and bring a lot of foreign investment into the country. Finally, the possibility of Turkey's accession is a deterrent, both for France and Germany, due to Turkey's population size, since in case of its admission it will be the largest country, which means that it will have the biggest number of votes in the European Council on decision-making, completely sidelining the German-French axis.

Demographic and Social Dynamics

Turkey has experienced significant population growth. From 21 million inhabitants in 1950, its population reached 84.7 million in 2021, with a continuing upward trend. This impressive population growth is primarily due to the very high fertility rates the country experienced in the early post-war decades. The recent census indicates an increase compared to previous measurements, confirming that Turkey remains one of the fastest-growing populations in both Europe and the Middle East (Türkiye İstatistik Kurumu, 2022). In the future, as Turkey is expected to complete its demographic transition around the mid-21st century, its population will continue to grow, but at a slower rate, projected to reach approximately 94 million by 2050 (United Nations, 2024).

According to demographic projections, Turkey is expected to acquire the characteristics of developed nations, with a relatively aged and numerically stable population. Currently, however, it maintains the youngest population in the region, with a median age of 30 years. Specifically, 25% of the population consists of children aged 0-14, approximately 19 million, while only 10% is over 60 years old (Türkiye İstatistik Kurumu, 2022).

It is noted that Turkey's population is not homogeneous: about 18% belong to the Kurdish ethnicity, 7%-12% consist of other minorities, while the remaining 70%-75% are Turks, according to a CIA study (The World Factbook, 2022). Furthermore, these population groups are not evenly distributed across the country.

The Kurdish issue in Turkey stems from the exclusion of Kurds from the national narrative of the Turkish state, which since its foundation has sought to assimilate them repressively, leading to their displacement from the rural areas of Southeastern Turkey and to their marginalization. Since 1984, the armed actions of the PKK have intensified the problem, causing a long-term and costly low-intensity war. Despite the inability to achieve military dominance, the insurgency has strengthened Kurdish national identity, making the issue of their political emancipation Turkey's most significant internal problem.

This demographic dynamic of Turkey affects three key areas:

a) Economy: A large and productive population enhances the country's self-sufficiency, reducing its dependence on Western investments and technologies. The Turkish leadership aims to transform the population into a strong internal market while promoting the development of domestic industry (Colibasanu, 2024).
b) Military Power: Turkey maintains one of the largest armies in NATO, with more than 750,000 military personnel and reserves, making it capable of conducting military operations independently of Western powers (Alonso-Trabanco, 2022).
c) Geopolitical Influence: Turkey uses its population as a means of exerting political influence, particularly through Turkish communities in Western Europe, and by granting citizenship to citizens from Middle Eastern and Central Asian countries, thereby expanding Ankara's influence in the wider region.

The Turkish government leverages its demographic dynamics as a tool for political pressure on European governments, strengthening its negotiating position and encouraging national pride and unity around the idea of a strong and independent Turkey. Through control of the educational system and mass media, the Turkish state seeks to reduce ideological dependence on the West, promoting an alternative identity based on neo-Ottomanism and pan-Turkism (Tokdoğan, 2024).

However, despite the opportunities provided by a large population, there are significant challenges. A large number of inhabitants requires sustainable economic growth and job creation, which is not easy in an economy facing issues such as unemployment and economic instability. Additionally, demographic diversity, with the presence of Kurdish and Alevi populations, creates internal tensions and challenges to social cohesion. Despite the youthful demographic structure of the country, Turkey is expected to face gradual population aging in the coming decades, which could be a limiting factor for its dynamism.

Arab Uprisings

The Arab uprisings of 2011 acted as a springboard for the realization of Turkey's geographical fantasies. The so-called "Arab Spring" highlighted the democratic deficits in the wider region, and Ankara began to project itself as a role model to the countries of the Arab world and the Balkans, due to its European policies, modernization reforms and gradual improvements in democratic principles. For the Arab world, Turkey was a state in very good economic condition, which respects cultural and religious values and guarantees freedoms to its people (Fuller, 2008:69-71). On the other hand, Turkey saw the Arab uprisings as an opportunity to promote itself, as a perfect model at the political and economic level, aiming to increase its geopolitical power in the Greater Middle East region, instrumentalizing historical, cultural and religious pillars.

Undoubtedly, since the Justice and Development Party (AKP) took over the government, Turkey has shown improvements in areas such as human, cultural and minority rights, the justice system, and limiting the military in state affairs (Hale & Özbudun, 2010:55-98). Additionally, the transformation of its economy, which combines the harmonization of Islam with democratic principles, combined with its long history of secularism and NATO membership, worked in its favor as a model country, as these characteristics were not possessed by the rebel Arab countries. (Korutürk, 2012). Until the end of 2013, this political model of Turkey remained popular in the Arab world, to a significant extent. In addition, the US promoted the Turkish model of governance in the countries of the Middle East and North Africa in order to mitigate regional instability, but also to limit Iran's influence in the region. It is noteworthy that Turkey and the USA also counted on the economic benefits that would arise from the future expected regional cooperation in the energy sector (Önis, 2014).

Turkey took advantage of this momentum gained mainly with the support of the US and, according to its regional ambitions, it strongly supported the insurgencies and the democratization processes, seeking to lead this geopolitical transformation of the region (Kardaş, 2011). Thus, the new landscape that emerged after the uprisings in the Arab world became a priority for Turkish foreign policy. After the end of the uprisings, Ankara offered financial aid in the form of loans to Tunisia, Egypt and Libya. In this way, it sought to maintain close ties with the pro-Islamic governments that emerged in Arab countries after the uprisings. In other words, Turkey tried to create a "Sunni zone" in the Greater Middle East, seeking to lead it, as it represents moderate Islam and supported the political parties associated with the Muslim Brotherhood (Korutürk, 2012). It is no coincidence that Ankara chose to distance itself from Israel, while supporting the Palestinians. Turkey seeked to maintain good relations with Arab countries and limit Israeli influence. However, Ankara tried to keep balance with Iran and maintain its credibility in the case of Syria vis-à-vis the Arab world.

As the focus of the Arab uprisings was intertwined with political reforms, Turkey could meddle with the demands of the Arab peoples. Moreover, it took seriously the religious background of the protestors, believing that the common cultural identity would contribute to Ankara's leading role in the emerging regional realignment.

However, when the insurgencies turned into ethno-religious conflicts, with regional and international ramifications, Turkey reconsidered its position, due to the changing attitudes of other international actors involved and the emergence of threats to both regional security and Turkey's internal security. Initially, the transformation of the Syrian crisis into a civil war and the overthrow of the government by the armed forces in Egypt (2013), were pivotal points of reversal of the changing mood of the Arab uprisings. Then, with the rise of Islamist militarism (DAESH, Al Nusra, etc) in Iraq and Syria, the international community prioritized regional security over democratic reforms, gradually withdrawing its support for opposition groups. In addition, Saudi Arabia and Iran supported opposing camps in the Syrian civil conflict, and in a short time the conflict turned into a proxy war, causing even further polarization in the Arab world, sharpening the regional rivalry between them. Finally, with the appearance of DAESH in Syria and Iraq, the separatist tendencies of the Kurds, mainly in Syria, in the northeast of the country, were strengthened, due to the shrinkage of the Syrian territory. The Kurdish militias were upgraded to a valuable partner of the West, in the eradication of DAESH, which encouraged the West to provide international legitimacy and military assistance, so they gained more bargaining power than Turkey (Ataman & Özdemir, 2018) On the other hand, after the collapse of the peace process between the Turkish government and the PKK (2013), terrorist attacks took place in Kurdish-majority cities in eastern and southeastern Turkey. Since then Ankara has prioritized its national security, despite its regional ambitions. At the same time, it has being attacked internally by DAESH, with suicide bombers, due to its decision to join the international alliance against it (Duman, 2016), something that caused significant effects on Turkey's regional policy in the region, which it sought to dominate.

In short, the events of the Arab uprisings first served as a trigger for Turkey's geographical fantasies, and then backfired, as Ankara began to be threatened in its southeastern soft underbelly by the Kurdish PKK and YPG militias, which found support from the US and its allies. Thus, the possibility of the emergence of a Kurdish state was no longer an internal issue, but an international issue affecting Turkey. Because of the US support for the Kurds, Turkey approached Russia and Iran, which also has a Kurdish population on its territory.

Discovery of Deposits in the Eastern Mediterranean

The Mediterranean is divided into three geographical areas: a) the western Mediterranean, which extends from Gibraltar to Malta, b) the Middle Mediterranean, which extends from Malta to the 27th longitude and c) the area east of it, called Eastern Mediterranean, which includes the states of Egypt, Turkey, Syria, Israel, Cyprus (South and North), Lebanon and the Palestinian Territories. In the Eastern Mediterranean, Turkey has a coastline of 569 miles (Villegas, 2020).

The geographical location of the Eastern Mediterranean occupies a prominent place on the world map, because, on the one hand, it is a gateway to the Aegean, the Black Sea, the Red Sea and the Atlantic Ocean. 30% of world trade passes through the Mediterranean basin. On the other hand, oil and natural gas deposits were discovered in the 2010s in the maritime zones of Israel, Egypt and the Republic of Cyprus. Thus, Turkey turned its attention to this region as well (Koray, 2020:128-131)

The first gas reserve was discovered in 1999 by Israel, in its geographical field called Leviathan. Between 2009 and 2011 exploration continued and natural gas deposits were found in the Tamar field of Israel and Aphrodite field of Cyprus (Fig. 1) Subsequently, the Republic of Cyprus invited global energy giants such as the American ExxonMobil - Noble, the French Total, the Italian Eni, Korean Kogas, Qatar Petroleum, in the region (Andreasyan, 2013) and at the same time signed agreements defining the EEZ with Egypt (2003), Lebanon (2007) and Israel (2010) sharing the Eastern Mediterranean with other states and ignoring the Turkish Cypriot side.

Figure 1. Gas Fields Levithian, Tamar, Aphrodite & Dali.

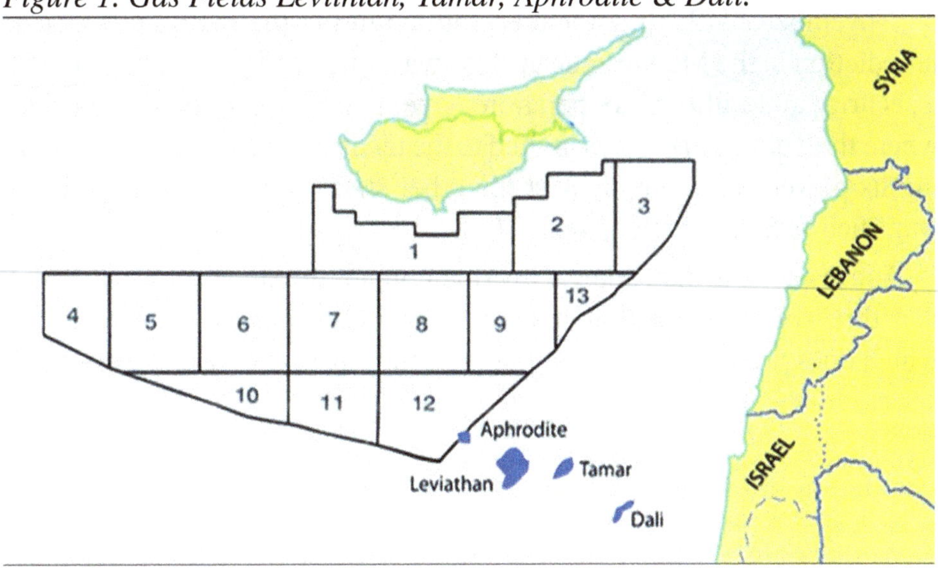

Source: alchetron.com

These actions caused Turkey's strong reactions and threats. In response, Ankara entered into a continental shelf demarcation agreement with the so-called "Turkish Republic of Northern Cyprus", recognized only by Ankara (International Crisis Group, 2012), which granted an exploration license for the discovery of oil and natural gas to Turkey's state-owned petroleum company TPAO. Seismographic research vessels Barbaros Hayrettin Paşa and Oruç Reis began operating in the area, and Turkish drillships Fatih, Yavuz and Kanuni began research activities. As mentioned, the transformation of the wider geopolitical environment, the strategic realignments in the changing power balances, strengthened Ankara's ambitions in order to emerge as a leading power in the post-Ottoman geopolitical and geocultural space. Turkey's revisionist aspirations created reactions from Greece, Cyprus, Israel and Egypt (Ozkan, 2014:119-140). Shared perceptions of insecurity about Turkish aspirations have led to closer cooperation at the economic, political, energy and military levels. This quadripartite alliance serves Turkey's regional balancing (Badarin & Schumacher, 2022).

Thus, in January 2019, the Republic of Cyprus, along with Greece, Italy, Israel, Egypt and Jordan, signed cooperation agreements during their meeting in Cairo, which sidelined Turkey from the Eastern Mediterranean.

Turkey, realizing its exclusion from the energy chessboard of the Eastern Mediterranean, signed with the Government of National Accord of Libya, on November 27, 2019, an agreement delimiting the maritime areas of jurisdiction in the Mediterranean. This was followed by the conclusion of a security and military cooperation agreement between the two parties, where the Turkish army was invited to the territory of Libya, thus upgrading its power projection against the other states involved in the Libyan war, such as Saudi Arabia, the UAE, France, Egypt, Russia and the USA.

As a response to the Turkey-Libya memorandum, Athens signed a partial maritime zone demarcation agreement with Cairo, at the 28th meridian, which does not include Kastelorizo, nor the entire Rhodes (Fig. 2).

Figure 2. Greece's agreement with Egypt on the EEZ

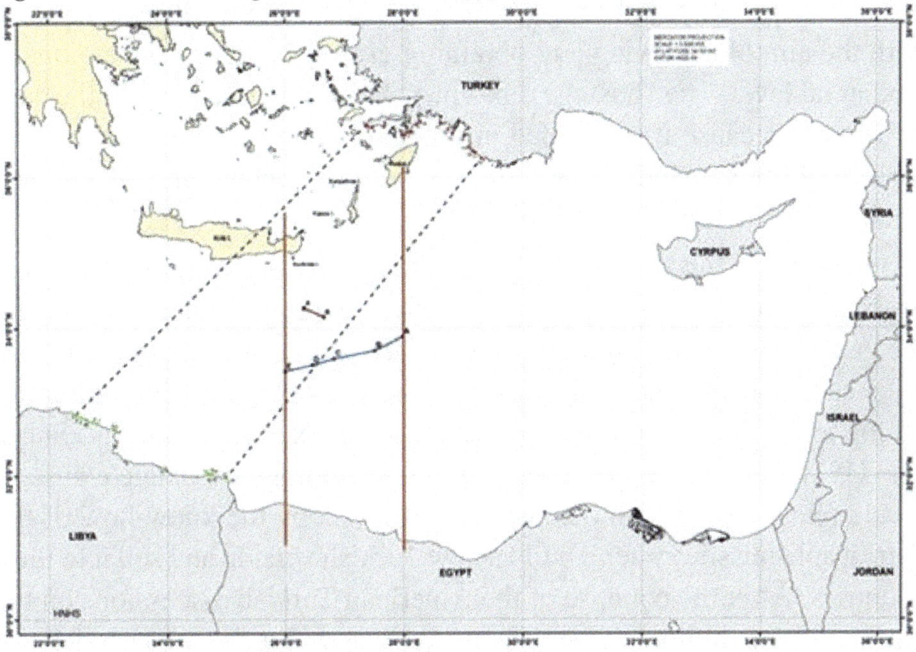

Source: Unofficial map as posted by Greek Media.

In this way, Greece and Egypt wanted to create a legal fait accompli, as their agreement overlaps the one between Ankara and the Libyan Government of National Accord, giving the parties involved (Athens and Cairo) the opportunity to appeal to the annulment of the illegal Turkish-Libyan treaty at the International Court of Justice in The Hague.

Autonomy Tendencies after the Coup Attempt

As mentioned, the failed coup attempt on July 15, 2016, caused a flurry of changes in Turkey's domestic and foreign policy, leading it to a series of tensions with the West, with the aim of its eventual self-reliance. Anti-Western rhetoric emerged in 2013, accusing foreign powers of inciting both the Gezi Park protests and the fall of the Muslim Brotherhood from Egypt's government. Turkey instrumentalized the detention of persons without evidence, citizens of the USA, Greece, Germany, France, Sweden, Finland, the Netherlands and Israel, under the pretext of either espionage or the risk of destabilizing the domestic legal order. These arrests were a means of negotiation with the governments of the aforementioned countries, with the aim of achieving and obtaining greater benefits-concessions at a bilateral level. The "hostage diplomacy" worked effectively in the case of Turkey, because it succeeded in dragging countries into negotiations by setting the demands, and not a few times by achieving the intended trade-offs (Erdemir & Edelman, 2018).

In addition, Turkey has long sought to acquire an anti-aircraft system in order to meet its defense needs. It initially expressed interest in buying the Patriot anti-aircraft system from the US NATO ally, but this offer was rejected by Ankara due to high fiscal costs, as it expected a hefty discount on the initial price and required a technology exchange-transfer clause. The US did not agree, because, with the technology exchange clause, it would allow the Turkish defense industry to copy the know-how of the Patriot anti-missile system, build a new Turkish version and sell it to third countries. After the collapse of the American-Turkish discussions on the Patriot system, a more advantageous alternative for the Turkish defense (accepted by NATO and the USA) was the acquisition of the long-range anti-missile system of the Franco-Italian group Eurosam, with which the Turkish side has signed a relevant agreement (Kibaroğlu, 2019).

Instead, Ankara went ahead with the S-400 purchase, opting for strategic rapprochement with Russia and disrupting relations with the US and NATO, citing as justification that its decision to purchase the S-400 does not pose a threat to any country, but it only concerns its defense, due to the various problems of instability that are developing in its wider region. This purchase caused tremors in the NATO alliance, on the one hand due to the operational approach between the two countries and on the other hand, due to the incompatibility of the system with NATO defense. The US reacted by activating the mechanism of sanctions against Ankara, provided by the Countering America's Adversaries Through Sanctions Act (CAATSA) and dismissed Turkey from the co-production of the F-35 fighter jets (Bozkurt, 2021). The imposition of sanctions has prompted the Turkish defense industry to look to Russia and China in order to cover its needs, trying to fill the void in the political, economic and military spheres.

Development of the Defense Industry

An impressive and at the same time important aspect of Turkey's shift towards greater strategic autonomy is the development of a national defense industry, which can cover almost 80% of its domestic needs. This transformation has its roots in the early 2000s, when Ankara envisioned the strategy of building a modern and autonomous defense sector and encouraging domestic investment (Demir, 2020). Turkey's rapidly growing defense industry is strengthening its global influence, as this sector is able to export billions of dollars worth of products.

It is worth noting that 2022 was a record year, as the Turkish Defense Industry and Aviation made exports worth 4.3 billion dollars. It is a fact that many Turkish companies in this industry have captured the attention of the international market, as they offer high quality products and are ranked among the top 100. Among them are BAYKAR, Aselsan and TAİ etc. (Göktürk-Çetinkaya & Koç, 2023)

In particular, the domestic production of armed drones has been tested and proved successful on many fronts, such as in Syria, Iraq, Libya and the Nagorno-Karabakh, as well as in Ukraine. So these good performances of defense technologies increased interest and sales, while also empowering Ankara to pursue a more active foreign policy (Sapmaz, 2023), improving relations with states such as Kazakhstan, Kyrgyzstan, Turkmenistan and Azerbaijan, or even creating new ties with various other countries such as Poland, Saudi Arabia and Tunisia (Yılmaz & Kılıçoğlu, 2018). Today, more than 30 countries have purchased Turkish drones and dozens have expressed interest in acquiring them.

However it must be taken into account that the most important thing that distinguishes Turkey from other producing countries is that Turkey is actively involved in conflicts and conducts extensive cross-border operations, simultaneously testing the weapons systems it produces.

CONCLUSIONS

Turkey's pursuit of geopolitical autonomy is a multifaceted and dynamic process shaped by historical, regional, and global factors. While its integration into Western structures such as NATO and its past EU accession aspirations once defined its strategic orientation, Ankara has increasingly sought to carve out an independent role in international politics. The decline of U.S. hegemony, growing regional instability, and shifting global power dynamics have provided Turkey with both opportunities and challenges in its pursuit of autonomy.

Turkey considers that it cannot be limited to the current narrow borders, as the global interaction of its economy is projected on a wider axis. The historical foundation of the doctrine is the view that, Turkey must acquire sea power in order to regain its rightful place. For this reason, it projects its power in the Eastern Mediterranean through the Turkish Navy, in order to acquire sovereign rights and maritime strategic interests, through the presence and display of the flag of its ships and the control of areas of its intended maritime jurisdiction. Exploitation of natural resources is only one part of the plan, the ultimate goal of which is to control the eastern sea transit routes to Europe and interconnect with the geopolitical space beyond the Eastern Mediterranean.

It is found that Turkey, taking advantage of the modern rearrangements of the international system - which is in a "post-Western transition", where would-be regional powers may have interests that are either conform or opposed to warring power centers (Dalay, 2021b) - seeks to systematically develop into a protagonist of the so-called energy diplomacy, with the ultimate goal of turning into a large transit hub for trade and energy in the Eurasian area. To achieve these goals, it seeks to acquire an enhanced strategic autonomy, fully adapted to the transformation of the new world order, projecting a more dynamic geopolitical identity, where it repositions itself as an active global actor, which will increase its capacity for autonomy in the geo-economic field. Turkey aims to be a self-sufficient country in the areas related to economy, trade, technology, industry, transport and defense industry and to act alone when the right circumstances allow.

This autonomy is interpreted as its ability to act unilaterally in order to defend its geostrategic interests, making use of military power, as in the case of the South-East Mediterranean, where it tries to eliminate all forms of risks and threats, so as not to find itself before a fait accompli that could exclude it from future energy plans. To serve these goals, it follows its own foreign policy, calculating the changes in the regional and international system. However, this does not mean that it moves away from the existing alliance relations, but rather that it implements independent policies, which ensure its vital interests and minimize the risks arising from the complexity and conflicting interests of the alliance, of which it is a member.

Turkey claims a more active role on the international stage, trying to become a more active player within the United Nations, which will help eliminate problems of global governance. From this point of view, it projects a new geopolitical face, showing that it is neither moving away from the Western alliance, nor approaching Eurasia. It simply does not identify with either pole. It seeks to become the Third Pole in the emerging international system (Tziarras, 2022), which will be the connecting link between the other two poles of confrontation and will trade with them on equal terms, maintaining ties with both.

Finally, despite these advancements, Turkey's future autonomy will depend on its ability to navigate economic uncertainties, maintain regional stability, and manage its diplomatic relationships with both Western and non-Western actors. Ultimately, while Turkey has made significant strides toward self-reliance, its geopolitical autonomy remains an evolving and contested process in a rapidly changing international order.

REFERENCES

Alonso-Trabanco, J. M. (2022). "Turkey as an Aspiring Great Power". *Geopolitical Monitor*. https://tinyurl.com/2uastnwv

Andreasyan, A. (2013). Gas Finds in the Eastern Mediterranean. *Journal of Palestine Studies*, *42*(3), 29–47. DOI: 10.1525/jps.2013.42.3.29

Ataman, M., & Özdemir, Ç. (2018). Turkey's Syria Policy: Constant Objectives, Shifting Priorities. *Turkish Journal of Middle Eastern Studies.*, *5*(2), 13–35. DOI: 10.26513/tocd.466046

Baç, M. M., & Taşkın, E. (2007). Turkey's accession to the European Union does culture and identity play a role? *Ankara Review of European Studies*, *6*(2), 31–50.

Badarin, E., & Schumacher, T. (2022). The Eastern Mediterranean Energy Bonanza: A Piece in the Regional and Global Geopolitical Puzzle, and the Role of the European Union. *Comparative Southeast European Studies*, *70*(3), 414–438. DOI: 10.1515/soeu-2022-0036

Bozkurt, A. (2021). "Turkey failed to convince Russia to share missile technology, agree to co-production". *Nordic Monitor*, available at: https://tinyurl.com/yeypb5vn

Colibasanu, A. (2024). (2024). *Turkey's evolving geopolitical strategy in the Black Sea.* Foreign Policy Research Institute. https://tinyurl.com/54mbvwkd

Dalay, G. (2021). *Turkish-Russian relations in light of recent conflicts: Syria, Libya, and Nagorno-Karabakh* Stiftung Wissenschaft und Politik. German Institute for International and Security Affairs. DOI: DOI: 10.18449/2021RP05

Danisi, C. (2017). Taking the 'Union' out of 'EU': The EU-Turkey Statement on the Syrian Refugee Crisis as an Agreement Between States under International Law. Blog of the European Journal of International Law, available at: https://tinyurl.com/yurb7k3w

Demir, I. (2020). Transformation of the Turkish Defense Industry. *Insight Turkey.*, *22*(3), 17–24. DOI: 10.25253/99.2020223.02

Duman, B. (2016). Turkey's fight against terrorism and the role of the Kurds. ORSA- Center for Middle Eastern Strategic Studies. Review of Regional Affairs. No 53, available at: https://orsam.org.tr/d_hbanaliz/53eng.pdf

Erdemir, A., & Edelman, E. (2018). *Erdogan's Hostage Diplomacy Western Nationals in Turkish Prisons*. Foundation for Defense of Democracies.

Erensü, S. & Karaman, O. (2017). "The Work of a Few Trees: Gezi, Politics and Space". *International Journal of Urban and Regional Research,* 2017, 41 (1), pp.19-36. DOI: ff10.1111/1468-2427.12387

Fuller, G. (2008). *The New Turkish Republic: Turkey as a Pivotal in the Muslim World.* United State Institute of Peace.

Göktürk-Çetinkaya, S. & Koç, M. (2023). "Türkiye'nin İnsansız Hava Araçları Serüveni". *Anadolu Strateji Dergisi.* Cilt 5, ss 1-27

Hale, W., & Özbudun, E. (2010). *Islamism, Democracy and Liberalism in Tukey*. Routledge.

Huseynov, Y. (2017). Geopolitics of the Republic of Turkey's Energy Policy. *International Journal of Energy Economics and Policy*, *7*(3), 337–344.

Kardaş Ş. (2011). Turkey and the Arab Spring: Coming to Terms with Democracy Promotion? October, The German Marshall Fund of The United States. Policy Brief. Foreign Policy Program.

Kibaroğlu, M. (2019). On Turkey's Missile Defense Strategy: The Four Faces of the S-400 Deal Between Turkey and Russia. Center For Strategic Research. Republic of Turkey Ministry of Foreign Affairs, available at: https://tinyurl.com/3dspvfzw

Kınıklıoğlu, S. (2022). *Necessary friends: Turkey's improving relationship with the West.* European Council of Foreign Relations. https://tinyurl.com/z83sx2yh

Koray, M. (2020). *Doğu Akdeniz'in jeopolitik ve jeostratejik önemi, teknolojik dönüşümler ve denizaltilarin rolü.* Yeni Deniz Güvenliği Ekosistemi ve Doğu Akdeniz. Istanbul: Türk Asya Stratejik Araştırmalar Merkezi.

Korutürk, O. (2012). Arab Revolution: Should We Still Call It a Spring? *Turkish Policy Quarterly*, *10*(4), 63–70.

Larabee, F. S., & Lesser, I. O. (2003). *Turkish Foreign Policy in an Age of Uncertainty*. RAND, National Security Research Division. Center for Middle East Public Policy.

Oğuzlu, H. T. (2020). 'Turkish Foreign Policy in a Changing World Order. Old alignments and new neighborhoods International Conference, Oxford 30 April – 2 May 2010. Published by *South East European Studies at Oxford* (SEESOX), European Studies Centre, St Antony's College University of Oxford, pp. 127-139

Önis, Z. (2014). Turkey and the Arab Revolutions: Boundaries of Regional Power Influence in a Turbulent Middle East. *Mediterranean Politics*, *19*(2), 203–219. DOI: 10.1080/13629395.2013.868392

Önis, Z., & Kutlay, M. (2017). The dynamics of emerging middle-power influence in regional and global governance: The paradoxical case of Turkey. *Australian Journal of International Affairs*, *71*(2), 167–183. DOI: 10.1080/10357718.2016.1183586

Ozkan, B. (2014). "Turkey, Davutoğlu and the Idea of Pan-Islamism". Survival. *Survival*, *56*(4), 119–140. Advance online publication. DOI: 10.1080/00396338.2014.941570

Pierini, M. (2019, May). Options for the EU-Turkey Relationship. Carnegie Europe, available at: https://tinyurl.com/228ws24b

Roubanis, I. (2019). "The European Crisis and Turkey's: Unpredictable Role in the Balkans". *Insight Turkey Spring*. Vol. 21, No 2, available at: https://tinyurl.com/h3wmx6h6

Tokdoğan, N. (2024). *Neo-Ottomanism as an Alternative Narrative of National Identity*. Palgrave Studies in Political Psychology., DOI: 10.1007/978-3-031-48723-1_3

Turan, I., Akçay, Y., & Kanat, S. (2019). An overview to Turkey-EU relations during the justice and development party period. *Suleyman Demirel University Visionary Journal, 10*(25), 658–666. DOI: 10.21076/vizyoner.563322

Türkiye İstatistik Kurumu. (2022). Nüfus ve demografi. TÜİK. https://tinyurl.com/mw7sfurz

Tziarras, Z. (2022). The Ukraine War and Turkey as a 'Third Pole' in a New International Order. In *PRIO Cyprus Centre Policy Brief, 1*. PRIO Cyprus Centre., available at https://tinyurl.com/2fupj8m6

United Nations, Department of Economic and Social Affairs, Population Division. (2024). World population prospects. https://tinyurl.com/4uedfpmb

Villegas, G. A. (2020): *The Mediterranean Sea: maritime power, conflicts and strategies*. Institute of Electrical and Electronics Engineers. Framework Document 03, available at: https://tinyurl.com/2w85zypj

World Bank. (2023). *Turkey Overview*, available at: https://tinyurl.com/3rbttvre

Yılmaz, A. N. & Kılıçoğlu, G (2018). "Türkiye'nin orta asya'daki yumuşak gücü ve kamu diplomasisi uygulamalarinin analizi". *Türk Dünyası Araştırmaları*. Cilt. 19 Sayı 235, ss 141-184.

Chapter 7
Turkey's Energy Needs: Geopolitical Stakes and Socio-Economic Sustainability

Konstantinos Bogiatzis
https://orcid.org/0009-0002-3136-4408
University of the Aegean, Greece

Athanasios Asmenoudis
University of the Aegean, Greece

Georgia Topaka
University of the Aegean, Greece

Spyros Anagnostou
University of the Aegean, Greece

ABSTRACT

According to Anglo-Saxon geopolitical theory, Turkey is a key part of Rimland. Its geographical position gives it the privilege of becoming a crossroads of Western markets, but also of many unstable, geostrategically and economically important regions, such as the Middle East, Russia and the Caspian Sea region. This paper analyses Turkey's energy needs and argues that in order to meet its growing energy demand, Turkey is trying to transform its energy mix by reaching out to global and regional actors

DOI: 10.4018/979-8-3373-8790-1.ch007

in order to become a focal point for energy trade in the region and a natural gas hub, taking advantage of its geographical position and access to energy-rich neighbors, without having hydrocarbon resources of its own. This energy dependence has an impact on its internal and foreign policy, as reforms will have to be designed and implemented to meet both its internal challenges and its geopolitical ambitions.

INTRODUCTION

The article focuses on Turkey's energy needs as an emerging and fast-growing economy and the role they play in its domestic and foreign policy and in its relations with its neighbors and allies.

The growth in Turkey's energy demand over the last two decades is due to its rapid economic and population growth. For this reason, it is seeking to restructure its energy sector, aiming to rationalize the growth in energy demand, reduce energy prices and restrict imports.

The main characteristics of the Turkish energy market are the ever-increasing energy needs and the dependence on imports. Therefore, Ankara's energy strategy includes, i) prioritizing energy security, ii) ensuring sustainable development, and therefore not neglecting environmental risks, iii) increasing efficiency and productivity through reforms and liberalization of the energy market, iv) increasing energy efficiency and, v) adding nuclear power and renewables to its energy mix (International Energy Agency, n.d.).

Figure 1. Total Energy Supply

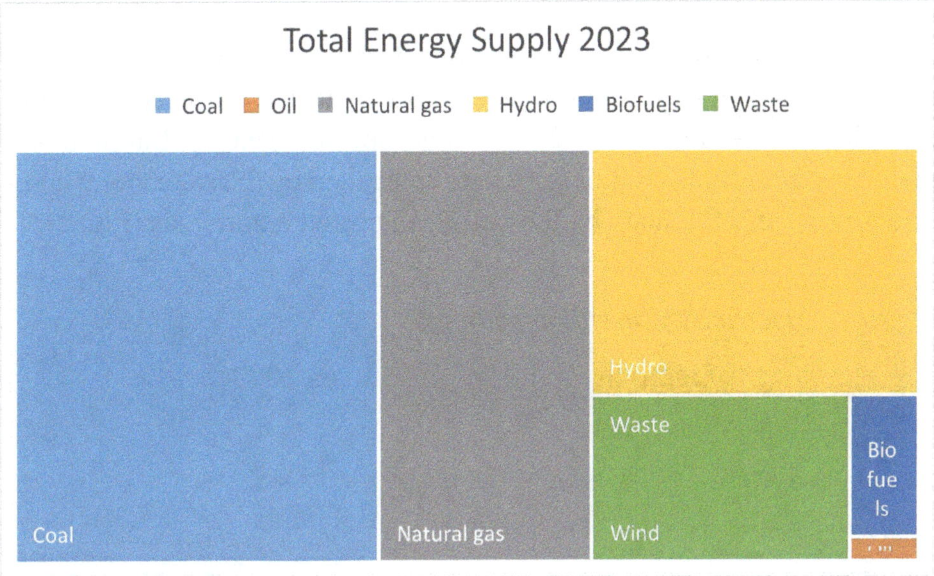

Source: International Energy Agency. License: CC BY 4.0

The growing demand for energy also determines its foreign policy and by practicing energy diplomacy, it is trying to strengthen its position and establish itself as an energy transit hub in the wider region. These ambitions have implications for allies and neighbors alike.

This paper aspires to answer the questions below: What is Turkey's energy mix? What is its energy mix? Why does its energy policy redefine its foreign policy?

ENERGY MIX

Turkey's energy mix is characterized by a combination of domestic and imported energy sources, with an emphasis on meeting the ever-increasing demand for energy due to rapid economic growth and a growing population. Turkey seeks to diversify its energy sources, reduce import dependence and promote domestic production, while developing renewable energy sources (Atay & Apak, 2024). The following is an analysis of the main sources contributing to Turkey's energy production?

Electricity

Electricity consumption per person in Turkey is higher than the world average, but lower than the European average. Most of the electricity from coal (36.3%), natural gas (21.2%) and hydropower (19.6%) (International Energy Agency, n.d.). Retail prices are controlled by the state, but wholesale prices are influenced by the cost of imported natural gas (Fig. 2).

Figure 2. Electricity generation sources

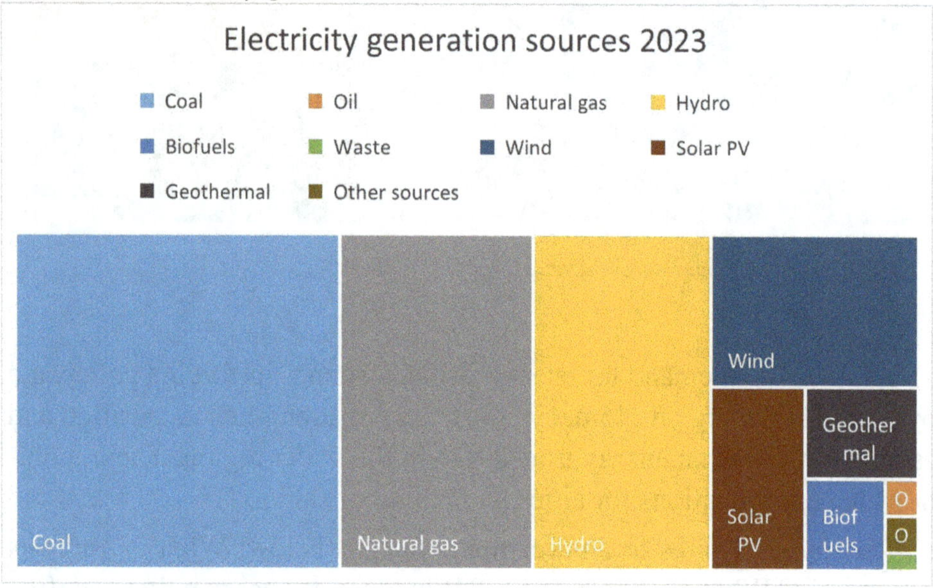

Source: International Energy Agency. License: CC BY 4.0

The sector of production, distribution and maintenance of electricity networks has largely followed the same development as in Western European countries. The Energy Market Regulatory Authority (EPDK[1]) was established in 2001, responsible for licensing companies involved in the generation, transmission and distribution of electricity on Turkish territory (Oral, 2022).

The previously state-owned electricity company (TEİAŞ[2]) was split into smaller transmission, distribution and trading companies in order to facilitate its partial - largely - privatization. The largest power generating company to date remains the state-owned EÜAŞ[3], which controls 50% of domestic production, with the remaining share distributed among smaller private companies operating under the supervision of EPDK (Kirmizioğlu, 2014).

Natural Gas and Liquefied Natural Gas (LNG)

Turkey is among the countries with the fastest growing demand for natural gas (Fig. 3). Globally, in 2022 it was the sixteenth largest consumer of natural gas, as a consequence of the growth its economy has experienced over the last twenty years. Natural gas is mainly used for electricity generation, heating, cooking and, to a lesser extent, for the production of chemicals used in the manufacture of fertilisers and plastics (Ağbulut et al, 2023).

Figure 3. Natural gas supply (TJ)

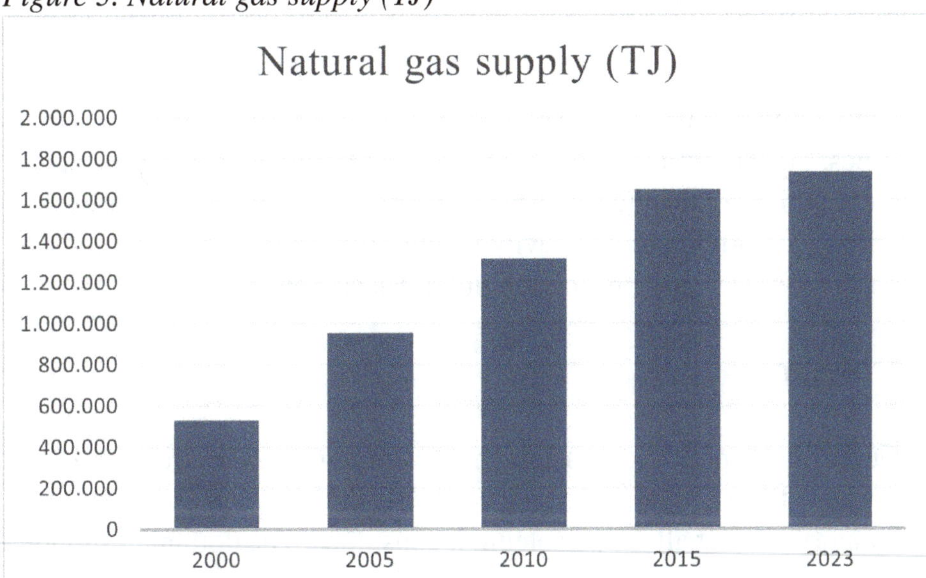

Source: International Energy Agency. License: CC BY 4.0

Russia is the main supplier of natural gas, although total exports have declined in recent years. Iran follows, while Azerbaijan and Algeria have a significant share of gas exports to Turkey (Trading Economics, n.d.)

The supply of natural gas from Russia should not come as a big surprise given the country's infrastructure networks, as two gas pipelines have been built between the countries, Blue Stream (2003) and Turk Stream (2020). Also, two other pipelines, of smaller capacity than the two Russian pipelines, connect Turkey to Azerbaijan (Baku-Tbilisi-Erzurum Natural Gas Pipeline, 2003 and Trans-Anatolian Natural Gas Pipeline Project, 2018) and with Iran (Iran–Turkey Natural Gas Pipeline, 2023).

According to available data for the year 2023, it imports 30% of its liquefied natural gas (LNG) needs (International Energy Agency, n.d.). There is an increase in LNG imports due to its strategic transformation in the energy sector, enhancing its energy security.

Turkey imports LNG from Algeria, Nigeria, the United States, Qatar, Egypt and Norway. So far 4 LNG terminals are operating (Marmara Ereglisi, Egegaz Aliaga, Etki-Aliaga and Dortyol-Hatay) with two floating terminals in operation, another terminal under construction in Saros Bay (Özdil, 2024).

As part of the energy transformation, it signed 10-year LNG supply agreements with Shell Plc (Shell, 2024) and Total Energies SE (Total Energies, 2024), with the possibility of redirecting cargoes to European markets, which contributes to Turkey's efforts to become a regional energy hub. It has already invested heavily in new storage and LNG facilities, as well as in research and production in the Black Sea.

Petroleum

Due to its dependence on external energy sources, petroleum is the second most important source of energy. It has few domestic resources and imports almost all the petroleum it consumes. The dominant supplier for the year 2023 is Venezuela (20%), followed by Saudi Arabia (17%), Canada (11%), Iran (9%), Iraq (8%), Russia (6%) and the USA (3%) and to a much lesser extent other countries (T.C. Turkish Ministry of Energy and Natural Resources, 2023).

Figure 4. Petroleum suppliers of Turkey

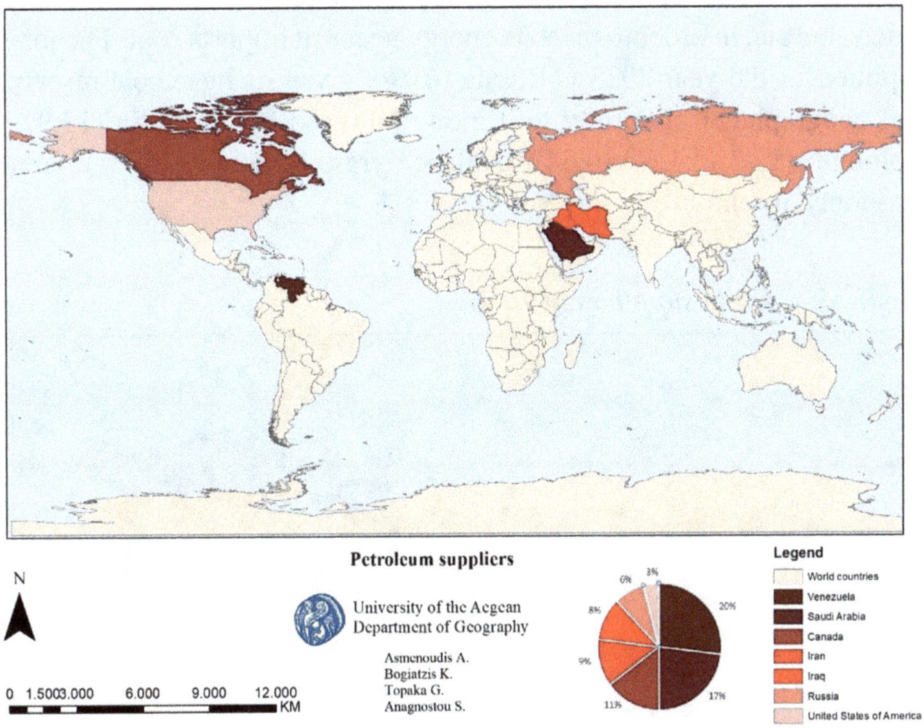

Source: Turkish Ministry of Energy and Natural Resources, 2023

However, Turkey plays a crucial role as an energy transit country. Its strategic geographical location (close to more than 70% of proven petroleum and gas reserves) makes Turkey a central transit hub for the transport of hydrocarbons from the Middle East, Russia and the Caspian Sea to Western markets. Transit crude petroleum pipelines (Kirkuk-Ceyhan Pipeline, Baku-Tbilisi-Ceyhan (BTC) Pipeline, Trans-Anatolian Pipeline (TANAP), Batman-Dörtyol Pipeline) connect it to global markets (Turkish Energy Ministry and Natural Resources, 2023) and strengthen its role in the global market and its strategic importance for energy security.

Carbon

Coal has a prominent place in Turkey's energy mix. Its main use is to generate electricity from domestically available lignite resources, but also from imported coal. Lignite and hard coal account for 26.1% of electricity generation. However, because domestic lignite reserves have a low calorific value and in order to meet its energy needs, it imports coal. The main supplier for the year 2023 is Russia (61%), given its huge coal reserves and geographical proximity to Turkey, followed by Australia (13.9%), Colombia (12.3%), USA (6.34%) and the Kyrgyz Republic (2.97%) (Trend Economy, n.d.).

Figure 5. Carbon suppliers of Turkey

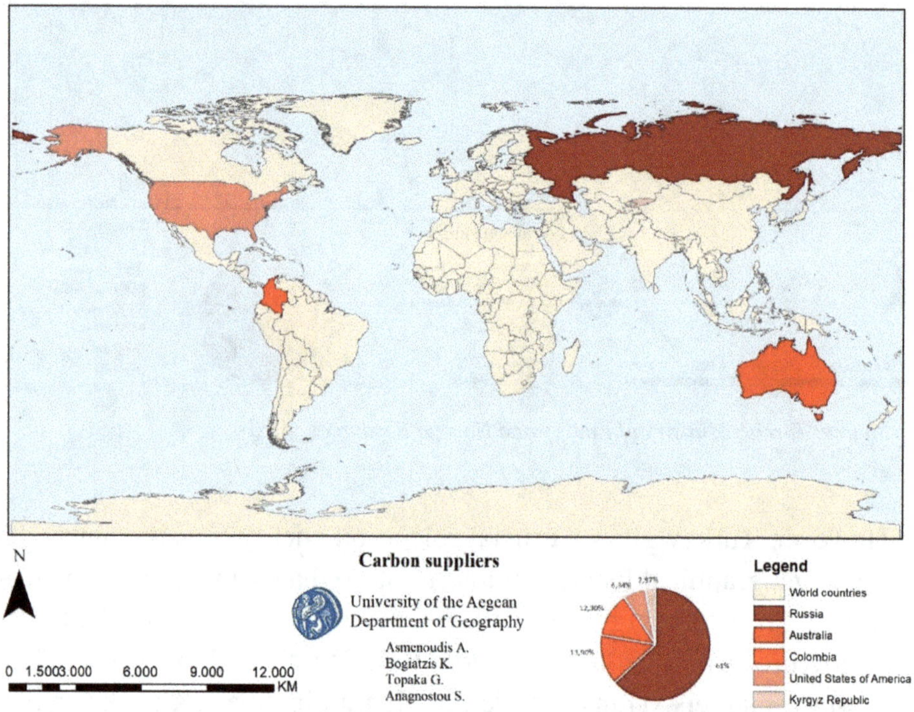

Source: Turkish Ministry of Energy and Natural Resources, 2023

In the context of efforts to reduce its energy dependence on natural gas, in recent decades, there has been a steady increase in coal consumption for electricity generation. In addition, the significant increase in imports is also due to the fact that the steel sector in Turkey is growing, as granulating coal is a critical component in steel production.

Due to its heavy dependence on coal, especially lignite, Ankara has been criticized for its greenhouse gas emissions and air pollution, while the global energy market is shifting towards renewable sources. Despite the criticisms, coal is expected to remain a key source of energy in the future, as government policy supports the development of new power plants, especially those using domestic lignite, both to boost local economies and to ensure its energy security (Gezen & Karaaslan, 2022).

Renewable Energy Sources

In recent years Turkey has experienced the fastest growth in electricity among Organization for Economic Co-operation and Development (OECD) countries and is therefore taking significant steps to reduce its dependence on imported fossil resources by increasing the use of domestic renewable resources for electricity generation. The country has significant potential in renewable energy sources such as wind, solar and hydropower, and has developed policies and investments to exploit them. Energy sources accounted for almost half of domestic electricity generation. This progress underscores Turkey's commitment to clean energy and its potential economic benefits (Ersoy & Ugurlu, 2024)

The economic benefits of this energy transition are undeniable, as it spends exorbitant amounts on petroleum and gas imports, with the 2022 bill reaching US$97 billion, while for 2023 import costs are not fully available, however they are expected to be equally high given geopolitical tensions and price volatility in energy markets (Temizer, 2024).

In fact, reducing this import dependence will significantly improve Turkey's financial stability and help manage its current account deficit. On the other hand, it is pursuing policies to reduce carbon emissions and ensure energy security through alternative sources.

Nuclear Energy

The planning of Turkey's nuclear program dates back to the 1960s, but its implementation started in the 2010s, with agreements signed with Russia and Japan to build nuclear power plants with pressurized water reactors in the Akkuyu region of Mersin province and in Sinope, on the Black Sea coast (Aydin, 2020).

The inauguration of the first reactor of the Akkuyu plant took place in April 2023, as part of Erdogan's election campaign and re-election. Construction of the other three reactors started in 2020 and are expected to be operational by 2026 (World Nuclear News, 2023).

According to government sources, when the Akkuyu plant becomes fully operational, it is expected to cover 10% of domestic electricity needs and will play a key role in diversifying Turkey's energy mix, in the context of its decoupling from fossil fuel imports (Kyriakides, 2022).

Despite the Turkish government's intentions to add nuclear energy to its energy mix, the implementation of the program is moving slowly. Due to the inflationary crisis it is experiencing, construction and financing costs have increased and it has cancelled the joint venture agreement with Japan to build the Sinope nuclear power plant (Dalton, 2020). In February 2023, South Korea's state-owned Korea Electric Power Corporation (Kepco) proposed to build another nuclear power plant in the north of the country[4] and, as part of the nuclear program implementation, started discussions with China to build a third nuclear power plant (World Nuclear Association, 2024).

ENERGY AND FOREIGN POLICY

The discovery of significant natural gas deposits in the Eastern Mediterranean, while initially raising hopes for European markets as an alternative source of natural gas, has subsequently created geopolitical tensions in the region, especially between Cyprus, Greece, Israel, Egypt, Israel and Turkey. Natural gas deposits found in the exclusive economic zones (EEZs) of countries in the region have the potential to change the balance of the energy market, as well as create new sources of income for these states.

During the 2000s and 2010s, Turkey challenged the delimitation agreements between Egypt, Israel, Cyprus, Cyprus and Lebanon, going so far as to deploy its navy to block drilling in maritime areas authorized by the Republic of Cyprus. Ankara considers that Cyprus' deposits should be shared with the Turkish Cypriots, and rejects the EEZ defined by Cyprus, making claims to maritime areas that it considers to belong to it (Mazis et al, 2022) or to the northern part of Cyprus, which only Turkey recognizes as a state.

In response, it has sent exploration and drilling vessels to areas that it considers to fall under its own jurisdiction, even if these areas overlap with the EEZs of other countries, such as Cyprus and Greece (Ioannides, 2018). This tactic has provoked mild reactions from the European Union, warning Turkey with sanctions, as well as from the United States and other countries that verbally condemn unilateral Turkish actions.

Fearing its energy isolation, Ankara has activated the Blue Homeland (Mavi Vatan) doctrine, which projects Ankara's claims across the Eastern Mediterranean. Within this framework, it has strengthened its relations with Libya, signing an agreement in 2019 to define maritime borders between the two countries. This agreement benefited Ankara both because it brought it out of regional isolation and revised the maritime border in Turkey's favour in exchange for military assistance to Libya. This agreement has been considered illegal by Greece and other countries, as it does not take into account the maritime zones of Greek islands such as Crete.

The growing demand for energy is a foreign policy priority, which is why Ankara often alters its geopolitical interests. Its energy needs push it towards rapprochement with global and regional actors such as Russia, Middle Eastern countries, Central Asian countries and the European Union (Yılmaz, 2023). However, its ardent desire is to become an energy distribution and trade center in energy, making itself a regional power.

This geopolitical vision of becoming an energy epicentre without having its own hydrocarbon energy resources has deep roots in foreign policy making. Turkey, fully aware of its important geographical position, has concluded agreements and built infrastructure to transport natural gas to European markets.

However, after Russia's invasion of Ukraine, Ankara has readjusted its energy policy as Europe seeks new gas suppliers. Ankara is seeking to reduce its energy dependence on imported gas by exploiting gas deposits in the Black Sea region and bringing the Akkuyu nuclear power plant online. In this way, it hopes to preserve Russian imported gas for domestic consumption and export the remaining quantities from domestic extraction or blend gas from various sources and make it available to energy-hungry Europe (Tüysüzoğlu, 2023).

In addition to its geopolitical ambitions, the dream of an energy hub causes strong reservations in Europe, which, since it is facing an energy problem, does not intend to be energy dependent on Turkey, as it has been in its recent past with Russia. For this reason, Europe is turning to green-renewable energy sources.

Nevertheless, as part of its ambition to become a regional energy player, in 2023 it signed gas export agreements with selected European countries (Bulgaria, Hungary, Romania and Moldova), which mark the energy diversification of these countries, reducing their vulnerability to supply disruptions and geopolitical pressures due to the ongoing Russia-Ukraine conflict (T.C. İletişim Başkanlığı, 2023).

For Turkey, these agreements provide significant economic benefits. With Europe's growing demand for gas from non-Russian sources, it can capitalize on transit fees and use energy as a tool in diplomatic negotiations with both the EU and the countries it supplies with gas (Göksel, 2023).

These agreements also ensure that Turkey can obtain gas from multiple suppliers and strengthen its domestic supply networks. Ankara, as an energy supplier or intermediate hub for Central and Eastern European countries, is likely to deepen political and economic ties with them. These agreements could serve as a basis for future cooperation in infrastructure, trade and diplomatic initiatives, enhancing its role in regional affairs (Üngör, 2024).

Turkey currently cannot limit its energy dependence on the Kremlin, as it imports coal, petroleum and gas through TurkStream and is working with Russia's Rosatom State Atomic Energy Corporation to build the Akkuyu nuclear power plant. However, it manages a delicate balance between Moscow and Brussels because Moscow's push to make Ankara a hub for Russian gas, with the low sales prices it offers, suggests increased dependence that will not change in the future (Kolay, 2023).

On the other hand, these agreements are in line with Europe's energy security policies and can play a role in the EU's smooth transition towards renewable energy sources. While these agreements concern natural gas, they emphasize the immediate need to convert energy supply from fossil fuels to renewable energy sources.

In summary, Turkey's gas export agreements signal its growing role as an energy corridor between Europe and the Middle East-Central Asia. They contribute to the diversification of Europe's energy sources, reduce Russian dominance, provide Turkey with economic and geopolitical advantages and strengthen its ties with Central and Eastern Europe, although they may create friction with Russia.

CONCLUSION

Turkey's dependence on energy resources makes it vulnerable to international prices and geopolitical developments, as its production and trade strategies are directly linked to its energy needs. Its independent energy policy choices had yielded tangible results both in its infrastructure network - such as gas-petroleum pipelines, liquefied natural gas (LNG) terminals - and in its international relations, through the conclusion of cooperation agreements with neighboring states, limiting in some way its dependence on Russian hydrocarbons. However, to this day the main energy supplier remains Russia (Andrei, 2022).

Turkey's dependence on imported energy is an important factor for both the stability of the economy and its position on the world stage, influencing decisions at the political, diplomatic and economic levels. Imported energy is a burden on its trade balance and directly affects production, business competitiveness and the cost of living. At the level of international relations, it shapes its foreign policy, influencing its ties with key suppliers such as Russia, Iran and Azerbaijan. Its need to ensure energy security leads it to seek alternative sources and methods of energy supply, investing in the development of renewable energy sources (wind, solar) and hydrocarbon exploration in the Black Sea and the Eastern Mediterranean (Siccardi, 2024).

Turkey's hydrocarbon exploration in the Eastern Mediterranean has led to increased tensions with neighboring countries such as Greece, Cyprus and Israel, as these areas are considered geostrategically critical for the region's energy security. Turkey is seeking to exploit the potential hydrocarbon deposits in the region to reduce its dependence and strengthen its energy independence. However, these explorations have raised serious questions about legitimacy and sovereignty, especially given the existing geopolitical disputes. With the potential hydrocarbon deposits in the Eastern Mediterranean being a promising resource, Turkey seeks to ensure its participation in the exploitation of these resources, even if it means confrontations with neighboring countries (Dilek, 2022).

However, tensions in the Eastern Mediterranean may lead to serious political and military complications if a diplomatic solution is not reached. Moreover, the ongoing conflict hampers efforts for regional cooperation on energy and security issues, as well as for the promotion of major energy projects that could benefit the entire region.

Its efforts to transform its energy policy, i.e. to wean itself off Russian imported hydrocarbons and coal, apart from the economic benefits to its budget, will redefine its relations with Europe and with its neighbors in the Eastern Mediterranean and the Caucasus, Central Asia and the Western Balkans.

The European strategy for energy diversification and decoupling from Russian energy, notably through the promotion of gas from other sources (such as Azerbaijan and the Eastern Mediterranean), gives Turkey the opportunity to play the role of an energy hub. The TANAP pipeline, which transports Azeri gas through Turkey to Europe, is an example of this role (Reka, 2023). If Turkey manages to develop more energy infrastructure and secure its energy self-sufficiency, its relations with Europe will be strengthened, offering new scope for cooperation.

Turkey's decoupling from traditional energy sources, combined with its pursuit of hydrocarbon deposits in the Eastern Mediterranean, will have a significant impact on its relations with Greece, Cyprus and Israel. Turkey may continue to seek alternatives through the development of its own energy resources or through partnerships with neighboring countries. However, the issue of sovereignty over maritime zones and disputes over EEZs will continue to be a source of tension.

The Caucasus and Central Asia are strategic regions for Turkey from both a geopolitical and energy point of view. Turkey already has strong ties with Azerbaijan through the TANAP pipeline, and aims to further strengthen cooperation with Central Asian countries such as Kazakhstan and Turkmenistan, which have significant energy reserves (Köstem, 2019). Reducing dependence on Russia will reinforce Turkey's need to maintain stable relations with these countries, both for energy supply and transit through its energy hubs.

The Western Balkan region, which is a strategic area for gas transit, will play a role in Turkey's energy game. The development of energy infrastructure linking Turkey with the Balkans and Central Europe could contribute to the energy diversification of the region. Turkey's participation in major energy projects, such as the TAP (Trans Adriatic Pipeline), which runs through Albania and North Macedonia, offers the possibility of strengthening cooperation with the Western Balkans (Reka, 2023).

In conclusion, it is evident that Turkey aims to become an energy hub in the Eastern Mediterranean region by investing in new infrastructure, pipelines, and partnerships, while simultaneously striving to increase domestic production and reduce dependence on imports. This effort to transform Turkey's energy policy not only has economic implications but could also redefine the country's geopolitical relations. Reducing dependence on Russian energy and developing new energy infrastructure could elevate Turkey's position as a regional energy player, bringing it closer to Europe and opening pathways for cooperation with neighboring countries in the Eastern Mediterranean, the Caucasus, and the Balkans. Given the ongoing tensions in the Eastern Mediterranean, where energy resources are directly linked to issues of national sovereignty and economic interests, the potential for further escalation of tensions remains ever-present. Therefore, diplomatic efforts remain crucial to finding solutions that promote cooperation and stability in the region.

REFERENCES

Andrei, R. (2022). Turkey's Energy Strategy. In *Search of an Upgraded Political and Energy Status". In Natural Gas at the Frontline Between the EU, Russia, and Turkey: A Conflict-Cooperation Perpetuum* (pp. 231–263). Springer International Publishing.

Atay, E., & Apak, S. (2024). The European Union and Turkey's Renewable Resources Versus Fossil Energy for the Sustainable Future. *New Approaches to CSR, Sustainability and Accountability*, *V*, 153–162. DOI: 10.1007/978-981-99-9145-7_8

Aydin, C. İ. (2020). Nuclear energy debate in Turkey: Stakeholders, policy alternatives, and governance issues. *Energy Policy*, *136*, 111041. Advance online publication. DOI: 10.1016/j.enpol.2019.111041

Dalton, D. (2020, January 2020). Turkey / Contract For Sinop Nuclear Station 'Has Been Cancelled. NucNet, The Independent Nuclear News Agency. https://shorturl.at/9Atu7

Dilek, E. (2022). Sovereignty Disputes and Resource Discoveries in the Eastern Mediterranean: A Conflict Analysis Perspective. *Journal of Middle East Perspectives*, *1*(2), 133–155.

Ersoy, E. A., & Ugurlu, A. (2024). Bioenergy's role in achieving a low-carbon electricity future: A case of Türkiye. *Applied Energy*, *372*, 123799. Advance online publication. DOI: 10.1016/j.apenergy.2024.123799

Gezen, M., & Karaaslan, A. (2022). *"Energy planning based on Vision-2023 of Turkey with a goal programming under fuzzy multi-objectives". Energy* (Vol. 261). Part A., DOI: 10.1016/j.energy.2022.124956

Göksel, O. (2023). Trading state or machiavellian state? Re-Evaluating the political economy of Turkish foreign policy under Erdoğan. *UPA Strategic Affairs*, *4*(2), 72–107.

İletişim Başkanlığı, T. C. (2023, September 29). *Türkiye, Moldova'ya doğal gaz ihraç edecek.* https://shorturl.at/gSAgG

International Energy Agency. (n.d.). *Energy system of Türkiye*. https://shorturl.at/SrIxI

Ioannides, N. (2018). *Rights and Obligations of States in Undelimited Maritime Areas: The Case of the Eastern Mediterranean Sea*. Stress Testing the Law of the Sea. [REMOVED HYPERLINK FIELD], DOI: 10.1163/9789004352926_014

Kirmizioğlu, E. (2014). Ülkemizin 2023 Stratejik Vizyonu Doğrultusunda Akıllı Şebekeye Geçilmesi için Öneriler. Uluslararası İstanbul Akıllı Şebekeler Kongre ve Fuarı, pp143-147. https://hdl.handle.net/11352/1910

Kolay, B. (2023). *Akkuyu Nuclear Power Plant and Energy Diplomacy: How Construction of the Akkuyu Power Plant affected Energy Diplomacy between Turkey and Russia? A Process Tracing Approach.*

Köstem, S. (2019). Geopolitics, identity and beyond: Turkey's renewed interest in the Caucasus and Central Asia. In *Turkey's Pivot to Eurasia* (pp. 111–128). Routledge. DOI: 10.4324/9780429023064-8

Kyriakides, K. (2022). The Akkuyu Nuclear Power Plant in Turkey: Some Causes for Concern. *Journal of Balkan & Near Eastern Studies*, *25*(3), 340–377. DOI: 10.1080/19448953.2022.2143855

Mazis, I., Sgouros, G. A., & Troulis, M. (2022). *The Chronicle of a Pre-announced Greek–Turkish Dialogue* (Vol. 9). Civitas Centium., https://shorturl.at/i4vYH

Oral, M. (2022). Türkiye Elektrik Enerjisi Piyasasının Kamu ve Özel Sektör Çerçevesinde Değerlendirilmesi. *Journal of Academic Social Science Studies*, *15*(90), 445–458. DOI: 10.29228/JASSS.62193

Özdil, E. (2024, September 13). Part 4. Turkey's geopolitical role in the Black Sea and European energy security: From pipelines to liquefied natural gas. Atlantic Council. https://shorturl.at/MzCnj

Reka, A. (2023). Energy and Regional Geopolitics in the Western Balkans and Eastern Mediterranean. In *Geopolitical Turmpetroleum in the Balkans and Eastern Mediterranean* (pp. 185–203). Springer International Publishing. DOI: 10.1007/978-3-031-34318-6_8

Shell (2024, September 2). Shell signs ten-year LNG supply agreement with Turkish energy company. https://shorturl.at/6msTx

Siccardi, F. (2024). *Understanding the Energy Drivers of Turkey's Foreign Policy*. Carnegie Endowment for International Peace. https://shorturl.at/v5Jco

T.C. Turkish Ministry of Energy and Natural Resources. (2023, July 12). *Crude Petroleum*. https://shorturl.at/LGaoT

Temizer, M. (2024, June 20). Türkiye's gas imports down 7.64% to 50.48 billion cubic meters in 2023. Anadolu Agency. https://shorturl.at/KiBJp

Total Energies. (2024, September 18). Long term LNG sales in Türkiye: TotalEnergies will supply 1.1 million tons per year to BOTAŞ for 10 years. https://shorturl.at/pNn6g

Trend Economy. (n.d.). Turkey | Imports and Exports | World | Coal | Value (US$) and Value Growth, YoY (%) | 2011 - 2023. https://shorturl.at/GXmdb

Tüysüzoğlu, G. (2023). The Impact of Eurasianism on Turkey's Role in the Ukraine War. *Middle East Policy*, *30*(4), 106–112. DOI: 10.1111/mepo.12715

Üngör, Ç. (2024). A 'bridge' pushed to the periphery?: Turkey's geopolitical significance in the Asia-Pacific century. *Turkish Studies*, •••, 1–23.

Üngör, Ç. (2024). A 'bridge' pushed to the periphery?: Turkey's geopolitical significance in the Asia-Pacific century. *Turkish Studies*, •••, 1–23.

World Nuclear Association. (2024, April 30). *Nuclear Power in Turkey*. https://shorturl.at/xHbcl

World Nuclear News. (2023, April 27). Presidents address ceremony inaugurating Turkey's first nuclear plant. https://shorturl.at/2qRVw

Yılmaz, Ş. (2023). *Facing new security threats in an era of global transformations: Turkey's challenges of energy security, climate change and sustainability*. Routledge.

ENDNOTES

1 Enerji Piyasası Düzenleme Kurumu

2 Türkiye Elektrik İletim Anonim Şirketi

3 Elektrik Üretim Anonim Şirketi

4 https://www.nucnet.org/news/south-korea-s-kepco-launches-bid-to-build-four-new-nuclear-reactors-2-4-2023

Chapter 8
The Democratization of Opportunity:
The Transforming State of Social Entrepreneurship for Disadvantaged Groups – The Cases of Italy and Spain

Nectarios Oudeniotis
https://orcid.org/0009-0006-0069-901X
University of the Aegean, Greece

George Odysseas Tsobanoglou
https://orcid.org/0000-0003-3006-2758
Hellenic Open University, Greece

ABSTRACT

Social enterprises are established upon the deliberative will of groups of citizens and through the use of entrepreneurial models they provide general interest services aiming at addressing social needs. Like any other civil society organization and in order to succeed in their social missions, they engage in establishing networks of people and organizations and in this respect, they generate social capital and collective action, what Field calls the "nursery of a democratic society" (Field, 2003:30). By engaging in

DOI: 10.4018/979-8-3373-8790-1.ch008

social innovation, they develop new working models and ethics and work opportunity for under-represented groups of people with a disadvantaged background (unemployed, Neets, disabled, immigrants, ex-convicts etc). This chapter is focusing on the Euro-Mediterranean countries of Italy and Spain, where the deliberative manifestations of civil society through social entrepreneurship endeavors has developed a stronghold for people belonging in disadvantaged groups, by deliberating and democratizing opportunity, promoting inclusive development and active citizenship

1. INTRODUCTION

Social enterprises are established upon the deliberative will of groups of citizens and through the use of entrepreneurial models they provide general interest services aiming at addressing social needs. Like any other civil society organization and in order to succeed in their social missions, they engage in establishing networks of people and organizations and in this respect, they generate social capital and collective action, what Field calls the "nursery of a democratic society" (Field, 2003:30). Most significantly, by engaging in social innovation, thus creating new services and products, they develop new working models and ethics and work opportunity for under-represented groups of people with a disadvantaged background (unemployed, Neets, disabled, immigrants, ex-convicts or substances abusers, Roma etc).

In this sense, they re-shape the landscape of work provision delimited primarily by public or for-profit organizations, by establishing new and sustainable work conditions for people having a difficulty in becoming absorbed in the context of the limited job offer provided within the public and even more limited within the private for-profit sectors. Since the 1970s, the emergence of an entrepreneurial and productive logic in third sector organizations has provided a new dynamic, as well as, a new way for addressing social challenges and unmet social needs in most of the Euro-Mediterranean countries (Italy, Spain, Greece, Portugal and Cyprus). The blooming of social entrepreneurial models based on European policies and state institutional arrangements (top-down), as well as, civil society's organization initiatives (bottom-up) have resulted to a transformation of labor market opportunities, through the creation of jobs and employment opportunities for people, which the public or for-profit sector failed, became incapable (because of financial, welfare crisis) or even didn't have an interest (no profit) to support. As it is argued in this chapter social entrepreneurial endeavors support and provide pluralism and choice, fundamental features of liberal democracies, particularly for social groups mostly in need. Although, most Euro-Mediterranean countries showcase an array of models and initiatives, the primary focus of this chapter is particularly in the countries of Italy and Spain as the countries with the greater development and evidence in terms of deliberative manifestations of civil society activation and engagement in social entrepreneurship and where social entrepreneurship endeavors have resulted in the development of a stronghold for people belonging in disadvantaged groups, by deliberating and democratizing opportunity in terms of generation of employment, as well as, promoting inclusive development and active citizenship.

2. THE TRANSFORMING STATE OF SOCIAL ENTREPRENEURSHIP FOR DISADVANTAGED GROUPS

Since the 1970's, crisis of the welfare state in Europe and the 2008 financial crisis, a great transformation takes place in societies both in Europe and elsewhere, in terms of the mobilization, involvement and the activation of civil society in all fields of social activity, establishing informal norms and cultures and most importantly engaged in the establishment of social enterprises and support the institutionalization of social entrepreneurship. The latter is taking place in the Euro-Mediterranean area since the 1990s and Italy and Spain consist particular cases, which we'll focus in this chapter, so as to highlight the significance that this new form of entrepreneurship has made particularly for people belonging in disadvantaged groups.

A cornerstone and central purpose of social entrepreneurship is to address social and emerging needs and find solutions for those in need and particularly the most vulnerable and disadvantaged people within a community or society at large. In this respect, it incorporates social business models that include the interplay of private, non-profit and public organizations for the attainment of endeavors, which have as a priority the establishment of a social impact and social value, than the generation of profit and economic value for those involved in the organizations (owners, members).

By focusing on the accomplishment of their social mission and the creation of social value, social entrepreneurs view wealth as "just a means to an end" (Dees, 1998:3). Social enterprises deliver services and produce goods using market and non-market resources in order to fulfill their social mission and achieve their objectives. Most crucially, they focus on the creation and supply of jobs and employability (*work integration*) particularly for those who have difficulties in accessing the job market such long-term-unemployed, young people belonging in vulnerable social groups or with low-skills between 18-29 years old - the so-called NEETS (Not in Employment, Education or Training) - disabled, immigrants, homeless, single-parent families or ex-prisoners seeking a second chance in life (Figure 1).

Figure 1. Areas of social enterprises intervention and activation

Source: OECD (2022)

Social entrepreneurship models and particular the Social Cooperative Model (SCM) of entrepreneurship is one, which witnessed a parallel development and institutionalization in many Euro-Mediterranean countries during the 1990's, namely Spain[1], Italy[2], Greece[3] and Portugal[4], particularly because of its cooperative, democratic governance, voluntary and open membership features, which can mostly be apprehended by groups of people aiming at cooperating and establish common endeavors. Although the model incorporates traditional cooperatives, which strive towards the implementation and fulfilment of its members mutual interest, "it goes beyond most conventional cooperatives in that it combines the pursuit of its members' interests with the pursuit of the interests of the whole community or of a specific target group" (. The implementation of activities of general interest, as well as, with a wider social impact characterizes and may also be part of the mission and operation of the organizations included in the Social Cooperative Model. Spain and Italy comprise two cases within the nexus of the Euro-Mediterranean countries, where the SCM have achieved a greater degree of impact concerning the employability, job generation and well-being for people belonging in vulnerable social groups aa the data gathered from statistical and secondary sources showcase and will be analyzed in the following sections.

2.1 Case A: Italy

It may be said, that Italy holds a special place in the historical evolution of social economy and entrepreneurship in the European Union, as well as the European continent as a whole, since it's the country, where the first national legislation concerning social enterprises *per se* was adopted in 1991 concerning the development of Social Cooperative Enterprises. Like most of the Euro-Mediterranean countries, Italy has a strong cooperative tradition ranging from agriculture, to worker and consumer cooperatives, as well as, in housing, transport and the banking sectors and seemed resilient as a sector in total during the latest economic crisis, by addressing "the crisis from within, without weighing upon local government funding and without claiming from the welfare state, but managing to save and create jobs instead" (Mertens et al 2017: 296).

Since 1970's onwards, the Italian civil society has taken initiatives so as to respond to numerous cases of support towards people from vulnerable social groups or in a disadvantaged position (unemployed, elderly, NEETs) and this fact can also be seen by the great numbers of third sector organizations, which have been emerged since, together with the emergence of social enterprises and the use of a new form of entrepreneurship and market-based initiatives in support of social ends and goals. The institution and organizational form of *Social Cooperative Enterprises (SCE)* in Italy[5], may be seen as the culmination of civil society efforts, which begun in the 1970's and particularly by "volunteer organizations engaged in an improved deployment of human resources and the integration of disadvantaged citizens into society (minors, the disabled, drug addicts, the elderly, former prison inmates, the mentally handicapped, and immigrants)" (Thomas, 2004:247).

Particularly, and as far as SCEs is concerned, during the crisis the number of employees has risen significantly providing jobs across all regions of Italy, with a special focus, on disadvantaged people. According to ISTAT, in 2015 the overall number of employees at SCEs was 439,621 people, having an increase of 17,29% (76.026 people) since 2011, showing a great degree of resilience alongside the cooperative sector (Table 2).

Table 1. Social Cooperative Enterprises in Italy, 2011-2015

2011		2015	
Number of SCEs	Number of employees at SCEs	Number of SCEs	Number of employees at SCEs
10.424	363.595	14.030	439.621

Source: ISTAT (2022)

The Third Sector and the number of social enterprises continue to grow in Italy even after the crisis and in 2020 among the 363.499 registered non-profit organizations, about 16.092 (4,43%) were social enterprises of which 14.984 where SCE's and 1.107 were so called de facto social enterprises, 38.500 (10,59%) were voluntary organizations, 21.085 (5,8%) were social promotion associations, 13.300 (3,66%) were considered as non-profit organizations of social utility (ONLUS) and 272.522 (75,52%) were other non-profit institutions (Table 3).

Table 2. Third sector organizations in Italy according to legal status in 2020

Types of Organizations	Organizations			Beneficiaries		
	no	%	Var: %2020/2019	no	%	Var: %2020/2019
Voluntary organizations	38.500	10.6	5.7	29.704	3.4	7.6
Social promotion associations	21.085	5.8	7.2	11.467	1.3	-7.1
Social enterprises	16.092	4.4	-1.8	471.199	54.2	1.6
Non-profit organizations of social utility	13.300	3.7	-2.7	81.048	9.3	-2.3
Other non-profit institutions	274.522	75.5	-0.7	276.765	31.8	0.5
Total	**363.499**	**100.0**	**0.2**	**870.183**	**100.0**	**1.0**

Source: ISTAT (2022)

Italy has been a pioneer during the 1980's and 90's onwards in the accommodation of welfare and employment needs of disadvantaged people, an overall effort which has received a great impetus after the enactment of legislation 381/91 'Regulation of Social Cooperatives' and the establishment off a legal form of social enterprise, the Social Cooperative Enterprise (SCE), which embodied on the one hand cooperative principles such as democratic participation, multi-stakeholder governance and solidarity and on the other, the purpose of the attainment of a socially oriented mission (social integration of citizens) and the development and promotion of services and goods of the general interest, which are thus aimed to benefit a community as a whole and not partially and unilaterally the members of an organization alone (as is profound case of for-profit enterprises).

It may be said that SCEs are the birth organizations (the first actually of their kind) of what has a little later on been coined as a term and proliferated throughout Europe and the Mediterranean, as a new form of social enterprise, the so-called Work Integration Enterprises (WISEs). WISEs in Italy belong primarily to the so-called," B-type Social Cooperatives" of Law 381/91 engaged with various activities such as agricultural, industrial, commercial or the delivery of services - aimed at the employment of disadvantaged people. From 2000 onwards it seems that there is a growing trend of disadvantaged persons finding employment in and through SCEs. The number of disadvantaged workers in rose from 23.587 persons in 2003, to 32.000 in 2017 having an increase of 36% (Table 4).

Table 3. Disadvantaged people employed by SCEs in Italy, 2003-2017

Social cooperatives	2003	2005	2011	2017	2003-2017 (percentage variations)
Number	5,515	7,363	11,264	15,770	+186%
Paid workforce	189,134	244,233	365,006	441,000	+133%
Disadvantaged workers	23,587	30,141	30,534*	32,000	+36%
Users	2,403,245	3,302,551	6,000,000	7,500,000*	+212%
Total turnover (million EUR	**4,826**	**6,381**	**10,000**	**11,900**	**+147%**

Source: Table adopted by Borzaga, 2020

2.2 Case B: Spain

Like Italy, Spain has a strong and long tradition of Third Sector initiatives and a large cooperative tradition (Mondragon). Whereas Italy pioneered with the enactment of the first Law in Europe regarding social entrepreneurship in 1991, Spain assumed the lead in legalization of the third sector by enacting the first Law specifically addressing social economy Law 5/2011 on March 29th 2011 (with Greece in the 2nd place, since it enacted a corresponding Law only six months later). However, the formal acknowledgment of social enterprises in Spain begun with the enactment of Law 27/1999 on Cooperatives, which included among its clauses the establishment of cooperatives with a social cause/mission, the so called 'Social Initiative Cooperatives' (cooperativa de iniciativa social). Cooperatives with a social mission, Special employment centers and Employment Integration Enterprises' (Empresas de Inserción) are the three forms of organizations, which emerged from the early 1980's in Spain, as a response from civil society focusing on excluded people or people at risk of exclusion, as well as, disabled and unemployed and they are considered as the "predecessors of social enterprises in Spain" (Diaz-Foncea et al 2016:5).

Like Greece, Spain entered a multi-year recession during the 2008-2013 financial crisis, however, the Spanish Third Sector and social enterprises displayed resilience and even an increase both in generation of employment and organizations. Associations seem to have the largest increase, with 2.712 organizations (37,6%), followed by Insertion companies with 55 organizations (26,83%), whereas in total social enterprises has seen an increase of 2.851 organizations (33,42%) during the crisis (Table 5).

Table 4. Social enterprises in Spain, 2004-2017

Year	Social Initiative Cooperatives (CIS)[1]	Employment Integration Enterprises[2]	Special Employment Centre for social initiative	Associations[3]	Foundations[4]	Total
2004	571	5	309	2,900	-	**3,785**
2005	578	60	760	2,900	-	**4,298**
2006	587	60	606	3,501	-	**4,754**
2007	599	108	700	4,001	12	**5,420**
2008	604	150	413	4,500	13	**5,680**
2009	566	154	440	5,001	16	**6,177**
2010	508	193	492	6,073	65	**7,331**
2011	-	200	490	6,059	46	**6,795**
2012	-	203	470	6,636	55	**7,364**
2013	600*	205	450	7,212	64	**8,531**
2014	621*	206	450	7,092	107	**8,476**
2015[5]	624*	-	-	-	-	**-**
2016	-	207	557	7,134	85	**7,983**
2017	647**	201	576	8,164	92	**9,680**

Source: European Commission, 2020

Despite the generalized difficulties, the response of the civil society and the third sector towards the pressing social needs that emerged during the crisis was "the flourishing of new models of business to try to satisfy the economic, social, environmental and cultural necessities" (Diaz et al 2021:16) particularly in the form on new cooperatives, as well as, with the establishment of organizations, such as social integration enterprises in the form of limited liabilities companies, renewable energy and housing cooperatives and social business companies focusing on services related to social impact and based on social innovation. Examples of these new form of cooperatives, which emerged as a response to the crisis, include according to 'Social Initiative Cooperatives', which emerged in social and health services, education mainly, but also professional activities, food, etc.

The role of civil society in support of both social entrepreneurship organizations and accommodation of the needs of disadvantaged has been pivotal in Spain. According to Vidal and Claver, the development of the first WISEs was the outcome of the actions of "leaders of local neighborhood and church associations" (Vidal and Claver, 2005:6), as well as, by "social activists *(which)* began working, without formal support and on a voluntary basis, on finding work for people with low levels of employability" *(ibid, parenthesis added).* Based on data from CEPES, all three forms of organizations namely Special Employment Centers (SECs), Employment Integration Enterprises (EIS) and Social Initiative Cooperatives have supported at a great degree the employment and inclusion of vulnerable social groups, as far as, the social and employment integration of disabled and socially excluded is concerned. It seems that there was a positive incremental trend regarding employment, which reached for EIs 15,24% in 2013 since the beginning of the crisis at 2008 and respectively 48,77% for SECs (Table 6).

Table 5. Employment is Special Employment Centers and Employment Integration Enterprises

YEAR	IN INSERTION	WITH DISABILITIES
2008	1,768	67,329
2010	1,589	125,157
2011	2,092	162,459
2013	2,086	131,424
2015	2,750	79,039
2016	2,750	73,620
2017	3,201	92,102
2018	3,439	84,946
2019	4,299	85,104
2020	4,299	85,104

Source: CEPES 2023[6], own elaboration

As seen in Table 6, the positive trend on employment for socially excluded continued until 2020, whereas the total employment in EIs is even larger in numbers and the provision of employment reaches other social groups too, showing that their operation has a greater social impact.

Finally, significant place in the development of inclusive employment through social entrepreneurship models in Spain has been the bottom-up emergence of social innovation models either at the private non-profit or at the local government level and in the autonomous and Basque Regions. According to Ramos "civil society has assumed a leading role in expanding and promoting SI" (Ramos, 2019:124) in Spain managing to create professional networks, establishing new enterprises, raising funds and mobilize market and non-market resources in a manner of articulating a well-established social innovation eco-system.

3. CONCLUSION

What the Italian and the Spanish cases has attested to is that social entrepreneurship models have the inherent capacity not just to withstand in critical socioeconomic conditions, but develop sustainable working conditions for people who have fewer opportunities and in a great sense *democratize the demand/supply* function of the labor market, which in the case of state and market failures, as the recent financial crisis has showed, may lead to unprecedented levels of poverty, unemployment, material deprivation and general social unrest.

Of particular importance is the dynamic and generation particularly of *Social Cooperatives Models* in the Euro-Mediterranean context (with Greece and Portugal showcasing also an advanced in terms of institutionalization and practice in the development of SCMs) and particularly in the cases of Italy and Spain, since as has been proved by year-long practice, it is the model most effectively supporting and accommodating the needs of people with fewer opportunities (vulnerable social groups), while equally enhances the role and activation of civil society in the development of those models. A strong civil society equals with high levels of social capital and bonds, common actions and cooperation within a community, as well as, more participatory and democratic decision-making processes at the local level.

This is also reflected in the cases of Italy and Spain, where bottom-up initiatives have achieved the development of new ways of addressing social challenges and have succeeded in becoming recognized, funded and even institutionalized by the state, resulting in becoming beacons of sustainable community development and sustainability not just for their specific national settings but across Europe.

REFERENCES

Dees, J. G. (1998). *The Meaning of Social Entrepreneurship*. The Kauffman Center for Entrepreneurial Leadership.

Díaz- Foncea. M., Marcuello, C., Marcuello, C., Solorzano, M., Navío, J., Guzmán, C., de la O Barroso, M., Rodríguez, M. J., Santos, F. J., Fisac, R., Alguacil, P., Chaves, R., Savall, T. & Villajos, E. (2016) "*Social Enterprise in Spain: A Diversity of Roots and a Proposal of Models*", ICSEM Working Papers, No. 29, Liege: The International Comparative Social Enterprise Models (ICSEM) Project.

European Commission. (2020). *"Social enterprises and their ecosystems in Europe. Comparative synthesis report", Authors: Carlo Borzaga, Giulia Galera, Barbara Franchini, Stefania Chiomento, Rocío Nogales and Chiara Carini*. Publications Office of the European Union.

Federazione Trentina della Cooperazione & Scuola Nazionale Servizi Foundation. (2017) "Italy", in *COOPilot Project: European Report*, by Sybille Mertens, Amélie Mernier, Lola Arpigny and Maxime Bouchat (eds), Center for Social Economy - University of Liege, pp. 291-315

ISTAT. (2022). *Struttura e profili del settore non profit Anno 2020*. Italian National Institute of Statistics.

OECD. (2022). *"Designing Legal Frameworks for Social Enterprises: Practical Guidance for Policy Makers", Local Economic and Employment Development (LEED)*. OECD Publishing., DOI: 10.1787/172b60b2-

Ramos, J. (2019) "Social innovation in Spain: the leading role of Civil Society", in *Atlas of Social Innovation – 2nd Volume: A World of New Practices,* in Jürgen Howaldt, Christoph Kaletka, Antonius Schröder, Marthe Zirngiebl (Eds), pp.124-126, Publisher: oekoem verlag, München.

Thomas, A. (2004). "The Rise of Social Cooperatives in Italy", in Voluntas. *Voluntas*, *15*(3), 243–263. DOI: 10.1023/B:VOLU.0000046280.06580.d8

Vidal, I., & Claver, N. (2005). *"Work Integration Social Enterprises in Spain", WP n. 04/05*. EMES Research Network.

ENDNOTES

1 Social initiative cooperative' (1999).

2 Law on social cooperatives' (381/1991).

3 Law 2716/99 (article 12) establishing Limited Liability Social Co-operatives' (Koi.S.P.E.).

4 'Social solidarity cooperative under Cooperative Code (Law No. 51/96), adopted in 1997.

5 According to Art. 1 par. 4 of the Legislative Decree No 112/2017 "Revision of the rules on social enterprises", SCEs and their consortia have acquired 'by right' the qualification of social enterprises.

6 La Confederación Empresarial Española de Economía Social (CEPES), https://www.cepes.es/estadisticas-generales-economia-social/datos-estadisticos, accessed in November 2023.

Chapter 9

The Role of Coaching in Education for People With Special Needs: The Effects for the Inclusion in the Labour Market

Eleni Prassa

https://orcid.org/0009-0002-4773-061X

University of the Aegean, Greece

ABSTRACT

The social inclusion of people with special needs remains one of the greatest challenges faced by contemporary societies. Despite the policies and programs of the EU and other organizations aiming to improve these individuals' access to education, employment, and society, social prejudices, limited opportunities, and labor market barriers continue to hinder their genuine inclusion.Coaching, as an individual or group practice, aims to offer guidance and support to individuals who need assistance in developing skills and overcoming challenges due to their disabilitiesIn the case of people with disabilities, coaching can be tailored to enhance their abilities, improve self-esteem, andfacilitate their integration into the labor market.This paper examines the role of coaching in the education and professional rehabilitation ofpeople with special needs,focusing particularly on the impact ofcoaching on their inclusion in the labor market.

DOI: 10.4018/979-8-3373-8790-1.ch009

1. THE IMPORTANCE OF COACHING FOR PEOPLE WITH DISABILITIES

Coaching refers to the process of enhancing both personal and professional development through guidance, boosting self-esteem, and developing strategies for achieving goals. Coaching differs from other forms of psychological support, such as psychotherapy or counseling, as it focuses on developing specific individual goals through practical strategies tailored to their needs (HSCB, 2014).

In the fields of education and employment, coaching can be applied to help individuals with disabilities develop skills that facilitate their integration into society and the labor market (Dillenburger et al., 2019). Coaching for people with disabilities may include various methods, particularly:

Life Coaching: Helps individuals in developing and managing their abilities, reinforcing them, and setting goals to achieve.

Career Coaching: Focuses on the development of professional skills, job search, job retention, and career management.

A coach can act as a supporter and guide at every level, providing strategies that empower individuals and help them overcome obstacles they face. Especially for individuals with disabilities, coaching can offer a safe framework to recognize and improve their skills, such as (Frey et al., 2022; Heft Sears, Jones & Strauser, 2014):

- Communication Skills
- Management
- Self-Esteem
- Self-Awareness
- Self-Confidence
- Decision
- Stress Management
- Leadership Skills
- Creativity and Innovation

2. LITERATURE REVIEW

The literature on coaching for people with disabilities and their integration into the labor market is limited. However, recent years have seen growing interest in studying the effects of coaching in these areas.

Research by Schur et al. (2013) highlights that individuals with disabilities face significant barriers in the labor market, such as lack of training opportunities, employer prejudices, and limited government support. Nonetheless, Gale et al. (Waxman, 2023) show that those participating in coaching programs for professional integration have increased chances of finding and maintaining employment.

The International Labour Organization's report (Moore & Huberty, 2020) underscores that policies combining professional training with coaching support can significantly enhance the employability of individuals with disabilities. The enhancement of self-esteem and social skills through coaching emerges as a critical factor for their successful inclusion in the labor market.

3. COACHING PRACTICES FOR PEOPLE WITH DISABILITIES

Applying coaching to individuals with disabilities requires tailored approaches, as their needs and goals can vary significantly. The main coaching strategies focus on developing personal and professional skills, boosting self-confidence, and supporting the management of challenges they may face in the workplace.

The effectiveness of coaching for individuals with disabilities depends on adapting strategies to their specific needs (Jurkovich & Wirtz, 2018). For example:

- **Time Management and Organization**: Coaches help individuals improve their organizational skills, manage their time, and set realistic goals (Frey et al., 2022). This approach is particularly useful for individuals with developmental or learning difficulties who may struggle to organize their daily lives.

- **Professional Skills Development**: Coaching aims to enhance skills such as communication, emotional management, teamwork, and problem-solving, which are essential for success in the professional arena.
- **Strategic Career Planning**: Coaching assists individuals in developing job search strategies and managing their careers (Heft Sears, Jones & Strauser, 2014). Coaches encourage them to recognize their strengths and choose positions that match their skills and interests.
- **Social Skills Training**: Individuals with disabilities may face challenges in social interactions, impacting their professional integration. Coaches use techniques to improve social skills, such as conflict management, developing empathy, and effective communication with colleagues and supervisors (HSCB, 2014).

One of the significant benefits of coaching is the increased self-esteem and self-confidence it provides to individuals with disabilities. Through empowerment, individuals feel more capable of facing labor market challenges. Support from a coach helps them recognize their value and overcome internal doubts or limiting beliefs that may hinder their goal achievement (Jurkovich & Wirtz, 2018).

4. BENEFITS OF COACHING FOR PROFESSIONAL INCLUSION OF PEOPLE WITH DISABILITIES

The application of coaching for the inclusion of individuals with disabilities in the labor market has proven particularly beneficial for these individuals. Some of the key benefits include (Carter, 2006):

Development of Social and Professional Skills: Individuals with disabilities enhance critical skills such as communication, collaboration, and time management, facilitating their smooth integration into the professional environment.

Increased Self-Esteem and Self-Confidence: Through coaching, individuals gain greater confidence in their abilities, which supports them in job searching and retention.

Creation of Strong Social Networks: Coaching encourages the creation and maintenance of professional networks, which help individuals identify new job opportunities and advance their careers.

Addressing Obstacles and Prejudices: Coaches provide strategies to overcome social and professional prejudices, which often serve as barriers to the professional inclusion of individuals with disabilities.

Coaching also offers multiple benefits for the labor market and employers. These benefits improve productivity and innovation. Specifically (Hagner et al., 2015):

Increased Productivity and Performance: One of the primary impacts of coaching is the improvement of employee productivity. When individuals with disabilities receive appropriate support, they feel more empowered and confident in their capabilities, leading to greater commitment and better job performance. The personalized nature of coaching allows them to focus on their personal and professional goals, thus enhancing overall performance for both the team and the business.

Creating an Inclusive Work Environment: Coaching also contributes to creating a work environment where diversity is valued and promoted. This fosters an atmosphere of acceptance and respect, enhancing collaboration and reducing workplace discrimination.

Enhancing Skills and Innovation: Coaching enables employees to develop new skills and improve existing ones. It supports continuous learning and personal development, making employees more adaptable to changes and challenges in the modern workplace (Carter, 2006). Additionally, promoting the inclusion of individuals with special needs can enhance creativity and innovation, as diverse perspectives can offer new solutions to problems and improve decision-making processes.

Coaching has been shown to significantly improve the mental health of employees. By providing a safe space for expressing concerns and developing strategies to cope with stress, it enhances emotional resilience. Improved mental well-being leads to fewer absences, increased job satisfaction, and higher performance.

Development of Leadership Skills and Employee Empowerment

Coaching is particularly effective in developing leadership skills, both for individuals with disabilities and other employees. It boosts self-confidence, self-awareness, and decision-making abilities, essential elements for emerging as a leader. This empowerment can promote their professional advancement.

Enhancing Team Collaboration and Social Cohesion

Coaching fosters open communication and effective collaboration. It helps employees strengthen their personal skills and become more adaptable, facilitating teamwork and conflict management.

5. CHALLENGES IN IMPLEMENTING COACHING FOR PEOPLE WITH DISABILITIES

Despite the significant benefits of coaching in the professional inclusion of individuals with disabilities, implementing these programs faces several critical challenges.

Social prejudices and perceptions about the abilities of individuals with disabilities often hinder their full inclusion in the labor market. Although coaching can boost individuals' self-confidence, the negative attitude of the social environment towards them may remain unchanged (Schur et al., 2017). Employers often fail to recognize the value that individuals with disabilities can offer, thus limiting their professional opportunities despite the support provided through coaching.

Additionally, coaches often lack the necessary expertise or training to address the specific needs of individuals with disabilities. The lack of adequate training can limit their effectiveness, reducing the likelihood of successful professional inclusion of these individuals in the labor market.

6. STRATEGIES TO OVERCOME CHALLENGES

To overcome the obstacles and enhance the inclusion of individuals with disabilities in the labor market through coaching, specific strategies are required. Some of these include:

- **Collaboration with Employers to Adapt Job Positions**: Collaboration between coaching bodies and employers is crucial for creating suitable job positions for individuals with disabilities. Employers need to be trained to understand these individuals' needs and adapt the work environment to make it more accessible and supportive (Frey, 2022). This may include adapting job positions, providing supportive equipment, and implementing flexible work forms.
- **Training and Continuous Support for Coaches**: The training of coaches is critical for the effectiveness of coaching programs. Coaches must have the necessary knowledge about the needs of individuals with disabilities and adapt their strategies according to the specific conditions of each person. Continuous support from specialized professionals is also necessary to ensure the high quality of the services provided (Hagner et al., 2015).
- **Social Inclusion and Support Policies**: Organizations must implement policies that promote the social inclusion and support of individuals with disabilities. This includes providing financial incentives for participation in coaching programs, promoting policies that facilitate professional inclusion, and raising public awareness about these individuals' potential. Additionally, these policies should offer incentives and resources to employers for hiring individuals with disabilities.
- **Development of Support and Collaboration Networks**: Creating support networks among individuals with disabilities, coaches, employers, and professional rehabilitation organizations is crucial for the success of coaching (Kaliris & Issari, 2022). These networks facilitate the exchange of experiences, offer continuous support, and contribute to developing new strategies for addressing challenges.

7. CONCLUSIONS

The application of coaching as a tool for the inclusion of individuals with disabilities in the labor market has proven extremely effective, offering benefits to both the employees and the businesses that hire them. Through personalized strategies and approaches, coaching contributes to developing critical professional and social skills, boosts self-esteem, and promotes professional success. Despite the challenges that may arise, collaboration with employers, continuous training of coaches, and support from society can create a more friendly and accessible work environment for individuals with disabilities.

To ensure the successful inclusion of these individuals in the labor market, a systematic effort is required from all stakeholders. Coaching, combined with appropriate policies and employer support, can facilitate their acceptance and integration into professional life, offering not only opportunities for career development but also for social integration. Coaching is a dynamic strategy that enhances employment opportunities for individuals with disabilities while promoting the creation of a more inclusive work environment.

8. REFERENCES

Carter, A. (2006). *Practical Methods for Evaluating Coaching. Institute for employment studies*. University of Sussex Campus.

Dillenburger, K., Matuska, E., de Bruijn, M., & Röttgers, H. R. (2019). *Job coaches for adults with disabilities: A practical guide*. Jessica Kingsley Publishers.

Frey, A., Bühler, E., & Ruppert, J. (2022). Conflict Management Strategies of Career Counsellors. *Psychology (Irvine, Calif.), 13*(1), 62–77. DOI: 10.4236/psych.2022.131005

Hagner, D., Dague, B., & Phillips, K. (2015). Including employees with disabilities in workplace cultures: Strategies and barriers. *Rehabilitation Counseling Bulletin, 58*(4), 195–202. DOI: 10.1177/0034355214544750

Heft Sears, S., Jones, A., & Strauser, D. R. (2014). Career counseling with people with disabilities. In Strauser, D. R. (Ed.), *Career development, employment and disability in rehabilitation: From theory to practice* (pp. 277–295). Springer Publishing Company.

HSCB. (2014). Coaching and Mentoring in Social Work – A Review of the Evidence: Commissioned by the HSCB.

Jurkovich, M., & Wirtz, R. A. (2018). Disability: Taking a turn for the better for labor markets. Fedgazette, 1–3.

Kaliris, A., & Issari, P. (2022). Exploring Narrative Ideas in Career Counseling. *Open Journal of Social Sciences, 10*(2), 365–380. DOI: 10.4236/jss.2022.102026

Moore, M. E., & Huberty, L. L. (2020). The Economic Impact of Employing Disabled Persons: Macro and Micro Perspectives. In Fielden, S. L., Moore, M. E., & Bend, G. L. (Eds.), *The Palgrave Handbook of Disability at Work*. DOI: 10.1007/978-3-030-42966-9_29

Schur, L., Han, K., Kim, A., Ameri, M., Blanck, P., & Kruse, D. (2017). Disability at work: A look back and forward. *Journal of Occupational Rehabilitation*, *27*(4), 482–497. DOI: 10.1007/s10926-017-9739-5 PMID: 29110160

Schur, L. A., Kruse, D., & Blanck, P. D. (2013). *People with disabilities*. Cambridge University Press. DOI: 10.1017/CBO9780511843693

Waxman, D. (2023). Disability and Employment Research: Mind the Gap. In Rioux, M. H., Viera, J., Buettgen, A., & Zubrow, E. (Eds.), *Handbook of Disability*. Springer. DOI: 10.1007/978-981-16-1278-7_94-1

Zappella, E. (2015). Job coaching in the workplace for people with disabilities: An Italian research. *Rehabilitation Counseling Bulletin*, *58*(4), 195–202.

Chapter 10
Rethinking Our Plate:
Sustainable Food Consumption in Greece and Its Role in Shaping a Greener Future

Panagiota Varela
https://orcid.org/0009-0002-5019-9209
University of the Aegean, Greece

Thanasis Kizos
https://orcid.org/0000-0002-1526-0919
University of the Aegean, Greece

ABSTRACT

This paper explores the vital role of sustainable food consumption within sustainable development, tracing its evolution from early development theories to its current importance. It addresses environmental, ethical, and economic issues, including organic products, animal welfare, meat reduction, fair trade, local and seasonal choices, plant-based diets, and food waste reduction. As global challenges grow, the shift toward sustainable food practices becomes urgent, with consumer awareness driving change. Focusing on Attica, Greece, the study examines consumer preferences and behaviors through statistical analysis, exploring how socio-demographic

DOI: 10.4018/979-8-3373-8790-1.ch010

factors shape purchasing decisions. The findings offer insights into the drivers and barriers of sustainable consumption, contributing to the global dialogue on responsible and ecologically sound practices.

1. INTRODUCTION

1.1. Linking Sustainable Development to Sustainable Food Consumption

Sustainable development was first defined in 1987 in the Brundtland Report, titled "Our Common Future," as development that "meets the needs of the present without compromising the ability of future generations to meet their own needs." (Brundtland, 1987). In light of today's global challenges, including biodiversity loss, environmental degradation, the climate and energy crisis, the COVID-19 pandemic, and the difficulty in achieving net-zero targets, the importance of adopting sustainable models is more critical than ever. Food systems, though complex and delicate, play a central role in this transition, and their proper management is key to sustainability. The connection between human well-being and sustainability underscores the need for such a transformation.

A crucial aspect of sustainable development is sustainable food consumption, which has garnered increasing attention in recent years. The various stages of food systems—including agricultural production, processing, distribution, and consumption—significantly contribute to environmental issues such as greenhouse gas emissions, biodiversity loss, water pollution, and soil degradation (Reisch et al., 2013). Consumers play a pivotal role in shaping the food system through their choices, making consumer awareness and responsibility essential components of sustainable food practices. Sustainable food consumption encompasses both individual behaviors and social responsibility, addressing local and global environmental impacts. As Reisch et al. (2013) explain, food consumption affects the environment, the economy, public and individual health, and social cohesion.

The 12th goal of the United Nations' Sustainable Development Goals (SDGs) emphasizes responsible consumption and production. It calls for sustainable practices across the entire food system—from production and processing to consumption—that are environmentally friendly and contribute to long-term sustainability. Similarly, Article 2 of the United Nations Framework Convention on Climate Change (UNFCCC) urges signatory nations to stabilize greenhouse gas concentrations to help ecosystems adapt to climate change, ensure food security, and promote sustainable economic development (United Nations, 1992).

Transforming food consumption patterns is essential for meeting global sustainability goals. According to the Food and Agriculture Organization (FAO, 2010), sustainable diets are those that have low environmental impacts while contributing to food and nutrition security and promoting a healthy lifestyle for present and future generations. These diets are protective of biodiversity and ecosystems, culturally acceptable, accessible, economically fair, and nutritionally adequate. Factors influencing food consumption include food availability, geography, demography, culture, urbanization, globalization, marketing, consumer behavior, and disposable income (Kearney, 2010). Notably, food consumption has the largest environmental footprint among all forms of consumption (Druckman & Jackson, 2010; Jackson & Papathanasopoulou, 2008; Lorek & Spangenberg, 2001). Over 60% of global greenhouse gas emissions are linked to domestic food consumption, making dietary changes a critical element in achieving sustainability (Ivanova et al., 2016).

Sustainable food consumption can be defined as food that meets basic human needs and enhances quality of life while minimizing the use of natural resources, toxic materials, and emissions of waste and pollutants across the lifecycle, without compromising the ability of future generations to meet their own needs (Oslo Roundtable on Sustainable Production and Consumption, 1994).

An alternative framework for an environmentally sustainable diet is the SHARP model, which stands for Sustainable (S), Healthy (H), Affordable (A), Reliable (R), and Preferable (P). This model emphasizes a diet that is environmentally sound, accessible to consumers, aligned with cultural norms, and reliable in terms of supply chain dynamics (Mertens et al., 2017).

The UK Sustainable Development Commission (2005; 2009) also defines sustainable food as that which is safe, healthy, and nutritious for consumers; accessible to all; and produced in ways that respect environmental limits. It should also support the livelihoods of workers in the food supply chain, uphold high standards of animal welfare, and promote local economies by minimizing food miles (Annunziata & Scarpato, 2014: 353–354).

Sustainable food consumption touches on a range of issues, including the purchase of organic products (Hughner et al., 2007; Magnusson et al., 2003; Scalvedi & Saba, 2018), increased consumption of fruits and vegetables (Cox et al., 1998), improved animal welfare (Hansen et al., 2003; Verbeke & Viaene, 1999), reduced meat consumption (Hoek et al., 2004; Mylan, 2018), support for fair trade products (Raynolds, 2002), and the preference for local and seasonal foods (Macdiarmid, 2014). Additionally, it involves reducing food waste (Derqui et al., 2018; Lagorio et al., 2018), decreasing the carbon and water footprint of food consumption, and adopting sustainable dietary patterns such as the Mediterranean diet, common in Greece, Italy, Spain, and North Africa (Bach-Faig et al., 2011; Pairotti et al., 2015).

1.2. Study Objectives

The main goal of this study is to explore how consumers perceive sustainable food consumption in their purchasing decisions within the Attica region. By examining these perceptions, the study aims to deepen our understanding of consumer attitudes towards sustainable food choices and how these attitudes can contribute to fostering sustainability in food systems. Attica was selected for the study because it includes the Athens metropolitan area, which is home to Athens, Greece's capital and largest city, making it an ideal location to assess urban consumer behavior in relation to sustainable food practices.

2. MATERIALS AND METHODS

The study combines a literature review and data from an online survey conducted between April and September 2022, targeting adult consumers in the Attica region. The survey was distributed via email (from exhibitions like HORECA, FoodExpo), municipalities, and social media (Instagram, Facebook, LinkedIn) to gather a broader sample. No financial incentives were provided, and 363 valid responses were collected. The survey, in Greek and administered via Qualtrics, included 26 questions covering socio-demographic data (gender, age, education, income, occupation, family status, children, and residence). The main goal was to analyze consumer perceptions and preferences on sustainable food consumption in Attica to inform better sustainability policies. Data were analyzed using SPSS with descriptive statistics, and factor analysis was employed to identify relationships between variables and create a composite for sustainable food preference. Reliability was confirmed with Cronbach's alpha (α = .856). Principal Component Analysis (PCA) was used for data reduction, identifying combinations of variables that maximize explained variance (Field, 2013; Raykov et al., 2017).

3. RESULTS AND DISCUSSION

3.1. Descriptive Statistics of the Sample

The survey data revealed that 61% of participants were female, while 39% were male. Regarding age, the largest group (32.5%) was aged 26-35, followed by 46-55 years old (24.2%), and smaller groups in the 36-45 (18.5%), 56-65 (15.2%), 18-25 (7.2%), and 65+ (2.5%) age brackets. In terms of education, 38.8% held a bachelor's degree, 35% had a master's/ MBA, 9.6% had completed high school, and 7.2% had doctorate degrees, with only 0.2% not completing high school. Regarding occupation, 47.9% worked in the private sector, while 19.8% were employed in the public sector, and 18.5% were freelancers. Smaller groups included students (6.6%), pensioners (4.1%), unemployed individuals (2.2%), and home-makers (0.8%). Family status data showed that 43.8% of respondents were single, 43.3% were married, 6.6% were divorced, and 2.8% were in civil partnerships or preferred not to answer. Only 0.8% were widowed. Additionally, 47.1% of participants had children, while 52.9% did not. Income levels showed that the largest group (39.7%) reported earning

€10,000-20,000 annually, followed by 21.5% earning below €10,000, 14.9% earning €20,000-30,000, 10.7% earning €30,000-40,000, and 11.8% earning above €40,000.

3.2. Key Factors in Food Purchasing Decisions

When asked to rank six factors—quality, price, health, taste, appearance, and origin (locality)—based on importance in food purchasing decisions, 37.7% of participants identified health as the most important attribute. Quality was close behind, with 37.2% of participants ranking it as their top priority. Taste was ranked as the most important factor by 11% of respondents, while 7.4% prioritized price. Origin (locality) was the top choice for 4.4% of participants, and appearance was considered the least important, with only 2.2% ranking it first.

These findings suggest that health and quality are the most significant factors influencing food purchasing decisions, whereas appearance and origin are less prioritized by consumers in Attica.

Table 1. Ranking of attributes when purchasing food products

	1	2	3	4	5	6
Quality	**37.2%**	36.4%	15.2%	7.7.%	2.2%	1.4%
Price	7.4%	13.8%	16.8%	**27.0%**	21.2%	13.8%
Health	**37.7%**	20.4%	20.9%	13.5%	6.1%	1.4%
Taste	11.0%	18.7%	**31.1%**	26.4%	11.0%	1.7%
Origin (locality)	4.4%	8.8%	12.4%	17.6%	**36.4%**	20.4%
Appearance	2.2%	1.9%	3.6%	7.7%	23.1%	**61.4%**

To identify sustainable consumers and understand their preferences, a series of questions were posed regarding food attributes such as organic products, fair trade, seasonal and Greek (local/regional) items, food waste, low environmental footprint, minimal or environmentally friendly packaging, and food miles (products that have not traveled long distances). Additional attributes included health, absence of preservatives, ease of preparation, low calorie content, affordability, and taste. Respondents' perceptions and attitudes were measured using a 6-point Likert scale, where 1 indicated "not important," 2 "slightly important," 3 "moderately important," 4 "important," 5 "very important," and 6 "do not know/no opinion." Responses marked as "do not know/no opinion" were excluded from the analysis.

Table 2. Evaluation of different attributes in sustainable food preference.

	1: not important	2: slightly important	3: moderately important	4: important	5: very important
No preservatives.	2.2%	6.3%	19%	40.5%	32%
To be organic.	4.4%	15.5%	35.4%	28.5%	16.3%
Not requiring preparation.	23.9%	25.8%	29.4%	15.3%	5.6%
Low in calories.	11.6%	14.6%	38.3%	24%	11.6%
Have a low environmental footprint.	3.6%	9.8%	26%	36%	24.6%
Good taste.	-	1.4%	8.5%	48.2%	41.9%
Not expensive.	0.8%	6.6%	33.9%	39.4%	19.3%
To be Greek or local.	2.5%	5%	22.6%	37.2%	32.8%
To be healthy.	0.6%	1.1%	7.5%	37.6%	53.3%
Fair Trade.	3.6%	8.7%	31.3%	32.8%	23.6%
To be packed in the least possible or environmentally friendly way.	3.9%	5.6%	24%	35.4%	31.2%
They must not have "travelled" long distances.	4.5%	14.5%	25.3%	31.5%	24.2%
Avoid food waste.	0.3%	1.9%	12.7%	40.6%	44.5%

3.3. Hypotheses Analysis

Table 3. Hypothesis 1: There is no relationship between gender and sustainable food consumption.

Preference for Sustainable Food Consumption	**Gender**	N	Mean	Std. Deviation	t	p
	Male	126	3.71	.69	-3.456	<.001
	Female	201	3.97	.64		

An independent sample t-test was conducted to assess gender differences in preferences for sustainable food consumption. The results showed that women had a significantly higher preference for sustainable food (M = 3.97, SD = 0.64) compared to men (M = 3.71, SD = 0.69), with a statistically significant difference ($t(325) = -3.456$, $p < .001$). The effect size, calculated using Cohen's d, was 0.393, suggesting a moderate relationship between gender and sustainable food consumption. Consequently, the null hypothesis was rejected, indicating that gender does influence attitudes toward sustainable food consumption. This finding suggests that female consumers may play a key role in driving sustainable food choices.

Table 4. Hypothesis 2: There is no relationship between income and sustainable food consumption.

ANOVA					
Preference for Sustainable Food Consumption					
Annual Income €	N	Mean	Std. Deviation	F	p
Below 10,000	68	3.71	.60	2.148	.075
10,000-20,000	127	3.85	.75		
20,000-30,000	50	3.93	.58		
30,000-40,000	36	4.01	.57		
Above 40,000	41	4.95	.68		
Total	322	3.88	.67		

A one-way ANOVA was conducted to examine the relationship between income and sustainable food consumption. The results showed no statistically significant difference between income levels and sustainable food consumption, as the test was only marginally significant ($F(4,317) = 2.148$, $p = .075$). Therefore, the null hypothesis is accepted, indicating that income does not significantly influence sustainable food consumption. However, the data suggests a trend where higher income levels are associated with a greater preference for sustainable food consumption, although this trend is not strong enough to reach statistical significance.

4. CONCLUSIONS

In conclusion, this study investigated sustainable food consumption in the Attica region by analyzing consumer preferences and behaviors. A range of attributes, including organic products, local goods, food waste, environmental impact, packaging, food miles, health, and price, were evaluated to understand how these factors influence consumer choices.

The findings revealed that women tend to have a stronger preference for sustainable food compared to men. Although there was a trend indicating that higher income is associated with greater preference for sustainable food, this relationship was not statistically significant. The results also indicated that health and quality are the most highly valued factors when purchasing food, whereas the origin (locality) of the food and its appearance were considered less important by consumers.

Consumers demonstrated significant concern for health and reducing food waste, yet organic and Fair Trade products received less attention than might be expected. Local products, especially those associated with the Mediterranean diet, were highlighted as an effective way to enhance sustainability by supporting regional production and consumption. This suggests that promoting locally sourced food could be an important strategy for fostering sustainable food practices.

Overall, while consumers in Attica show an interest in sustainability, there is still room for improvement, particularly in raising awareness about organic and Fair Trade products, as well as the environmental footprint of food. To foster more sustainable consumption patterns, targeted policies and information campaigns are essential. Such initiatives should aim to provide consumers with the tools and knowledge they need to make informed choices that align with sustainable food practices, thereby promoting greater environmental awareness and supporting the transition to more sustainable food systems.

REFERENCES

Annunziata, A., & Scarpato, D. (2014). 'Factors affecting consumer attitudes towards food products with sustainable attributes', *Agricultural Economics - Czech*, 60, 353-363.

Bach-Faig, A., Berry, E., Lairon, D., Reguant, J., Trichopoulou, A., Dernini, S., & Serra-Majem, L. (2011). Mediterranean diet pyramid today: Science and cultural updates. *Public Health Nutrition, 14*(12A), 2274–2284. DOI: 10.1017/S1368980011002515

Brundtland, G. (1987). 'Report of the World Commission on Environment and Development: Our Common Future'. [online]. Available at: <http://www.un-documents.net/our-common-future.pdf> (Accessed 9 April 2023).

Druckman, A., & Jackson, T. (2010). The bare necessities: How much household carbon do we really need? *Ecological Economics*, *69*(9), 1794–1804. DOI: 10.1016/j.ecolecon.2010.04.018

FAO. (2010). 'Sustainable diets and biodiversity: directions and solutions for policy, research and action'. *Proceedings of the International Scientific Symposium: Biodiversity and sustainable diets against hunger.*

Field, A. (2013). *Discovering Statistics Using IBM SPSS Statistics*. SAGE Publications.

Hansen, J., Holm, L., Frewer, L., Robinson, P., & Sandøe, P. (2003). Beyond the knowledge deficit: Recent research into lay and expert attitudes to food risks. *Appetite*, *41*(2), 111–121. DOI: 10.1016/S0195-6663(03)00079-5

Hoek, A. C., Luning, P. A., Stafleu, A., & de Graaf, C. (2004). Food-related lifestyle and health attitudes of Dutch vegetarians, non-vegetarian consumers of meat substitutes, and meat consumers. *Appetite*, *42*(3), 265–272. DOI: 10.1016/j.appet.2003.12.003

Hughner, R., McDonagh, P., Prothero, A., Shultz, C. J.II, & Stanton, J. (2007). Who are organic food consumers? A compilation and review of why people purchase organic food. *Journal of Consumer Behaviour*, *6*(2-3), 94–110. DOI: 10.1002/cb.210

Ivanova, D., Stadler, K., Steen-Olsen, K., Wood, R., Vita, G., Tukker, A., & Hertwich, E. G. (2016). Environmental impact assessment of household consumption. *Journal of Industrial Ecology*, *20*(3), 526–536. DOI: 10.1111/jiec.12371

Jackson, T., & Papathanasopoulou, E. (2008). 'Luxury or 'lock-in'? An exploration of unsustainable consumption in the UK: 1968 to 2000′. *Ecological Economics*, *68*(1-2), 1–2, 80–95. DOI: 10.1016/j.ecolecon.2008.01.026

Kearney, J. (2010). Food consumption trends and drivers. *Philosophical Transactions of the Royal Society of London. Series B, Biological Sciences*, *365*(1554), 2793–2807. DOI: 10.1098/rstb.2010.0149

Lagorio, A., Pinto, R., & Golini, R. (2018). Food Waste Reduction in School Canteens: Evidence from an Italian Case. *Journal of Cleaner Production*, *199*, 77–84. DOI: 10.1016/j.jclepro.2018.07.077

Lorek, S., and Spangenberg, J. (2001). 'Indicators for environmentally sustainable household consumption', *International Journal of Sustainable Development*, 4:1, 101.

Macdiarmid, J. I. (2014). Seasonality and dietary requirements: Will eating seasonal food contribute to health and environmental sustainability? *The Proceedings of the Nutrition Society*, *73*(3), 368–375. DOI: 10.1017/S0029665113003753

Magnusson, M., Arvola, A., Hursti, U., Åberg, L., & Sjödén, P. (2003). Choice of organic foods is related to perceived consequences for human health and to environmentally friendly behaviour. *Appetite*, *40*(2), 109–117. DOI: 10.1016/S0195-6663(03)00002-3

Mertens, E., van't Veer, P., Hiddink, G. J., Steijns, J. M. J. M., & Kuijsten, A. (2017). Operationalising the health aspects of sustainable diets: A review. *Public Health Nutrition*, *20*(4), 739–757. DOI: 10.1017/S1368980016002664

Mylan, J. (2018). Sustainable Consumption in Everyday Life: A Qualitative Study of UK Consumer Experiences of Meat Reduction. *Sustainability (Basel)*, *10*(7), 2307. DOI: 10.3390/su10072307

Oslo Roundtable on Sustainable Production and Consumption. (1994). 'The Imperative of Sustainable Production and Consumption'. [online]. Available at: <https://enb.iisd.org/consume/oslo004.html> (Accessed 19 October 2024).

Pairotti, M. B., Cerutti, A. K., Martini, F., Vesce, E., Padovan, D., & Beltramo, R. (2015). Energy consumption and GHG emission of the Mediterranean diet: A systemic assessment using a hybrid LCA-IO method. *Journal of Cleaner Production, 103*, 507–516. DOI: 10.1016/j.jclepro.2013.12.082

Raynolds, L. T. (2002). Consumer/producer links in fair trade coffee networks. *Sociologia Ruralis, 42*(4), 404–424. DOI: 10.1111/1467-9523.00224

Reisch, L., Eberle, U., and Lorek, S. (2013). 'Sustainable food consumption: an overview of contemporary issues and policies', *Sustainability: Science, Practice and Policy*, 9:2, 7-25.

Scalvedi, M. L., & Saba, A. (2018). Exploring local and organic food consumption in a holistic sustainability view. *British Food Journal, 120*(4), 749–762. DOI: 10.1108/BFJ-03-2017-0141

United Nations. (1992). 'United Nations Framework Convention on Climate Change'. [online]. Available at: < https://unfccc.int/resource/docs/convkp/conveng.pdf> (Accessed 19 October 2024).

Verbeke, W., & Viaene, J. (1999). Consumer Attitude to Beef Quality Labeling and Associations with Beef Quality Labels. *Journal of International Food & Agribusiness Marketing, 10*(3), 45–65. DOI: 10.1300/J047v10n03_03

Chapter 11

Geopolitical Analysis of Greece and Turkey: Strategic Depth and Blue Homeland in Foreign Policy

Spyros Anagnostou
https://orcid.org/0009-0001-3930-3223
University of the Aegean, Greece

Konstantinos Bogiatzis
https://orcid.org/0009-0002-3136-4408
University of the Aegean, Greece

ABSTRACT

This article analyzes the transformation of the foreign policy of Turkey in the light of the shift in doctrines, from Strategic Depth to Blue Homeland. Initially, the "Strategic Depth" doctrine, introduced by Ahmet Davutoğlu, emphasized Turkey's central geopolitical role as a bridge between Europe, Asia and Africa, leveraging its Ottoman heritage to claim influence across the Middle East, the Balkans, and Central Asia. However, this doctrine faded after 2011, due to regional instability, internal political shifts and the failure of the "zero problems with neighbors" policy. Following Davutoğlu's resignation and the 2016 coup attempt, the "Blue Homeland" doctrine emerged, prioritizing maritime sovereignty and energy resources

DOI: 10.4018/979-8-3373-8790-1.ch011

in the Aegean, the Eastern Mediterranean, and the Black Sea. This doctrine, initiated by Cem Gürdeniz, reflects Turkey's maritime ambitions, including disputed claims over Greek and Cypriot waters. The shift from "Strategic Depth" to "Blue Homeland" highlights Turkey's transition from soft power diplomacy to a more assertive and militarized foreign policy.

INTRODUCTION

The Turkish nation-state emerged from the collapse of the Ottoman Empire and the rise of Turkish nationalist forces. From the power vacuum resulting from the cooperation of the Sublime Gate with the Entente forces, a figure emerged who led the Turkish national movement (1919-1922), Mustafa Kemal Atatürk. With the signing of the Treaty of Lausanne (July 24, 1923), the new Turkish state was established, independent, sovereign and with full territorial sovereignty. Thus, the Turks, after achieving international recognition of their statehood, begin the process of establishing a Western-type nation-state with a simultaneous and vertical break with the Ottoman past.

Mustafa Kemal Atatürk, founder of the Turkish Republic, implemented radical and revolutionary reforms from 1923 to his death (1938) aiming at modernizing the country, establishing a one-party and authoritarian regime. The main feature of Turkish foreign policy during this period was isolationism, as the primary concern of the newly formed state was internal reconstruction and national homogenization.

After his death, his close associate and very important figure in the National War of Independence, İsmet İnönü, took over the government of the country, during World War II, until the first multi-party elections held in 1950. It is a fact that throughout World War II, İnönü maintained a policy of equidistance from the warring sides in order to ensure the country's territorial integrity. However, he declared war on Germany after it ended.

The Cold War caused antagonism at the geopolitical, military and economic levels between two main groups of countries, the capitalist bloc, led by the USA and the communist bloc, led by the USSR. Turkey joined the capitalist camp during the Cold War period, becoming a member of

NATO (1952), associate of the European Economic Community (1963) and contributing on the one hand to the containment strategy vis-a-vis the USSR, as a strong bastion, due to its important geographical position for the security architecture of the capitalist camp, and on the other hand strengthening the feeling of security within it against the threat from the communist camp. Ankara provided the NATO alliance with reliable military support, although there were instances of rupture in relations between them, such as the invasion of Cyprus in 1974 and the military coups of 1960 and 1980.

The end of the Cold War, the dissolution of the USSR and the collapse of the communist regimes in Eastern Europe, changed the international environment for Turkey, as the threat from the Soviet Union, which was the main reason for Turkey's attachment to the capitalist alliance in the first place, virtually disappeared. Russia found itself territorially reduced, and a number of smaller successor states emerged in the Central Asian, Black Sea, and Caucasus regions. Thus, Turkey found itself surrounded by smaller neighboring states, weaker than itself, both militarily and economically. Throughout the 1990s, Ankara tried to readjust its geopolitical orientation, having lost its role as the cornerstone of NATO security in the Eastern Mediterranean. Thus, it sought new opportunities with post-Soviet Russia and with the newly created states of the Black Sea and Central Asia.

Another notable aspect of Turkey's geopolitical plans, observed in the 2000s, was Turkey's accession to the EU, which, however, did not prosper, to the fault of both sides. At the same time, the terrorist attacks of September 11 and the subsequent invasion of Iraq (2003) shook the foundations of global security. Furthermore, the assumption of power in Turkey by an Islamic and pro-Western government, ushered in a new period of coupling relations between Ankara and the West, where the geopolitical orientation is defined by the doctrine of Strategic Depth, which is to be examined in the next chapter.

THE DOCTRINE OF STRATEGIC DEPTH

Since 2002, the Justice and Development Party (AKP) has ruled Turkey under the leadership of Recep Tayyip Erdogan, who held the prime ministership from 2002 to 2014, and is the president of Turkey from 2017 to the present, under full executive power. Ahmet Davutoglu, an academic specializing in political science and international relations, initially a foreign policy adviser to Erdogan, later minister of Foreign Affairs, from 2009 to 2014, and then Prime Minister of the country until 2016, was an influential figure with the greater influence in shaping Turkey's geopolitical aspirations and geographical fantasies. His book "Strategic Depth: The International Position of Turkey", published in 2000, before the AKP came to power, is still a guide to understanding both the strategic choices of Turkish diplomacy, as well as the philosophical and worldview background of Turkish politics leadership of the last twenty years, as it became a guideline of the ruling party's foreign policy.

The sources of the doctrine of strategic depth can be traced to the Turkish-Islamic synthesis proposed by the former president Turgut Özal and to the pan-Islamist ideology of the "National Vision" of Necmettin Erbakan (Murison, 2006), and they conceivably unite the aforementioned with Davutoglu, without leaving Erdogan out of this chain.

With the doctrine of strategic depth, Davutoglu claims that Turkey, due to its history and geographical position, being a geopolitical link between Europe, Africa and Asia, should develop a proactive foreign policy commensurate with its historical and geographical depth, enhanced by its Ottoman heritage. The strategic depth offers valuable opportunities for Turkey to become a "central power" country, able to exert influence in the Middle East, the Balkans, the Caucasus, Central Asia, the Caspian, the Mediterranean, the Arabian Gulf and the Black Sea, claiming a global strategic role in the international system (Kaya, 2020).

Turkey should not content with a regional role in the Balkans or the Middle East, because it is not a regional, but a central power. As such, it should aspire to play a leading role in various regions, which could endow it with global strategic importance. He explicitly emphasizes that Turkey should not act as a connecting link between Islam and the West, as this would make it a mouthpiece for the geopolitical interests of other countries. Instead, Turkey will possess a leading role in the Islamic world, taking advantage of its historical and geographical depth of the Ottoman period (Davutoğlu, 2010:189-194).

In order to materialize his strategic vision, Davutoglu, as foreign minister, made regional use of soft power dynamics, such as promoting solidarity, shared historical and cultural ties, as well as promoting democratic institutions and increasing trade relations, pursuing strategic cooperation with neighboring countries, which he described as a "policy of zero problems with neighbors". While, at the international level, he tried to promote Turkey, as part of the solution to local conflicts, he reinforced regional economic cooperation, seeking to prevent the intervention of the great powers, making Turkey a leading power in the region (Donelli & Levaggi, 2016).

Undoubtedly, in the first decade, of the 2000s, the application of the doctrine of strategic depth met with relative success, but this policy was weakened by its counterproductive execution and the non-compliance of several neighboring states, which criticized Ankara for seeking the reconstitution of the Ottoman Empire. However, since 2011, this doctrine has been eroded by a variety of factors, which will be analyzed later in this paper, forcing Turkey to reshape its strategic choices, leaving behind the soft power approach and taking into account the ever-changing geopolitical situation of the region, as for example the events of the "Arab Spring" and the discovery of natural gas deposits in the Eastern Mediterranean (Benhaïm & Öktem, 2015). Therefore, Turkey has ended up with the so-called "precious solitude" in the international system, applying a tougher approach and claiming greater strategic autonomy from the West, especially after the coup attempt on July 15, 2016.

The forced resignation of Davutoglu in May 2016, due to his disputes with President Erdogan, and the coup attempt in July 2016, led Turkey to readjust its strategic options, which now mostly reflect elements of its ideology of " Blue Homeland", rather than that of the "Strategic Depth".

THE DOCTRINE OF THE BLUE HOMELAND

During the first years of the Justice and Development Party's rule, Davutoglu's policy was implemented, which aimed to increase Turkey's geopolitical influence in countries that had been territories of the Ottoman Empire. However, "Strategic Depth" was called into question after the resignation of Davutoglu and the attempted coup in July 2016, and was replaced by the so-called "Blue Homeland" doctrine, which is Turkey's current geographical fantasy. The "Blue Homeland", introduced as a doctrine by Kemalist Admiral Cem Gürdeniz in 2006, constitutes the plan of Turkish maritime geopolitics for the 21st century, and consists of two pillars: First, the identification of maritime jurisdictional areas under Turkish sovereignty (territorial waters, EEZ). Secondly, the foundation of a maritime worldview for Turkey.

The geopolitical goal of the "Blue Homeland" is to control the three seas that surround Turkey (Aegean Sea, Southeast Mediterranean and Black Sea) by creating an Exclusive Economic Zone, covering 462,000 km2, (Fig. 1), seeking on the one hand the regional and international projection of Ankara's power and on the other hand access to energy resources, which will contribute to its economic development, reducing its dependence on Russia and strengthening its position in the wider geographical environment, as it attempts to become an energy transit hub (Gürdeniz, 2017:35).

The "Blue Homeland" doctrine actually represents the maritime zones of Turkish interests in the waters between the 25th and 45th east meridians and the 33rd and 43rd north parallels (Fig. 1) (Gürdeniz, 2020). However, it should be clarified that in the Black Sea region, the maritime zone corresponds to the EEZ, which Turkey has demarcated, applying the principles of equidistance with the littoral states, but in the Aegean and Eastern Mediterranean region, it encroaches on the EEZ claimed by Greece and Cyprus. Thus, Turkey's jurisdiction would extend to the eastern half of the Aegean, without the annexation of the Greek islands, but allowing them to have territorial waters of 6 nautical miles. According to the "Blue Homeland", Turkey's EEZ will adjoin the EEZs of Libya and Egypt, based on the principle of equidistance between the coastal states, but completely ignoring the potential claims of Greece in this area. Finally, part of the EEZ between the Republic of Cyprus, Syria and Lebanon is also claimed by the self-proclaimed "Turkish Republic of Northern Cyprus", where Ankara and its Northern Cypriot ally will extend over a maritime area of 462,000 square kilometers. So according to the "Blue Homeland", these claims should constitute the base for any negotiation with the rest of the Eastern Mediterranean states, especially with Greece and the Republic of Cyprus (Denizeau, 2021).

Figure 1. The Blue Homeland Doctrine.

Source: mavivatan.net

These geopolitical ambitions are part of a broader strategic vision to make Turkey a regional power. Just as the Anatolia region, according to Ahmet Davutoglu's "Strategic Depth", functions as a geographical link between Europe, Asia and Africa, in the same way, the Eastern Mediterranean plays a similar role in the "Blue Homeland" concept. The core of this doctrine is Ankara's dominance in the Mediterranean in order to regain maritime power, once held by the Ottoman Empire (Yanarocak, 2021). Its main pursuit is the geopolitical supremacy in the Eastern Mediterranean, which is a key crossing point for trade routes connecting Europe with the Indian Ocean, and by extension with Southeast Asia. Additionally, the Eastern Mediterranean connects the Near East with the Mashreq. That is why Cyprus, due to its geographical position, has a high geopolitical and geostrategic value for Ankara. Through the control of the maritime zones stretching from the Black Sea and the Suez Canal to the Central Mediterranean, Turkey will have under its supervision all the main transit routes to European markets (Alaranta, 2021).

FROM 'STRATEGIC DEPTH' TO THE 'BLUE HOMELAND'

The first years of the Justice and Development Party rule saw the implementation of Ahmet Davutoglu's "zero problems with neighbors" policy, which aimed to increase Turkey's geopolitical influence through soft power in the former Ottoman territories. In short, it highlighted a more dynamic presence of Turkey at the international level, instrumentalizing geographical, historical and cultural characteristics (Alekseevich, 2018). The rapid improvement of the Turkish economy, combined with the development of commercial and cultural ties with neighboring countries, helped Turkey to improve its position in the international system, making it primarily a commercial and secondarily an energy hub.

For Davutoglu, the decline of the Ottoman Empire is due to the loss of control of the seas, and in order not to repeat the same historical mistakes, Turkey must ensure a permanent and dynamic commercial and naval fleet from the Black Sea to the Red Sea and to the Indian Ocean.

In the first decade of the 2000s, these policies of Davutoglu were successfully implemented, while Western countries applauded these efforts. But, in the following decade the "Strategic Depth" declined, due to various factors and current developments that arose.

Davutoglu considered Anatolia as a geographical unifying bridge between Europe, Africa and Asia. The Eastern Mediterranean plays an identical role in the "Blue Homeland" doctrine, as it straddles the Mediterranean basin and the Middle East. The discoveries of natural gas reserves in Israel and Egypt, and the Republic of Cyprus' conclusion of an agreement demarcating maritime zones with neighboring countries, combined with Turkey's increased energy needs, have intensified Ankara's geopolitical fears of being left out of future energy designs.

Another key turning point was the publication of the scientific article "Maritime Europe and EU enlargement: A geopolitical perspective", popularly known as "the Map of Seville". This is a study published in 2006 by the academic geographers from the University of Seville, Juan Luis Suárez de Vivero and Juan Carlos Rodríguez Mateos, at the request of the European Union, which sought to carry out maritime spatial planning, for the implementation of the Law of the Sea and the protection of the marine environment, in the context of the vision of European enlargement, i.e. the process by which a state joins the European Union, after having fulfilled a set of political and economic criteria. In other words, it is a map that included Exclusive Economic Zones of the EU member states, which validate the territorial claims of the Republic of Cyprus and Greece's sovereignty in the Aegean, -something that Turkey strongly disputes- completely disregarding Ankara's claims in the Aegean and the Eastern Mediterranean (Fig. 2).

Figure 2. EU members maritime jurisdictions {EEZ declared/hypothetical}.

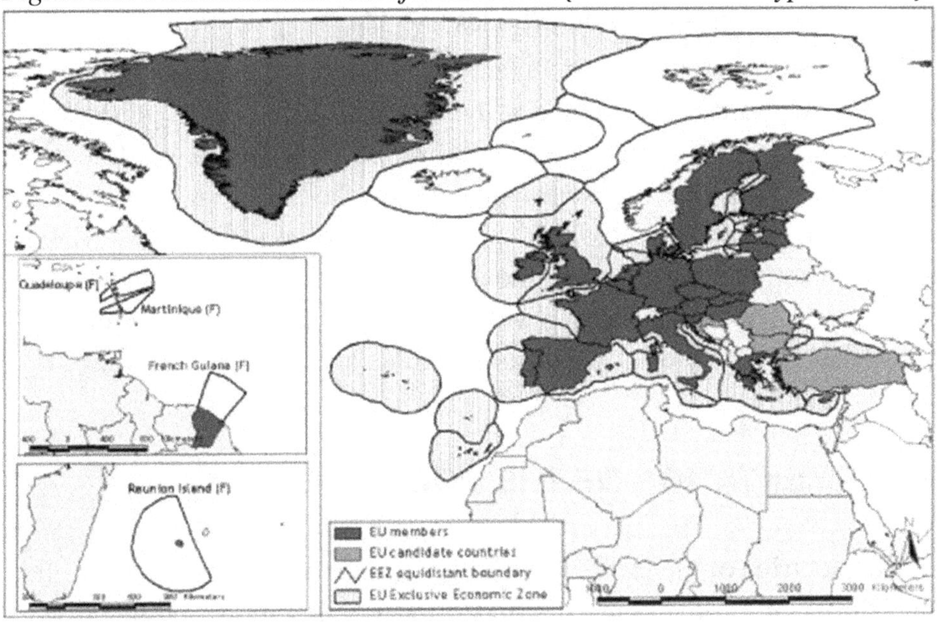

Source: Juan Luis Suárez de Vivero και Juan Carlos Rodríguez Mateos

Ankara, outraged, reacted by claiming that the map in question is "a conspiracy plan of the European Union and the US, without legal basis", with the aim of cutting off Turkey from the Aegean and the Mediterranean, with the exception of the Gulf of Antalya. In Ankara, on October 14, 2006, at a conference organized by the commanders of the Turkish Navy, Admiral Cem Gürdeniz, who was in charge of maritime strategic planning, presented the doctrine of the "Blue Homeland" in response to the map of Seville, according to which, Turkey is motivated to claim a larger economic zone in the Aegean and the Eastern Mediterranean (Deriziotis, 2021).

Subsequently, another admiral of the Turkish navy, Cihat Yaycı, and a retired colonel of the Turkish armed forces, Ali Karamahmut, based on the theory of Cem Gürdeniz, authored the treatise "Fundamental maritime law for naval officers: in times of peace and of war", further developing the concept and interpretation of the United Nations Convention on the Law of the Sea and the Delimitation of Maritime Zones, expanding Turkey's maritime zones to such a point that it adjoins a common maritime border with Libya, without taking into account and violating the territorial waters of the Greek islands of Crete, Rhodes and Megisti.

This construction of the doctrine helps Turkey to legitimize, both in the domestic political scene and at the international level, its geopolitical fears, in order not to limit its territorial waters in Anatolia, but to extend them to the Black Sea, the Aegean and also to the Eastern Mediterranean, where it intends to play a leading role. For this reason, Turkey is trying to redefine itself as a naval power, modernizing its navy and coast guard and resetting its s, not fully aligning with the Western countries and approaching, for its own geopolitical purposes, China and Russia (Dalay, 2021).

IMPLEMENTATION OF THE DOCTRINE

The doctrine of the "Blue Homeland" is undoubtedly now a geopolitical priority of Turkish foreign policy, proceeding with the publication of maps with claims to maritime zones. Until 1972, Turkey had no claim to sovereign rights of the Greek islands, while to this day its claims extend from the Aegean to the Eastern Mediterranean. Ankara's revisionist attitude begins in 1973-74, when it announces its claims in the Aegean and the Eastern Mediterranean, publishing corresponding maps and granting licenses for research on the Greek continental shelf, to the Turkish Petroleum Company (TRAO) in the Northern Aegean in 1973, and between of the Greek islands of Rhodes and Megisti in 1974. In the 1980s, its claims intensified by trying to usurp Search and Rescue (SAR) areas of responsibility, up to the 25th meridian, effectively bisecting the Aegean, while in the 1990s it challenged the territorial integrity of islands and islets of the Aegean, describing them as "indeterminate ownership" (Başak, 2021). In 2004, it claimed all the sea areas west of 32° 16΄18΄΄ Meridian seeking to secure rights west of Cyprus, up to Crete. Since September 21, 2011, Turkey and the self-proclaimed "Turkish Republic of Northern Cyprus" signed an agreement on the delimitation of the continental shelf, which they equate with the EEZ, based on the principle of equality and not the median line, and submitted to the United Nations the geographic coordinates (Klokkaris, 2015). In July 2012, Ankara re-granted licenses to the state-owned Turkish Oil Company (TPAO) in parts of the potential continental shelf of the Greek islands of Rhodes, Karpathos, Megisti and the western part of the Cypriot EEZ (Gürel et al, 2013:61-73).

After the July 2016 coup attempt, President Recep Tayyip Erdoğan, in order to assert himself within his country, is hardening his policy in order to project his hegemonic agenda at the region. In more detail, in February 2018, Turkish naval vessels were ordered to obstruct and prevent drilling by the Italian Energy Company (ENI) in plot 3 of the Cypriot EEZ, stating on the one hand that Turkey also has sovereign rights in the EEZ of Eastern Cyprus and on the other hand, that no research and exploitation of energy resources can be carried out in the Eastern Mediterranean without its own participation. In October 2018, in accordance with the "Blue Homeland" doctrine, it carried out the first drilling off the Gulf of Antalya, with the Fatih drillship, in an undemarcated area, but without violating the sovereign rights of the Republic of Cyprus (Andrei, 2019).

Subsequently, from May 2019 to July 2020, Turkey, using gun boat diplomacy, continued to assert its claims in the Eastern Mediterranean by sending Turkish drillships Fatih and Yavuz and violating the Cyprus Republic EEZ, while its claims in the Aegean continued systematically and escalated in the summer of 2020, with the dispatch of the research vessel Oruç Reis for research within the potential continental shelf of Greece (Gurcan, 2020).

An offshoot of the "Blue Homeland" doctrine is the signing of the Memorandum of Agreement between the Government of the Republic of Turkey and the Government of National Accord of Libya on the delimitation of maritime jurisdictions in the Mediterranean, on November 27, 2019. Two weeks earlier, Ankara had prepared the ground by sending a letter to the UN, setting out its claims for the boundaries of its maritime zones. Actually, the Turkish claims up to the 28th meridian were disclosed (Kansu, 2020), but also further west, without taking into account the influence of the Dodecanese and Crete (Fig. 3).

Figure 3. Libya (GNA)–Turkey maritime deal.

Source: moderndiplomacy.eu

Subsequently, on March 18, 2020, the Permanent Representative of Turkey to the United Nations Feridun Hadi Sinirlioğlu submitted in a letter to the Secretary General of the United Nations the geographical coordinates [points F (34° 16′ 13.72″ N – 026° 19′ 11.64″ E) and E (34° 09′ 07.90″ N – 026° 39′ 06.30″ E)] of the Turkish continental shelf as derived from the memorandum of understanding which defines the Turkey-Libya median line (United Nations A/74/757, 2020). Cyprus, Egypt and Greece rejected the agreement as illegal and geographically unreasonable, however the said memorandum was annulled on 27 January 2021 by the Court of Appeal of Al-Bayda, Libya (Waala, 2021) (Fig. 4).

Figure 4. Geographical coordinates of the outer limits of the Turkish continental shelf, as agreed by the Memorandum of Understanding Between the Government of Republic of Turkey and the Government of National.

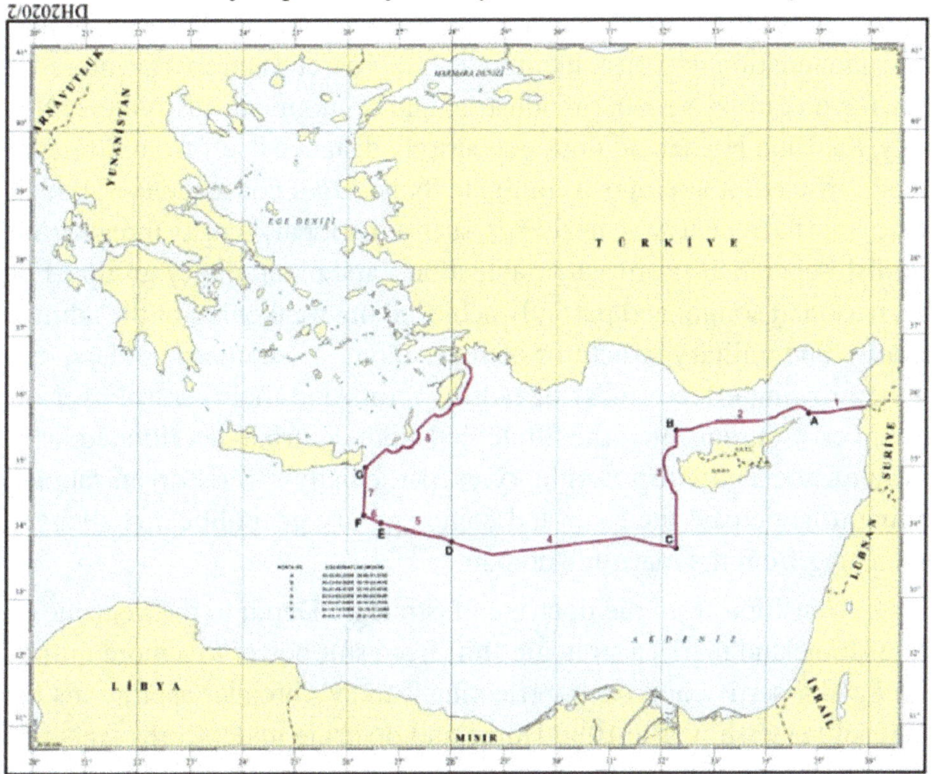

DH2020/2

Source: The letter from the Permanent Representative of Turkey to the United Nations addressed to the Secretary-General Accord-State of Libya on Delimitation of Maritime Jurisdiction Areas in the Mediterranean.

CONCLUSION

The doctrines of Strategic Depth and Blue Homeland have served as the pillars of Turkey's foreign policy, which has undergone significant transformations over the past two decades due to shifting geopolitical dynamics and domestic political changes. It should be clarified that the Strategic Depth doctrine was rooted in the historical geographical space of the Ottoman Empire, utilizing political and cultural pillars, and primarily aimed to enhance Turkey's geopolitical power in the land domain, namely in the Balkans, the Greater Middle East, and Central Asia, while focusing secondarily on the maritime domain.

In contrast, the Blue Homeland doctrine was not purely based on historical foundations but on contemporary commercial and energy interests, drawing on Turkey's modern industrial and economic infrastructure. Notably, the Blue Homeland does not entirely distance itself from Strategic Depth; instead, it attempts to mitigate its negative consequences, which arose from the recent Arab uprisings, such as national security threats from Kurdish separatists, terrorist organizations, and paramilitary groups. For this reason, it sought and partially achieved the weakening of the administrative and military structures of states along its southern borders, due to the growing effectiveness of radical actors and their control over oil resources. Consequently, the Strategic Depth doctrine deteriorated, as it became associated with paramilitary and particularly terrorist organizations, failing to anticipate the risks and contemporary geopolitical challenges emanating from the maritime domain.

The transition from the doctrine of Strategic Depth to the doctrine of Blue Homeland marks a strategic shift from soft power to a more militarized and assertive approach, reflecting Turkey's broader aspirations for regional leadership. The Blue Homeland doctrine underscores Ankara's maritime ambitions and its determination to control key energy routes and maritime zones, challenging neighboring states and the established international order.

This evolution reveals Turkey's intent to reaffirm its historical influence and geopolitical autonomy, particularly in the Eastern Mediterranean. However, these ambitions have exacerbated tensions with Greece, Cyprus, and other regional actors, raising concerns about regional stability. Moving forward, Turkey's ability to balance its revisionist goals with the need for constructive engagement will determine its role in the international system and its relations with both regional and global powers.

REFERENCES

Alaranta, T. (2021). "The Eastern Mediterranean conflict from TURKEY-Greece confrontation to regional power struggles". Finnish Institute of International Affairs, available at: https://tinyurl.com/mr32ekxn

Alekseevich, A. V. (2018, September). Neo-Ottomanism as a Key Doctrine of Modern Turkey. *Communication and Public Diplomacy*, *1*(1), 80–88. DOI: 10.17265/2160-6579/2018.01.007

Andrei, R. (2019, September 2). "The Cyprus Issue and Natural Gas in the Eastern Mediterranean". *Geopolitical Monitor*, available at: https://tinyurl.com/bddrwckm

Başak, Ü. (2021). "Yunanistan'da tersanelerin özelleştirme süreçleri ve bunun yunan deniz kuvvetlerine etkileri. Mavi Vatan'dan Açık Denizlere Dergisi". *Deniz Harp Enstitüsü. Milli Savunma Üniversitesi*, Sayı 9, ss. 72-87

Benhaïm, Y., & Öktem, K. (2015). The rise and fall of Turkey's soft power discourse: Discourse in foreign policy under Davutoğlu and Erdoğan. *European Journal of Turkish Studies, 21*. Advance online publication. DOI: 10.4000/ejts.5275

Dalay, G. (2021, January). "Turkey, Europe, and the Eastern Mediterranean: Charting a Way Out of the Current Deadlock". *Brookings Doha Center Policy Briefing*.

Davutoğlu, A. (2010) *Το Στρατηγικό βάθος, Η διεθνής θέση της Τουρκίας* (Ν. Ραπτόπουλος, μτφ & Ν. Σαρρής, επίμ.). Αθήνα: Ποιότητα

Denizeau, A. (2021). *Mavi Vatan, the "Blue Homeland" The Origins, Influences and Limits of an Ambitious Doctrine for Turkey*. Etudes de l'Ifri.

Deriziotis, A. (2021). "The "Blue Homeland" and Erdoğan's Rhetoric: State Doctrine or Populist Narrative? Convergence and Confrontation" *The Balkans and the Middle East in the 21st Century. Article*, *1*, 9–32. DOI: 10.18485/iipe_conv_conf.2021.ch1

Donelli, F., & Levaggi, A. G. (2016). Becoming Global Actor: The Turkish Agenda for the Global South. *SSRN*, *1*(2), 93–115. DOI: 10.2139/ssrn.3462255

Gurcan, M. (2020). "Turkey expands gas exploration efforts to Libya's offshore waters". Al Monitor, Independent, trusted coverage of the Middle East, available at: https://tinyurl.com/yruf3sft

Gürdeniz, C. (2017). *Mavi Vatan Yazıları*. Kırmızı Kedi Yayınevi.

Gürdeniz, C. (2020). "What is the Blue Homeland in the 21st century?" *United World*, available at: https://tinyurl.com/mhpf94pv

Gürel, A., Mullen, F., & Tzimitras, H. (2013). "Turkish and Turkish Cypriot response to roc exploration. The Cyprus Hydrocarbons Issue: Context, Positions and Future Scenarios". *Peace Research Institute* Oslo (PRIO). PCC Report 1/2013, Cyprus Centre, available at: https://tinyurl.com/5n7eynmv

Kansu, Z. N. (2020). "An assesment of Eastern Mediterranean maritime boundary delimitation agreement between Turkey and Libya". Kara Harp Okulu Bilim Dergisi. *Science Journal of Turkish Military Academy*, *30*(1), 51–84.

Kaya, K. (2020, January). "Book Review: A Look Back and Forward at Turkey's "Strategic Depth" Foreign Policy Doctrine". Foreign Military Studies Office (FMSO).

Murison, A. (2006, November). The Strategic Depth Doctrine of Turkish Foreign Policy. *Middle Eastern Studies*, *42*(6), 945–964. DOI: 10.1080/00263200600923526

United Nations (2020). A/74/757. Letter dated 18 March 2020 from the Permanent Representative of Turkey to the United Nations addressed to the Secretary-General.

Waala, A. (2021). "Libyan court cancels border demarcation and security cooperation agreement between Al-Wefaq and Turkey". *Egypt Today*, available at: https://tinyurl.com/276v64f6

Yanarocak, H. E. C. (2021). *Turkish Irredentism and the Greater Middle East.* The Jerusalem Institute for Strategy and Security, available at: https://tinyurl.com/rzpe8tw5

Compilation of References

Alaranta, T. (2021). "The Eastern Mediterranean conflict from TURKEY-Greece confrontation to regional power struggles". Finnish Institute of International Affairs, available at: https://tinyurl.com/mr32ekxn

Alberola, E., Arslan, Y., Cheng, G., & Moessner, R. 2020, The fiscal response to the COVID-19 crisis in advanced and emerging market economies. Available at https://www.bis.org/publ/bisbull23.htm (accessed 20 January 2022).

Alekseevich, A. V. (2018, September). Neo-Ottomanism as a Key Doctrine of Modern Turkey. *Communication and Public Diplomacy*, *1*(1), 80–88. DOI: 10.17265/2160-6579/2018.01.007

Alonso, L. E., & Rodríguez, C. J. (2020). Crisis and sacrifice in Spain, International Karl Polanyi Society, Debate: Crisis in Southern Europe, Available at: https://www.karlpolanyisociety.com/2020/06/29/crisis-and-sacrifice-in-spain/

Alonso-Trabanco, J. M. (2022). "Turkey as an Aspiring Great Power". *Geopolitical Monitor*. https://tinyurl.com/2uastnwv

Anastasiadis, G. (2003). Alexandros Papanastasiou. His important contribution towards Democracy and the Constitution. In: Anastasiadis, G. (Edit.) *The Creative relationship of Alexandros Papanastasiou with Thessaloniki and her University*. Athens: Foundation of the Greek Parliament for Parliamentarism and Democracy. (In Greek).

Andreasyan, A. (2013). Gas Finds in the Eastern Mediterranean. *Journal of Palestine Studies*, *42*(3), 29–47. DOI: 10.1525/jps.2013.42.3.29

Andrei, R. (2019, September 2). "The Cyprus Issue and Natural Gas in the Eastern Mediterranean". *Geopolitical Monitor*, available at: https://tinyurl.com/bddrwckm

Andrei, R. (2022). Turkey's Energy Strategy. In *Search of an Upgraded Political and Energy Status". In Natural Gas at the Frontline Between the EU, Russia, and Turkey: A Conflict-Cooperation Perpetuum* (pp. 231–263). Springer International Publishing.

Annunziata, A., & Scarpato, D. (2014). 'Factors affecting consumer attitudes towards food products with sustainable attributes', *Agricultural Economics - Czech*, 60, 353-363.

Ataman, M., & Özdemir, Ç. (2018). Turkey's Syria Policy: Constant Objectives, Shifting Priorities. *Turkish Journal of Middle Eastern Studies.*, *5*(2), 13–35. DOI: 10.26513/tocd.466046

Atay, E., & Apak, S. (2024). The European Union and Turkey's Renewable Resources Versus Fossil Energy for the Sustainable Future. *New Approaches to CSR, Sustainability and Accountability*, *V*, 153–162. DOI: 10.1007/978-981-99-9145-7_8

Aydin, C. İ. (2020). Nuclear energy debate in Turkey: Stakeholders, policy alternatives, and governance issues. *Energy Policy*, *136*, 111041. Advance online publication. DOI: 10.1016/j.enpol.2019.111041

Bach-Faig, A., Berry, E., Lairon, D., Reguant, J., Trichopoulou, A., Dernini, S., & Serra-Majem, L. (2011). Mediterranean diet pyramid today: Science and cultural updates. *Public Health Nutrition*, *14*(12A), 2274–2284. DOI: 10.1017/S1368980011002515

Baç, M. M., & Taşkın, E. (2007). Turkey's accession to the European Union does culture and identity play a role? *Ankara Review of European Studies*, *6*(2), 31–50.

Badarin, E., & Schumacher, T. (2022). The Eastern Mediterranean Energy Bonanza: A Piece in the Regional and Global Geopolitical Puzzle, and the Role of the European Union. *Comparative Southeast European Studies, 70*(3), 414–438. DOI: 10.1515/soeu-2022-0036

Barber, B. (1983). *The Logic and Limits of Trust*. New Rutgers University Press.

Başak, Ü. (2021). "Yunanistan'da tersanelerin özelleştirme süreçleri ve bunun yunan deniz kuvvetlerine etkileri. Mavi Vatan'dan Açık Denizlere Dergisi". *Deniz Harp Enstitüsü. Milli Savunma Üniversitesi*, Sayı 9, ss. 72-87

Benhaïm, Y., & Öktem, K. (2015). The rise and fall of Turkey's soft power discourse: Discourse in foreign policy under Davutoğlu and Erdoğan. *European Journal of Turkish Studies, 21*. Advance online publication. DOI: 10.4000/ejts.5275

Bijl, M. (2020). The Covid-19 crisis is exacerbating gender inequalities—But who cares? *Social Europe*, •••, 5.

Bockmann, M. W. (2024, October 23). Greece-owned ships are top Houthi target. Lloyd's List. https://lloydslist.com/LL1151096/Greece-owned-ships-are-top-Houthi-target

Borgerson, S. G. (2009). The national interest and the law of the sea (Council Special Report No. 46). Council on Foreign Relations.

Bourdieu, P. (1986). The forms of capital. In Richardson, J. G. (Ed.), *Handbook of theory and research for the sociology of education* (pp. 241–258). Greenwood Press.

Bozkurt, A. (2021). "Turkey failed to convince Russia to share missile technology, agree to co-production". *Nordic Monitor*, available at: https://tinyurl.com/yeypb5vn

Brundtland, G. (1987). 'Report of the World Commission on Environment and Development: Our Common Future'. [online]. Available at: <http://www.un-documents.net/our-common-future.pdf> (Accessed 9 April 2023).

Bueger, C., & Edmunds, T. (2017). Beyond seablindness: A new agenda for maritime security studies. *International Affairs*, *93*(6), 1293–1311. DOI: 10.1093/ia/iix174

Burawoy, M. (2021). Letter from Oakland, 15th International Karl Polanyi Conference: The Role of the State in the post-COVID 21st Century, Concordia University, Montreal

Calhoun, C. (2011). From the Current Crisis to Possible Futures. In Calhoun, C., & Derluguian, G. (Eds.), *Business as Usual: The Roots of the Global Financial Meltdown*. New York University Press.

Cangiani, M. (2020). Italy: New Problems are not New, International Karl Polanyi Society, Debate: Crisis in Southern Europe. Available at: https://www.karlpolanyisociety.com/2020/06/29/new-problems-are-not-new-i/

Carter, A. (2006). *Practical Methods for Evaluating Coaching. Institute for employment studies*. University of Sussex Campus.

Cavallo, A. F., & Cai, T. 2020, HBS COVID-19 global policy tracker. Available at https://www.hbs.edu/covid-19-business-impact/Insights/Economic-and-Financial-Impacts/Global-Policy-Tracker (accessed 20 January 2022).

Chatziiosif, Ch. (2002). History of Greece during the 20th Century. The Interwar period 1922-1940. In Chatziiosif, Ch. (Ed.), *The Refugee Problem, the constants and the Changes in the Greek Economy* (Vol. B1). Bibliorama. (In Greek)

Chen, C., Shi, Y., Zhang, P., & Ding, C. (2021). A Cross-Country Comparison of Fiscal Policy Responses to the COVID-19 Global Pandemic. *Journal of Comparative Policy Analysis*, *23*(2), 262–273. Retrieved January 20, 2022, from. DOI: 10.1080/13876988.2021.1878885

Cohen Yanarocak, H. E. (2021, November 8). Turkish irredentism and the Greater Middle East. Jerusalem Institute for Strategy and Security. https://jiss.org.il/en/yanarocak-turkish-irredentism-and-the-greater-middle-east/

Cohen, D., & Economicus, H. (2014). *The (Lost) Prophet of Modern Times*. Polity Press.

Coleman, J. (1988). Social Capital in the Creation of Human Capital. *American Journal of Sociology*, *94*, S95–S120. DOI: 10.1086/228943

Colibasanu, A. (2024). (2024). *Turkey's evolving geopolitical strategy in the Black Sea*. Foreign Policy Research Institute. https://tinyurl.com/54mbvwkd

Corbett, J. S. (2012). *Principles of maritime strategy*. Dover Publications. (Original work published 1911)

Cottarelli, C., Gerson, P., & Senhadji, A. (Eds.). 2014, Post-Crisis Fiscal Policy (Cambridge, MA: MIT pressF)

Dalay, G. (2021, January). "Turkey, Europe, and the Eastern Mediterranean: Charting a Way Out of the Current Deadlock". *Brookings Doha Center Policy Briefing*.

Dalay, G. (2021). *Turkish-Russian relations in light of recent conflicts: Syria, Libya, and Nagorno-Karabakh* Stiftung Wissenschaft und Politik. German Institute for International and Security Affairs. DOI: DOI: 10.18449/2021RP05

Dalton, D. (2020, January 2020). Turkey / Contract For Sinop Nuclear Station 'Has Been Cancelled. NucNet, The Independent Nuclear News Agency. https://shorturl.at/9Atu7

Daniel, R., & Lindenstrauss, G. (2023). Nationalism and Turkish foreign policy following the May 2023 elections. Strategic Assessment, 26(2), 117–124. https://inss.org.il/wp-content/uploads/2023/08/Daniel_Lindenstrauss.pdf

Danisi, C. (2017). Taking the 'Union' out of 'EU': The EU-Turkey Statement on the Syrian Refugee Crisis as an Agreement Between States under International Law. Blog of the European Journal of International Law, available at: https://tinyurl.com/yurb7k3w

Dasgupta, P. (1999). Economic progress and the idea of social capital. In *S. I. in Dasgupta. P., Social Capital. A Multifaceted Perspective*. The World Bank. DOI: 10.1596/0-8213-4562-1

Davutoğlu, A. (2010) *Το Στρατηγικό βάθος, Η διεθνής θέση της Τουρκίας* (Ν. Ραπτόπουλος, μτφ & Ν. Σαρρής, επίμ.). Αθήνα: Ποιότητα

De Matos, A. P., & Pusceddu, A. M. (2021). Austerity, the state and common sense in Europe: A comparative perspective on Italy and Portugal. *Anthropological Theory*, *21*(4), 21. DOI: 10.1177/1463499621991326

Dees, J. G. (1998). *The Meaning of Social Entrepreneurship*. The Kauffman Center for Entrepreneurial Leadership.

Degli Antoni, G., & Grimalda, G. (2024). Is social capital bridging or bonding? Evidence from a field experiment with association members. *Theory and Decision*, *97*(1), 167–190. DOI: 10.1007/s11238-023-09971-7

Demir, I. (2020). Transformation of the Turkish Defense Industry. *Insight Turkey.*, *22*(3), 17–24. DOI: 10.25253/99.2020223.02

Denizeau, A. (2021). *Mavi Vatan, the "Blue Homeland" The Origins, Influences and Limits of an Ambitious Doctrine for Turkey*. Etudes de l'Ifri.

Deriziotis, A. (2021). "The "Blue Homeland" and Erdoğan's Rhetoric: State Doctrine or Populist Narrative? Convergence and Confrontation" *The Balkans and the Middle East in the 21st Century. Article*, *1*, 9–32. DOI: 10.18485/iipe_conv_conf.2021.ch1

Díaz- Foncea. M., Marcuello, C., Marcuello, C., Solorzano, M., Navío, J., Guzmán, C., de la O Barroso, M., Rodríguez, M. J., Santos, F. J., Fisac, R., Alguacil, P., Chaves, R., Savall, T. & Villajos, E. (2016) "*Social Enterprise in Spain: A Diversity of Roots and a Proposal of Models*", ICSEM Working Papers, No. 29, Liege: The International Comparative Social Enterprise Models (ICSEM) Project.

Dilek, E. (2022). Sovereignty Disputes and Resource Discoveries in the Eastern Mediterranean: A Conflict Analysis Perspective. *Journal of Middle East Perspectives*, *1*(2), 133–155.

Dillenburger, K., Matuska, E., de Bruijn, M., & Röttgers, H. R. (2019). *Job coaches for adults with disabilities: A practical guide*. Jessica Kingsley Publishers.

Dionellis, M. Not everyone is safe at home. Efsyn Newspaper, 22.11.2020 (In Greek). Available at: https://www.efsyn.gr/efkriti/koinonia/269727_den-menoyn-oles-asfaleis-otan-menoyn-sto-spiti

Donelli, F., & Levaggi, A. G. (2016). Becoming Global Actor: The Turkish Agenda for the Global South. *SSRN*, *1*(2), 93–115. DOI: 10.2139/ssrn.3462255

Dörre, K. (2015). Social Capitalism and Crisis: from the internal to the external Landnahme. 2015). Sociology-Capitalism-Critique, 247-277.

Druckman, A., & Jackson, T. (2010). The bare necessities: How much household carbon do we really need? *Ecological Economics*, *69*(9), 1794–1804. DOI: 10.1016/j.ecolecon.2010.04.018

Duman, B. (2016). Turkey's fight against terrorism and the role of the Kurds. ORSA- Center for Middle Eastern Strategic Studies. Review of Regional Affairs. No 53, available at: https://orsam.org.tr/d_hbanaliz/53eng.pdf

ECB (European Central Bank). (2012). Speech by M. Draghi, President of the ECB at the Global Investment Conference in London. Available at: https://www.ecb.europa.eu/press/key/date/2012/html/sp120726.en.html

Erdemir, A., & Edelman, E. (2018). *Erdogan's Hostage Diplomacy Western Nationals in Turkish Prisons*. Foundation for Defense of Democracies.

Erensü, S. & Karaman, O. (2017). "The Work of a Few Trees: Gezi, Politics and Space". *International Journal of Urban and Regional Research,* 2017, 41 (1), pp.19-36. DOI: ff10.1111/1468-2427.12387

Ersoy, E. A., & Ugurlu, A. (2024). Bioenergy's role in achieving a low-carbon electricity future: A case of Türkiye. *Applied Energy*, *372*, 123799. Advance online publication. DOI: 10.1016/j.apenergy.2024.123799

Estanque, E. (2020). Commodification and Countermovements: Portugal against the Trend, International Karl Polanyi Society, Debate: Crisis in Southern Europe, Available at: https://www.karlpolanyisociety.com/2020/06/21/commodification-and-countermovements-portugal-against-the-trend/

Estanque, E., Costa, H. A., Fonseca, D., & Santos, A. (2019). Are Trade Unions Trapped? Precarious Movements and Labour Struggles at the Left Turn in Portugal. In Schmalz, S., & Sommer, B. (Eds.), *Confronting Crisis and Precariousness*. Organized Labour and Social Unrest in the European Union, Rowman and Littlefield.

ETUC. (2021). Anticipating and managing the COVID-19 crisis impact on jobs and workplaces: Swift action needed to enforce rights to worker involvement. Available at: https://www.etuc.org/sites/default/files/page/file/2020-06/ETUFs%20ETUC%20letter%20to%20Mr%20Schmit_Enforcement%20of%20ICP%20rights_20%20May%202020.pdf

European Commission. (2020). *"Social enterprises and their ecosystems in Europe. Comparative synthesis report", Authors: Carlo Borzaga, Giulia Galera, Barbara Franchini, Stefania Chiomento, Rocío Nogales and Chiara Carini*. Publications Office of the European Union.

European Commission. (2023). EU Blue Economy Observatory: Country profiles. https://blue-economy-observatory.ec.europa.eu/country-profiles/greece_en

Eurostat, C. I., & Engelbert, A. (2013). Coastal regions: People living along the coastline, integration of NUTS 2010 and latest population grid (KS-SF-13-030-EN-N). https://ec.europa.eu/eurostat/statistics-explained/index.php?title=Archive:Coastal_regions_-_population_statistics

FAO. (2010). 'Sustainable diets and biodiversity: directions and solutions for policy, research and action'. *Proceedings of the International Scientific Symposium: Biodiversity and sustainable diets against hunger.*

Federazione Trentina della Cooperazione & Scuola Nazionale Servizi Foundation. (2017) "Italy", in *COOPilot Project: European Report*, by Sybille Mertens, Amélie Mernier, Lola Arpigny and Maxime Bouchat (eds), Center for Social Economy - University of Liege, pp. 291-315

Ferguson, N., Laydon, D., Nedjati-Gilani, G., Imai, N., Ainslie, K., Baguelin, M., ... (2020). Impact of non-pharmaceutical interventions [NPIs] to reduce COVID-19 mortality and healthcare demand. https://doi.org/ DOI: 10.25561/77482

Field, A. (2013). *Discovering Statistics Using IBM SPSS Statistics*. SAGE Publications.

Flaxman, S., Mishra, S., Gandy, A., Unwin, H. J. T., Mellan, T. A., Coupland, H., Whittaker, C., Zhu, H., Berah, T., Eaton, J. W., Monod, M., Perez-Guzman, P. N., Schmit, N., Cilloni, L., Ainslie, K. E. C., Baguelin, M., Boonyasiri, A., Boyd, O., Cattarino, L., & Bhatt, S. (2020). Estimating the effects of non-pharmaceutical interventions on COVID-19 in Europe. *Nature*, *584*(7820), 257–261. DOI: 10.1038/s41586-020-2405-7 PMID: 32512579

Freedman, L. (2005). The official history of the Falklands campaign: Vol. II. War and diplomacy. Routledge.

Freedman, L. (2013). *Strategy: A history*. Oxford University Press.

Frey, A., Bühler, E., & Ruppert, J. (2022). Conflict Management Strategies of Career Counsellors. *Psychology (Irvine, Calif.)*, *13*(1), 62–77. DOI: 10.4236/psych.2022.131005

Fuchs, C. (2021). *Communicating COVID-19: Everyday Life, Digital Capitalism, and Conspiracy Theories in Pandemic Times*. Emerald Publishing Limited. DOI: 10.1108/9781801177207

Fukuyama, F. (1995). *Trust. The Social Virtues and the Creation of Prosperity*. Free Press.

Fukuyama, F. (2002). Social Capital and Development: The Coming Agenda. *SAIS Review (Paul H. Nitze School of Advanced International Studies)*, *XXII*(1), 23–37. DOI: 10.1353/sais.2002.0009

Fuller, G. (2008). *The New Turkish Republic: Turkey as a Pivotal in the Muslim World.* United State Institute of Peace.

Germond, B. (2015). The maritime dimension of European security: Seapower and the European Union. Palgrave Macmillan.

Gezen, M., & Karaaslan, A. (2022). *"Energy planning based on Vision-2023 of Turkey with a goal programming under fuzzy multi-objectives". Energy* (Vol. 261). Part A., DOI: 10.1016/j.energy.2022.124956

Ghaddar, H., Nadimi, F., & Schenker, D. (2024, June 21). Hezbollah threatens Cyprus: Capabilities, intentions, and potential consequences. Washington Institute for Near East Policy. https://washingtoninstitute.org/policy-analysis/hezbollah-threatens-cyprus-capabilities-intentions-and-potential-consequences

Göksel, O. (2023). Trading state or machiavellian state? Re-Evaluating the political economy of Turkish foreign policy under Erdoğan. *UPA Strategic Affairs*, *4*(2), 72–107.

Göktürk-Çetinkaya, S. & Koç, M. (2023). "Türkiye'nin İnsansız Hava Araçları Serüveni". *Anadolu Strateji Dergisi.* Cilt 5, ss 1-27

Government of the Russian Federation. (2022). Directive No. 1998-r of 20 July 2022. https://publication.pravo.gov.ru/document/0001202409200036?index=2

Greek Institute of Labour (INE/GSEE). (2018). Greek Economy and Employment: Annual Report. Athens [In Greek]. Available at: https://www.inegsee.gr/ekdosi/etisia-ekthesi-2018-ine-gsee-i-elliniki-ikonomia-ke-i-apascholisi/

Gundelach, K. (1981). *Die deutsche Luftwaffe im Mittelmeer 1940–1945* (Vol. 1). Lang.

Gurcan, M. (2020). "Turkey expands gas exploration efforts to Libya's offshore waters". Al Monitor, Independent, trusted coverage of the Middle East, available at: https://tinyurl.com/yruf3sft

Gürdeniz, C. (2020). "What is the Blue Homeland in the 21st century?" *United World*, available at: https://tinyurl.com/mhpf94pv

Gürdeniz, C. (2017). *Mavi Vatan Yazıları*. Kırmızı Kedi Yayınevi.

Gürel, A., Mullen, F., & Tzimitras, H. (2013). "Turkish and Turkish Cypriot response to roc exploration. The Cyprus Hydrocarbons Issue: Context, Positions and Future Scenarios". *Peace Research Institute* Oslo (PRIO). PCC Report 1/2013, Cyprus Centre, available at: https://tinyurl .com/5n7eynmv

Hagner, D., Dague, B., & Phillips, K. (2015). Including employees with disabilities in workplace cultures: Strategies and barriers. *Rehabilitation Counseling Bulletin, 58*(4), 195–202. DOI: 10.1177/0034355214544750

Hale, W., & Özbudun, E. (2010). *Islamism, Democracy and Liberalism in Tukey*. Routledge.

Hansen, J., Holm, L., Frewer, L., Robinson, P., & Sandøe, P. (2003). Beyond the knowledge deficit: Recent research into lay and expert attitudes to food risks. *Appetite, 41*(2), 111–121. DOI: 10.1016/S0195-6663(03)00079-5

Heft Sears, S., Jones, A., & Strauser, D. R. (2014). Career counseling with people with disabilities. In Strauser, D. R. (Ed.), *Career development, employment and disability in rehabilitation: From theory to practice* (pp. 277–295). Springer Publishing Company.

Hoek, A. C., Luning, P. A., Stafleu, A., & de Graaf, C. (2004). Food-related lifestyle and health attitudes of Dutch vegetarians, non-vegetarian consumers of meat substitutes, and meat consumers. *Appetite, 42*(3), 265–272. DOI: 10.1016/j.appet.2003.12.003

Höpner, M., Petring, A., Seikel, D., & Werner, B. (2014). Liberalization policy: An empirical analysis of economic and social interventions in western democracies.

HSCB. (2014). Coaching and Mentoring in Social Work – A Review of the Evidence: Commissioned by the HSCB.

Hughner, R., McDonagh, P., Prothero, A., Shultz, C. J.II, & Stanton, J. (2007). Who are organic food consumers? A compilation and review of why people purchase organic food. *Journal of Consumer Behaviour*, *6*(2-3), 94–110. DOI: 10.1002/cb.210

Huseynov, Y. (2017). Geopolitics of the Republic of Turkey's Energy Policy. *International Journal of Energy Economics and Policy*, *7*(3), 337–344.

İletişim Başkanlığı, T. C. (2023, September 29). *Türkiye, Moldova'ya doğal gaz ihraç edecek.* https://shorturl.at/gSAgG

ILO (International Labour Organization). (1998). Declaration on Fundamental Principles and Rights at Work and its Follow-up. Available at: https://www.ilo.org/wcmsp5/groups/public/---ed_norm/---declaration/documents/normativeinstrument/wcms_716594.pdf

ILO (International Labour Organization). (2021). Issue paper on COVID-19and fundamental principles and rights at work, Available at: https://www.ilo.org/wcmsp5/groups/public/@ed_norm/@ipec/documents/publication/wcms_757247.pdf

International Energy Agency. (n.d.). *Energy system of Türkiye*. https://shorturl.at/SrIxI

International Monetary Fund (IMF)'s Tracker of Policy Responses to COVID-19. (2020). Available at https://www.imf.org/en/Topics/imf-and-covid19/Policy-Responses-to-COVID-19 ((accessed 20 January 2022).

Ioannides, N. (2018). *Rights and Obligations of States in Undelimited Maritime Areas: The Case of the Eastern Mediterranean Sea.* Stress Testing the Law of the Sea. [REMOVED HYPERLINK FIELD], DOI: 10.1163/9789004352926_014

ISTAT. (2022). *Struttura e profili del settore non profit Anno 2020.* Italian National Institute of Statistics.

Ivanova, D., Stadler, K., Steen-Olsen, K., Wood, R., Vita, G., Tukker, A., & Hertwich, E. G. (2016). Environmental impact assessment of household consumption. *Journal of Industrial Ecology*, *20*(3), 526–536. DOI: 10.1111/jiec.12371

Jackson, T., & Papathanasopoulou, E. (2008). 'Luxury or 'lock-in'? An exploration of unsustainable consumption in the UK: 1968 to 2000'. *Ecological Economics*, *68*(1-2), 1–2, 80–95. DOI: 10.1016/j.ecolecon.2008.01.026

Jessop, B. (2002). *The Future of the Capitalist State*. Polity Press.

Jurkovich, M., & Wirtz, R. A. (2018). Disability: Taking a turn for the better for labor markets. Fedgazette, 1–3.

Kaliris, A., & Issari, P. (2022). Exploring Narrative Ideas in Career Counseling. *Open Journal of Social Sciences*, *10*(2), 365–380. DOI: 10.4236/jss.2022.102026

Kansu, Z. N. (2020). "An assesment of Eastern Mediterranean maritime boundary delimitation agreement between Turkey and Libya". Kara Harp Okulu Bilim Dergisi. *Science Journal of Turkish Military Academy*, *30*(1), 51–84.

Karamanoli, M. (2024). Fiscal response in covid-19 crisis – The case of the Eurozone. *Acta Scientiarum Polonorum. Oeconomia*, *23*(3), 5–18. DOI: 10.22630/ASPE.2024.23.3.9

Karamanos, A. (2020). Skirtings of Creativity in Late Greece. The Life and Work of Ioannis Karamanos. In Kontogiorgis, E. (Ed.), *Ioannis Karamanos and the agrarian settlement of the refugees*. Papazisi. (In Greek)

Kardaş Ş. (2011). Turkey and the Arab Spring: Coming to Terms with Democracy Promotion? October, The German Marshall Fund of The United States. Policy Brief. Foreign Policy Program.

Kaya, K. (2020, January). "Book Review: A Look Back and Forward at Turkey's "Strategic Depth" Foreign Policy Doctrine". Foreign Military Studies Office (FMSO).

Kearney, J. (2010). Food consumption trends and drivers. *Philosophical Transactions of the Royal Society of London. Series B, Biological Sciences, 365*(1554), 2793–2807. DOI: 10.1098/rstb.2010.0149

Kibaroğlu, M. (2019). On Turkey's Missile Defense Strategy: The Four Faces of the S-400 Deal Between Turkey and Russia. Center For Strategic Research. Republic of Turkey Ministry of Foreign Affairs, available at: https://tinyurl.com/3dspvfzw

Kınıklıoğlu, S. (2022). *Necessary friends: Turkey's improving relationship with the West*. European Council of Foreign Relations. https://tinyurl.com/z83sx2yh

Kirmizioğlu, E. (2014). Ülkemizin 2023 Stratejik Vizyonu Doğrultusunda Akıllı Şebekeye Geçilmesi için Öneriler. Uluslararası İstanbul Akıllı Şebekeler Kongre ve Fuarı, pp143-147. https://hdl.handle.net/11352/1910

Kolay, B. (2023). *Akkuyu Nuclear Power Plant and Energy Diplomacy: How Construction of the Akkuyu Power Plant affected Energy Diplomacy between Turkey and Russia? A Process Tracing Approach.*

Koray, M. (2020). *Doğu Akdeniz'in jeopolitik ve jeostratejik önemi, teknolojik dönüşümler ve denizaltilarin rolü.* Yeni Deniz Güvenliği Ekosistemi ve Doğu Akdeniz. Istanbul: Türk Asya Stratejik Araştırmalar Merkezi.

Korutürk, O. (2012). Arab Revolution: Should We Still Call It a Spring? *Turkish Policy Quarterly, 10*(4), 63–70.

Köstem, S. (2019). Geopolitics, identity and beyond: Turkey's renewed interest in the Caucasus and Central Asia. In *Turkey's Pivot to Eurasia* (pp. 111–128). Routledge. DOI: 10.4324/9780429023064-8

Kounias, S. (2016). Ioannis Papadakis (Jean Papadakis) (1903-1997). In: Proceedings 29th PanHellenic Conference of Statistical Analysis of Risk in the Environment and the Economy, Thessaloniki & Naousa: Greek Statistical Institute. (In Greek).

Kyriakides, K. (2022). The Akkuyu Nuclear Power Plant in Turkey: Some Causes for Concern. *Journal of Balkan & Near Eastern Studies, 25*(3), 340–377. DOI: 10.1080/19448953.2022.2143855

Lagorio, A., Pinto, R., & Golini, R. (2018). Food Waste Reduction in School Canteens: Evidence from an Italian Case. *Journal of Cleaner Production, 199*, 77–84. DOI: 10.1016/j.jclepro.2018.07.077

Larabee, F. S., & Lesser, I. O. (2003). *Turkish Foreign Policy in an Age of Uncertainty*. RAND, National Security Research Division. Center for Middle East Public Policy.

Le Mière, C. (2014). *Maritime diplomacy*. Routledge. DOI: 10.4324/9780203555590

Lloyd's List. (2024, October 28). The week in charts: Container shipping rates show signs of life; Black Sea attacks threaten global food security; Greece-owned ships are top Houthi target. https://lloydslist.com/LL1151148/The-week-in-charts-Container-shipping-rates-show-signs-of-life--Black-Sea-attacks-threaten-global-food-security--Greece-owned-ships-are-top-Houthi-target

Lorek, S., and Spangenberg, J. (2001). 'Indicators for environmentally sustainable household consumption', *International Journal of Sustainable Development*, 4:1, 101.

Luhmann, N. (2002). *La Fiducia*. Il Mulino.

Macdiarmid, J. I. (2014). Seasonality and dietary requirements: Will eating seasonal food contribute to health and environmental sustainability? *The Proceedings of the Nutrition Society*, *73*(3), 368–375. DOI: 10.1017/S0029665113003753

Magnusson, M., Arvola, A., Hursti, U., Åberg, L., & Sjödén, P. (2003). Choice of organic foods is related to perceived consequences for human health and to environmentally friendly behaviour. *Appetite*, *40*(2), 109–117. DOI: 10.1016/S0195-6663(03)00002-3

Mahan, A. T. (1918). The influence of sea power upon history, 1660–1783 (12th ed.). Little, Brown & Co. (Project Gutenberg edition, updated 2007). https://classicsofstrategy.com/2022/02/09/alfred-thayer-mahan-the-influence-of-sea-power-upon-history-as-strategy-grand-strategy-and-polemic/

Mahan, A. T. (1905). *Sea power and its relations to the War of 1812* (Vol. 1). Sampson Low, Marston & Company.

Markantonatou, M. (2013). *Diagnosis, Treatment, and Effects of the Crisis in Greece: A" Special Case" or a.* Test Case.

Mavrogordatos, G. (1992). The unrepeatable achievement. [Athens.]. *Bulletin of the Center Asia-Minor Studies*, *9*, 9–12.

Mazaraki, H. (2012). *Health: Public or Private Good? Achaiki Medicine, 31 (1).* Patra.

Mazis, I., Sgouros, G. A., & Troulis, M. (2022). *The Chronicle of a Pre-announced Greek–Turkish Dialogue* (Vol. 9). Civitas Centium., https://shorturl.at/i4vYH

Mazower, M. (2002). *Greece and the economic crisis of the interwar period.* MIET. (In Greek)

Mazower, M. (2014). *Power networks in modern Greece.* Alexandreia Publishing. (In Greek)

Mertens, E., van't Veer, P., Hiddink, G. J., Steijns, J. M. J. M., & Kuijsten, A. (2017). Operationalising the health aspects of sustainable diets: A review. *Public Health Nutrition*, *20*(4), 739–757. DOI: 10.1017/S1368980016002664

Messenger, J. (2019). Introduction: Telework in the 21st century – an evolutionary perspective. In Messenger, J. C. (Ed.), *Telework in the 21st Century, The ILO Future of Work series.* DOI: 10.4337/9781789903751.00005

Mitsopoulos, D. (2024, July 29). Greek shipyard delivers blocks for France's second FDI. Naval News. https://navalnews.com/naval-news/2024/07/greek-shipyard-delivers-blocks-for-frances-second-fdi/

Moore, M. E., & Huberty, L. L. (2020). The Economic Impact of Employing Disabled Persons: Macro and Micro Perspectives. In Fielden, S. L., Moore, M. E., & Bend, G. L. (Eds.), *The Palgrave Handbook of Disability at Work*. DOI: 10.1007/978-3-030-42966-9_29

Murison, A. (2006, November). The Strategic Depth Doctrine of Turkish Foreign Policy. *Middle Eastern Studies*, *42*(6), 945–964. DOI: 10.1080/00263200600923526

Mylan, J. (2018). Sustainable Consumption in Everyday Life: A Qualitative Study of UK Consumer Experiences of Meat Reduction. *Sustainability (Basel)*, *10*(7), 2307. DOI: 10.3390/su10072307

Nahapiet, J. G. (1998). "Social Capital, intellectual capital and the creation of value in firms". *Accademy of Management Best Paper Proceedings*, 242.

Nowak, M. A. (2006). Five rules for the evolution of cooperation. *Science*, *314*(5805), 1560–1563. DOI: 10.1126/science.1133755 PMID: 17158317

OECD. (2020). OECD territorial reviews: Regional policy for Greece post-2020. OECD Publishing. https://www.oecd.org/content/dam/oecd/en/publications/reports/2020/10/regional-policy-for-greece-post-2020_bb991164/cedf09a5-en.pdf

OECD. (2022). *"Designing Legal Frameworks for Social Enterprises: Practical Guidance for Policy Makers", Local Economic and Employment Development (LEED)*. OECD Publishing., DOI: 10.1787/172b60b2-

OECD. 2020, Tax and fiscal policy in response to the Coronavirus crisis: Strengthening confidence and resilience. Available at https://www.oecd.org/ctp/tax-policy/tax-and-fiscal-policy-in-response-to-thecoronavirus-crisis-strengthening-confidence-and-resilience.htm (accessed 20 January 2022).

Oğuzlu, H. T. (2020). 'Turkish Foreign Policy in a Changing World Order. Old alignments and new neighborhoods International Conference, Oxford 30 April – 2 May 2010. Published by *South East European Studies at Oxford* (SEESOX), European Studies Centre, St Antony's College University of Oxford, pp. 127-139

Önis, Z. (2014). Turkey and the Arab Revolutions: Boundaries of Regional Power Influence in a Turbulent Middle East. *Mediterranean Politics, 19*(2), 203–219. DOI: 10.1080/13629395.2013.868392

Önis, Z., & Kutlay, M. (2017). The dynamics of emerging middle-power influence in regional and global governance: The paradoxical case of Turkey. *Australian Journal of International Affairs, 71*(2), 167–183. DOI: 10.1080/10357718.2016.1183586

Oral, M. (2022). Türkiye Elektrik Enerjisi Piyasasının Kamu ve Özel Sektör Çerçevesinde Değerlendirilmesi. *Journal of Academic Social Science Studies, 15*(90), 445–458. DOI: 10.29228/JASSS.62193

Oslo Roundtable on Sustainable Production and Consumption. (1994). 'The Imperative of Sustainable Production and Consumption'. [online]. Available at: <https://enb.iisd.org/consume/oslo004.html> (Accessed 19 October 2024).

Özdil, E. (2024, September 13). Part 4. Turkey's geopolitical role in the Black Sea and European energy security: From pipelines to liquefied natural gas. Atlantic Council. https://shorturl.at/MzCnj

Ozkan, B. (2014). "Turkey, Davutoğlu and the Idea of Pan-Islamism". Survival. *Survival, 56*(4), 119–140. Advance online publication. DOI: 10.1080/00396338.2014.941570

Pairotti, M. B., Cerutti, A. K., Martini, F., Vesce, E., Padovan, D., & Beltramo, R. (2015). Energy consumption and GHG emission of the Mediterranean diet: A systemic assessment using a hybrid LCA-IO method. *Journal of Cleaner Production, 103*, 507–516. DOI: 10.1016/j.jclepro.2013.12.082

Papadakis, J. (1987). The increase of the income of peasants as a basis of economic development: The Greek model of Papanastasiou-Koryzis. Proceedings Academy of Athens, vol. 62, series A, pg. 59-77. (In Greek).

Papadakis, I. (1988). Ioannis Papadakis for Ioannis Karamanos. In Karamanos, A. (Ed.), *Enlightened Ideas in Modern Greece. The Life and Work of Ioannis Karamanos*. Papazisi. (In Greek)

Papagaroufali, E. (1985-1986). Greek Female Farmer and women's cooperatives. Athens: Research Centre for the Women of the Mediterranean. (In Greek).

Pelagidis, E. *The Refugees of Macedonia in the economic life of the country*, Thessaloniki: Society for Macedonia Studies. (In Greek).

Pellagra, V. (2002). "Rispondenza fiduciaria: principi e implicazioni per la progettazione istituzionale". *in Stato e Mercato, n. 65*, 335-357.

Pierini, M. (2019, May). Options for the EU-Turkey Relationship. Carnegie Europe, available at: https://tinyurl.com/228ws24b

Posidonia International Shipping Exhibition. (2024, April 10). Posidonia 2024 marks the rebirth of the Greek shipbuilding industry [Press release]. https://posidonia-events.com/press-releases/posidonia/article/140/posidonia-2024-marks-the-rebirth-of-the-greek-shipbuilding-industry/

Psaraftis, H., & Pallis, A. A. (2012). Concession of the Piraeus container terminal: Turbulent times and the quest for competitiveness. *Maritime Policy & Management*, *39*(1), 27–43. DOI: 10.1080/03088839.2011.642316

Putnam, R. D. (2000). *Bowling Alone: The Collapse and Revival of American Community*. Touchstone Books.

Ramos, J. (2019) "Social innovation in Spain: the leading role of Civil Society", in *Atlas of Social Innovation – 2nd Volume: A World of New Practices,* in Jürgen Howaldt, Christoph Kaletka, Antonius Schröder, Marthe Zirngiebl (Eds), pp.124-126, Publisher: oekoem verlag, München.

Raynolds, L. T. (2002). Consumer/producer links in fair trade coffee networks. *Sociologia Ruralis*, *42*(4), 404–424. DOI: 10.1111/1467-9523.00224

Reisch, L., Eberle, U., and Lorek, S. (2013). 'Sustainable food consumption: an overview of contemporary issues and policies', *Sustainability: Science, Practice and Policy*, 9:2, 7-25.

Reka, A. (2023). Energy and Regional Geopolitics in the Western Balkans and Eastern Mediterranean. In *Geopolitical Turmpetroleum in the Balkans and Eastern Mediterranean* (pp. 185–203). Springer International Publishing. DOI: 10.1007/978-3-031-34318-6_8

Reuters. (2025, January 20). Chevron expresses interest in Greek energy exploration. https://reuters.com/business/energy/chevron-expresses-interest-hydorcarbons-exploration-greece-energy-ministry-says-2025-01-20/

Rosanvallon, P. (2013). *The society of equals*. Harvard University Press. DOI: 10.4159/harvard.9780674726444

Roubanis, I. (2019). "The European Crisis and Turkey's: Unpredictable Role in the Balkans". *Insight Turkey Spring*. Vol. 21, No 2, available at: https://tinyurl.com/h3wmx6h6

Ryan, N. E., & El Ayadi, A. M. (2020). A call for a gender-responsive, intersectional approach to address COVID-19. *Global Public Health: An International Journal for Research, Policy and Practice*, *15*(9), 1404–1412.

Scalvedi, M. L., & Saba, A. (2018). Exploring local and organic food consumption in a holistic sustainability view. *British Food Journal*, *120*(4), 749–762. DOI: 10.1108/BFJ-03-2017-0141

Scharpf, F. W. (2011). Monetary Union, Fiscal Crisis and the Pre-Emption of Democracy, Zeitschrift Für Staats- und Europawissenschaften (ZSE). *Journal for Comparative Government and European Policy*, *9*(2).

Schelling, T. C. (2020). Arms and influence (A. M. Slaughter, Intro.; Original work published 1966). Yale University Press.

Schur, L. A., Kruse, D., & Blanck, P. D. (2013). *People with disabilities*. Cambridge University Press. DOI: 10.1017/CBO9780511843693

Schur, L., Han, K., Kim, A., Ameri, M., Blanck, P., & Kruse, D. (2017). Disability at work: A look back and forward. *Journal of Occupational Rehabilitation*, *27*(4), 482–497. DOI: 10.1007/s10926-017-9739-5 PMID: 29110160

Shell (2024, September 2). Shell signs ten-year LNG supply agreement with Turkish energy company. https://shorturl.at/6msTx

Siccardi, F. (2024). *Understanding the Energy Drivers of Turkey's Foreign Policy*. Carnegie Endowment for International Peace. https://shorturl.at/v5Jco

Speller, I. (2024). *Understanding naval warfare* (3rd ed.). Routledge.

Streeck, W. (2014). The politics of public debt: Neoliberalism, capitalist development and the restructuring of the state. *German Economic Review*, *15*(1), 143–165.

T.C. Turkish Ministry of Energy and Natural Resources. (2023, July 12). *Crude Petroleum*. https://shorturl.at/LGaoT

Tajfel, H., Billig, M. G., Bundy, R. P., & Flament, C. (1971). Social categorization and intergroup behaviour. *European Journal of Social Psychology*, *1*(2), 149–178. DOI: 10.1002/ejsp.2420010202

Tangredi, S. (2013). *Anti-access warfare: Countering A2/AD strategies*. Naval Institute Press.

Temizer, M. (2024, June 20). Türkiye's gas imports down 7.64% to 50.48 billion cubic meters in 2023. Anadolu Agency. https://shorturl.at/KiBJp

Thomas, A. (2004). "The Rise of Social Cooperatives in Italy", in Voluntas. *Voluntas*, *15*(3), 243–263. DOI: 10.1023/B:VOLU.0000046280.06580.d8

Till, G. (2018). *Seapower: A guide for the twenty-first century* (4th ed.). Routledge. DOI: 10.4324/9781315621210

Tokdoğan, N. (2024). *Neo-Ottomanism as an Alternative Narrative of National Identity*. Palgrave Studies in Political Psychology., DOI: 10.1007/978-3-031-48723-1_3

Total Energies. (2024, September 18). Long term LNG sales in Türkiye: TotalEnergies will supply 1.1 million tons per year to BOTAŞ for 10 years. https://shorturl.at/pNn6g

Trend Economy. (n.d.). Turkey | Imports and Exports | World | Coal | Value (US$) and Value Growth, YoY (%) | 2011 - 2023. https://shorturl.at/GXmdb

Tsai, W., & Ghoshal, S. (1998). Social Capital and value creation: The role of intrafirm networks. *Academy of Management Journal*, *41*(4), 464–476. DOI: 10.2307/257085

Turan, I., Akçay, Y., & Kanat, S. (2019). An overview to Turkey-EU relations during the justice and development party period. *Suleyman Demirel University Visionary Journal*, *10*(25), 658–666. DOI: 10.21076/vizyoner.563322

Türkiye İstatistik Kurumu. (2022). Nüfus ve demografi. TÜİK. https://tinyurl.com/mw7sfurz

Tüysüzoğlu, G. (2023). The Impact of Eurasianism on Turkey's Role in the Ukraine War. *Middle East Policy*, *30*(4), 106–112. DOI: 10.1111/mepo.12715

Tziarras, Z. (2022). The Ukraine War and Turkey as a 'Third Pole' in a New International Order. In *PRIO Cyprus Centre Policy Brief, 1*. PRIO Cyprus Centre., available at https://tinyurl.com/2fupj8m6

Üngör, Ç. (2024). A 'bridge'pushed to the periphery?: Turkey's geopolitical significance in the Asia-Pacific century. *Turkish Studies*, •••, 1–23.

Union of Greek Shipowners. (2023). Greek shipping: A strategic sector for the European economy. https://www.ugs.gr/en/greek-shipping-and-economy/greek-shipping-and-economy-2023/greek-shipping-a-strategic-sector-for-the-european-economy

United Nations (2020). A/74/757. Letter dated 18 March 2020 from the Permanent Representative of Turkey to the United Nations addressed to the Secretary-General.

United Nations Organization, NATO, WTO, OECD, Council of Europe, IMO, OSCE, BSEC, UNESCO, ICOMOS, UNT, IHRA, & Union for the Mediterranean. (n.d.). Membership list of international organizations. [Publisher unspecified].

United Nations, Department of Economic and Social Affairs, Population Division. (2024). World population prospects. https://tinyurl.com/4uedfpmb

United Nations. (1992). 'United Nations Framework Convention on Climate Change'. [online]. Available at: < https://unfccc.int/resource/docs/convkp/conveng.pdf> (Accessed 19 October 2024).

United Nations. Policy Brief: The impact of COVID-19 on children, 2020, Available at: https://unsdg.un.org/sites/default/files/2020-04/160420_Covid_Children_Policy_Brief.pdf

Uphoff, N. (1999). Understanding Social Capital: Learning from the Analysis and Experience of Participation. In *P. Dasgupta, & I. Serageldin, (a cura di), Social Capital. A Multifaceted Perspective*. The World Bank.

Van Creveld, M. (1999). *The Rise and the Decline of the State*. Cambridge University Press. DOI: 10.1017/CBO9780511497599

Vego, M. (2005). *Naval strategy and operations in narrow seas* (2nd ed.). Frank Cass.

Vego, M. (2019). *Maritime strategy and sea denial: Theory and practice*. Routledge.

Verbeke, W., & Viaene, J. (1999). Consumer Attitude to Beef Quality Labeling and Associations with Beef Quality Labels. *Journal of International Food & Agribusiness Marketing*, *10*(3), 45–65. DOI: 10.1300/J047v10n03_03

Vidal, I., & Claver, N. (2005). *"Work Integration Social Enterprises in Spain", WP n. 04/05*. EMES Research Network.

Villegas, G. A. (2020): *The Mediterranean Sea: maritime power, conflicts and strategies*. Institute of Electrical and Electronics Engineers. Framework Document 03, available at: https://tinyurl.com/2w85zypj

Vitale, M. C. (1995). Jointness by design, not accident. *Joint Force Quarterly*, (Autumn), 24–30.

Vranken, M. (2018). *Labour Law Reform in France: The Macron Effect* (Vol. 24). Comparative Law Journal of the Pacific.

Waala, A. (2021). "Libyan court cancels border demarcation and security cooperation agreement between Al-Wefaq and Turkey". *Egypt Today*, available at: https://tinyurl.com/276v64f6

Waxman, D. (2023). Disability and Employment Research: Mind the Gap. In Rioux, M. H., Viera, J., Buettgen, A., & Zubrow, E. (Eds.), *Handbook of Disability*. Springer. DOI: 10.1007/978-981-16-1278-7_94-1

World Bank. (2023). *Turkey Overview*, available at: https://tinyurl.com/3rbttvre

World Nuclear Association. (2024, April 30). *Nuclear Power in Turkey*. https://shorturl.at/xHbcl

World Nuclear News. (2023, April 27). Presidents address ceremony inaugurating Turkey's first nuclear plant. https://shorturl.at/2qRVw

Yanarocak, H. E. C. (2021). *Turkish Irredentism and the Greater Middle East*. The Jerusalem Institute for Strategy and Security, available at: https://tinyurl.com/rzpe8tw5

Yılmaz, A. N. & Kılıçoğlu, G (2018). "Türkiye'nin orta asya'daki yumuşak gücü ve kamu diplomasisi uygulamalarinin analizi". *Türk Dünyası Araştırmaları*. Cilt. 19 Sayı 235, ss 141-184.

Yılmaz, Ş. (2023). *Facing new security threats in an era of global transformations: Turkey's challenges of energy security, climate change and sustainability*. Routledge.

Zappella, E. (2015). Job coaching in the workplace for people with disabilities: An Italian research. *Rehabilitation Counseling Bulletin*, *58*(4), 195–202.

Zoiopoulos, P. (2003), The Epos od Sitikon, in Historika Eleythrotypia Newspaper, Vol. 185, May 2003.

Zoiopoulos, P. (2014). *Two blades of grass. The agrarian miracle*. Armos. (In Greek)

Related References

To continue our tradition of advancing information science and technology research, we have compiled a list of recommended IGI Global readings. These references will provide additional information and guidance to further enrich your knowledge and assist you with your own research and future publications.

Abdel-Hameid, S. O., & Wilson, E. (2018). Gender, Organization, and Change in Sudan. In Mahtab, N., Haque, T., Khan, I., Islam, M., & Wahid, I. (Eds.), *Handbook of Research on Women's Issues and Rights in the Developing World* (pp. 107–120). Hershey, PA: IGI Global. DOI: 10.4018/978-1-5225-3018-3.ch007

Abdullahi, R. B. (2018). Volunteerism in Urban Development the Case of Non-Cash, Non-Digital Crowdfunding Growth in Nigeria. In Benna, U., & Benna, A. (Eds.), *Crowdfunding and Sustainable Urban Development in Emerging Economies* (pp. 188–210). Hershey, PA: IGI Global. DOI: 10.4018/978-1-5225-3952-0.ch010

Abioye, T. O., Oyesomi, K., Ajiboye, E., Omidiora, S., & Oyero, O. (2017). Education, Gender, and Child-Rights: Salient Issues in SDGS Years in ADO-ODO/OTA Local Government Area of Ogun State, Nigeria. In Nelson, O., Ojebuyi, B., & Salawu, A. (Eds.), *Impacts of the Media on African Socio-Economic Development* (pp. 141–154). Hershey, PA: IGI Global. DOI: 10.4018/978-1-5225-1859-4.ch009

Adalı, G. K. (2022). Measuring the Attitudes of Governmental Policies and the Public Towards the COVID-19 Pandemic. In Omeraki Çekirdekci, Ş., İngün Karkış, Ö., & Gönültaş, S. (Eds.), *Handbook of Research on Interdisciplinary Perspectives on the Threats and Impacts of Pandemics* (pp. 163–187). IGI Global. https://doi.org/10.4018/978-1-7998-8674-7.ch009

Adisa, W. B. (2018). Land Use Policy and Urban Sprawl in Nigeria: Land Use and the Emergence of Urban Sprawl. In Eneanya, A. (Ed.), *Handbook of Research on Environmental Policies for Emergency Management and Public Safety* (pp. 256–274). Hershey, PA: IGI Global. DOI: 10.4018/978-1-5225-3194-4.ch014

Afolabi, O. S., Amao-Kolawole, T. G., Shittu, A. K., & Oguntokun, O. O. (2018). Rule of Law, Governance, and Sustainable Development: The Nigerian Perspective. In Teshager Alemu, K., & Abebe Alebachew, M. (Eds.), *Handbook of Research on Sustainable Development and Governance Strategies for Economic Growth in Africa* (pp. 273–290). Hershey, PA: IGI Global. DOI: 10.4018/978-1-5225-3247-7.ch015

Agyemang, O. S. (2018). Institutional Structures and the Prevalence of Foreign Ownership of Firms: Empirical Evidence From Africa. In Teshager Alemu, K., & Abebe Alebachew, M. (Eds.), *Handbook of Research on Sustainable Development and Governance Strategies for Economic Growth in Africa* (pp. 455–479). Hershey, PA: IGI Global. DOI: 10.4018/978-1-5225-3247-7.ch024

Aham-Anyanwu, N. M., & Li, H. (2017). E-State: Realistic or Utopian? *International Journal of Public Administration in the Digital Age*, *4*(2), 56–76. DOI: 10.4018/IJPADA.2017040105

Al Balushi, T., & Ali, S. (2020). Theoretical Approach for Instrument Development in Measuring User-Perceived E-Government Service Quality: A Case of Oman E-Government Services. *International Journal of Electronic Government Research*, *16*(1), 40–58. DOI: 10.4018/IJEGR.2020010103

Al-Jamal, M., & Abu-Shanab, E. (2018). Open Government: The Line between Privacy and Transparency. *International Journal of Public Administration in the Digital Age*, *5*(2), 64–75. DOI: 10.4018/IJPADA.2018040106

Alsaç, U. (2017). EKAP: Turkey's Centralized E-Procurement System. In Shakya, R. (Ed.), *Digital Governance and E-Government Principles Applied to Public Procurement* (pp. 126–150). Hershey, PA: IGI Global. DOI: 10.4018/978-1-5225-2203-4.ch006

Amadi, L. A., & Igwe, P. (2018). Open Government and Bureaucratic Secrecy in the Developing Democracies: Africa in Perspective. In Kok, A. (Ed.), *Proliferation of Open Government Initiatives and Systems* (pp. 1–28). Hershey, PA: IGI Global. DOI: 10.4018/978-1-5225-4987-1.ch001

Arble, E., & Arnetz, B. B. (2021). Four Fundamental Principles to Enhance Police Performance and Community Safety. In Arble, E., & Arnetz, B. (Eds.), *Interventions, Training, and Technologies for Improved Police Well-Being and Performance* (pp. 231–245). IGI Global. https://doi.org/10.4018/978-1-7998-6820-0.ch015

Arora, G. C. (2020). The Problem of Climate-Induced Displacement: Analyzing the International Framework on Protection of Rights of Climate Migrants. In Das, R., & Mandal, N. (Eds.), *Interdisciplinary Approaches to Public Policy and Sustainability* (pp. 67–82). IGI Global. https://doi.org/10.4018/978-1-7998-0315-7.ch004

Arora, T., & Mehra, N. (2021). Administration of Civil Justice in India: Ancient and Modern Perspectives. In Yin, E., & Kofie, N. (Eds.), *Advancing Civil Justice Reform and Conflict Resolution in Africa and Asia: Comparative Analyses and Case Studies* (pp. 17–45). IGI Global. https://doi.org/10.4018/978-1-7998-7898-8.ch002

Arteta, A. (2019). *Democracy and Government: Making Decisions*. IGI Global. DOI: 10.4018/978-1-5225-7558-0.ch001

Asante, M., & Botchway, T. P. (2021). Shielding Members of Parliament Against Court Summons: Interrogating the Question of Parliamentary Immunity. In Yin, E., & Kofie, N. (Eds.), *Advancing Civil Justice Reform and Conflict Resolution in Africa and Asia: Comparative Analyses and Case Studies* (pp. 210–229). IGI Global. https://doi.org/10.4018/978-1-7998-7898-8.ch012

Ateş, V. (2021). Critical Antecedents of Trust in E-Government Services in Turkey. In Babaoğlu, C., Akman, E., & Kulaç, O. (Eds.), *Handbook of Research on Global Challenges for Improving Public Services and Government Operations* (pp. 94–116). IGI Global. https://doi.org/10.4018/978-1-7998-4978-0.ch006

Ayeni, A. O. (2018). Environmental Policies for Emergency Management and Public Safety: Implementing Green Policy and Community Participation. In Eneanya, A. (Ed.), *Handbook of Research on Environmental Policies for Emergency Management and Public Safety* (pp. 40–59). Hershey, PA: IGI Global. DOI: 10.4018/978-1-5225-3194-4.ch003

Ayodele, J. O. (2017). The Influence of Migration and Crime on Development in Lagos, Nigeria. In Afolayan, G., & Akinwale, A. (Eds.), *Global Perspectives on Development Administration and Cultural Change* (pp. 192–230). Hershey, PA: IGI Global. DOI: 10.4018/978-1-5225-0629-4.ch009

Baarda, R. (2017). Digital Democracy in Authoritarian Russia: Opportunity for Participation, or Site of Kremlin Control? In Luppicini, R., & Baarda, R. (Eds.), *Digital Media Integration for Participatory Democracy* (pp. 87–100). Hershey, PA: IGI Global. DOI: 10.4018/978-1-5225-2463-2.ch005

Balakrishnan, K. (2017). The Rationale for Offsets in Defence Acquisition from a Theoretical Perspective. In Burgess, K., & Antill, P. (Eds.), *Emerging Strategies in Defense Acquisitions and Military Procurement* (pp. 263–276). Hershey, PA: IGI Global. DOI: 10.4018/978-1-5225-0599-0.ch015

Banerjee, S. (2017). Globalization and Human Rights: How Globalization Can Be a Tool to Protect the Human Rights. In Akrivopoulou, C. (Ed.), *Defending Human Rights and Democracy in the Era of Globalization* (pp. 1–16). Hershey, PA: IGI Global. DOI: 10.4018/978-1-5225-0723-9.ch001

Bessant, J. (2017). Digital Humour, Gag Laws, and the Liberal Security State. In Luppicini, R., & Baarda, R. (Eds.), *Digital Media Integration for Participatory Democracy* (pp. 204–221). Hershey, PA: IGI Global. DOI: 10.4018/978-1-5225-2463-2.ch010

Bhat, M. Y. (2020). Environmental Problems of Delhi and Governmental Concern. In Merviö, M. (Ed.), *Global Issues and Innovative Solutions in Healthcare, Culture, and the Environment* (pp. 133–167). IGI Global. https://doi.org/10.4018/978-1-7998-3576-9.ch008

Bhat, R. A. (2021). Identification of Various Dimensions and Indicators of Immigrant Integration Into Global Scenarios. In Mafukata, M. (Ed.), *Impact of Immigration and Xenophobia on Development in Africa* (pp. 247–260). IGI Global. https://doi.org/10.4018/978-1-7998-7099-9.ch014

Boachie, C. (2017). Public Financial Management and Systems of Accountability in Sub-National Governance in Developing Economies. In Schoburgh, E., & Ryan, R. (Eds.), *Handbook of Research on Sub-National Governance and Development* (pp. 193–217). Hershey, PA: IGI Global. DOI: 10.4018/978-1-5225-1645-3.ch009

Boachie, C., & Adu-Darko, E. (2018). Socio-Economic Impact of Foreign Direct Investment in Developing Countries. In Malepati, V., & Gowri, C. (Eds.), *Foreign Direct Investments (FDIs) and Opportunities for Developing Economies in the World Market* (pp. 66–81). Hershey, PA: IGI Global. DOI: 10.4018/978-1-5225-3026-8.ch004

Bogdanoski, M., Stoilkovski, M., & Risteski, A. (2020). Novel First Responder Digital Forensics Tool as a Support to Law Enforcement. In I. Management Association (Ed.), *Improving the Safety and Efficiency of Emergency Services: Emerging Tools and Technologies for First Responders* (pp. 239-270). IGI Global. https://doi.org/10.4018/978-1-7998-2535-7.ch011

Borràs, S. (2017). Rights of Nature to Protect Human Rights in Times of Environmental Crisis. In Akrivopoulou, C. (Ed.), *Defending Human Rights and Democracy in the Era of Globalization* (pp. 225–261). Hershey, PA: IGI Global. DOI: 10.4018/978-1-5225-0723-9.ch010

Bouaziz, F. (2021). E-Government and Digital Transformation: A Conceptual Framework for Risk Factors Identification. In Sandhu, K. (Ed.), *Disruptive Technology and Digital Transformation for Business and Government* (pp. 67–90). IGI Global. https://doi.org/10.4018/978-1-7998-8583-2.ch004

Bradford, A. C., McElroy, H. K., & Rosenblatt, R. (2019). Social Climate Change and the Modern Police Department: Millennials, Marijuana, and Mass Media. In I. Management Association (Ed.), *Police Science: Breakthroughs in Research and Practice* (pp. 34-51). IGI Global. https://doi.org/10.4018/978-1-5225-7672-3.ch003

Brusca, I., Olmo, J., & Labrador, M. (2018). Characterizing the Risk Factors for Financial Sustainability in Spanish Local Governments. In Rodríguez Bolívar, M., & López Subires, M. (Eds.), *Financial Sustainability and Intergenerational Equity in Local Governments* (pp. 206–223). Hershey, PA: IGI Global. DOI: 10.4018/978-1-5225-3713-7.ch009

Budd, J. R., & Littrell, M. W. (2021). Law Enforcement Challenges to Gathering Intelligence in the Street: The Fourth Amendment. In de Silva, E., & Abeyagoonesekera, A. (Eds.), *Intelligence and Law Enforcement in the 21st Century* (pp. 18–40). IGI Global. https://doi.org/10.4018/978-1-7998-7904-6.ch002

Bush, C. L. (2021). Policing Strategies and Approaches to Improving Community Relations: Black Citizens' Perceptions of Law Enforcement Efforts to Intentionally Strengthen Relationships. In Pittaro, M. (Ed.), *Global Perspectives on Reforming the Criminal Justice System* (pp. 56–75). IGI Global. https://doi.org/10.4018/978-1-7998-6884-2.ch004

Canto Moniz, G. (2020). Is There Anything Left of the Portuguese Law Implementing the GDPR?: The Decision of the Portuguese Supervisory Authority. In Tzanou, M. (Ed.), *Personal Data Protection and Legal Developments in the European Union* (pp. 125–139). IGI Global. https://doi.org/10.4018/978-1-5225-9489-5.ch007

Casoria, M., & AlSarraf, E. M. (2020). The Impact of the GDPR on Extra-EU Legal Systems: The Case of the Kingdom of Bahrain. In Tzanou, M. (Ed.), *Personal Data Protection and Legal Developments in the European Union* (pp. 224–237). IGI Global. https://doi.org/10.4018/978-1-5225-9489-5.ch011

Chaves, A. (2022). Government Response Capacity to the COVID-19 Pandemic: Estimating the Impact of Lockdown Measures in Colombia. In Antošová, G. (Ed.), *Innovative Strategic Planning and International Collaboration for the Mitigation of Global Crises* (pp. 114–137). IGI Global. https://doi.org/10.4018/978-1-7998-8339-5.ch008

Chen, M., & Su, F. (2017). Global Civic Engagement as an Empowering Device for Cross-Ethnic and Cross-Cultural Understanding in Taiwan. In Shin, R. (Ed.), *Convergence of Contemporary Art, Visual Culture, and Global Civic Engagement* (pp. 24–45). Hershey, PA: IGI Global. DOI: 10.4018/978-1-5225-1665-1.ch002

Chigwata, T. C. (2017). Fiscal Decentralization: Constraints to Revenue-Raising by Local Government in Zimbabwe. In Schoburgh, E., & Ryan, R. (Eds.), *Handbook of Research on Sub-National Governance and Development* (pp. 218–240). Hershey, PA: IGI Global. DOI: 10.4018/978-1-5225-1645-3.ch010

Chowdhury, M. A. (2017). The Nexus Between Institutional Quality and Foreign Direct Investments (FDI) in South Asia: Dynamic Heterogeneous Panel Approach. In Dorożyński, T., & Kuna-Marszałek, A. (Eds.), *Outward Foreign Direct Investment (FDI) in Emerging Market Economies* (pp. 293–310). Hershey, PA: IGI Global. DOI: 10.4018/978-1-5225-2345-1.ch015

Christopher, M. E., & Tsushima, V. G. (2017). Police Interactions with Persons-in-Crisis: Emergency Psychological Services and Jail Diversion. In Mitchell, C., & Dorian, E. (Eds.), *Police Psychology and Its Growing Impact on Modern Law Enforcement* (pp. 274–294). Hershey, PA: IGI Global. DOI: 10.4018/978-1-5225-0813-7.ch014

Ciftci, D. (2022). Digital Citizenship and E-Government Integration: The Case of North Cyprus. In Öngün, E., Pembecioğlu, N., & Gündüz, U. (Eds.), *Handbook of Research on Digital Citizenship and Management During Crises* (pp. 34–55). IGI Global. https://doi.org/10.4018/978-1-7998-8421-7.ch003

Citro, F., Lucianelli, G., & Santis, S. (2018). Financial Conditions, Financial Sustainability, and Intergenerational Equity in Local Governments: A Literature Review. In Rodríguez Bolívar, M., & López Subires, M. (Eds.), *Financial Sustainability and Intergenerational Equity in Local Governments* (pp. 101–124). Hershey, PA: IGI Global. DOI: 10.4018/978-1-5225-3713-7.ch005

Correa de Mello, M. B. (2019). The Information Access Law as a Full Constitutional Citizenship Instrument. In Melro, A., & Oliveira, L. (Eds.), *Constitutional Knowledge and Its Impact on Citizenship Exercise in a Networked Society* (pp. 55–72). IGI Global. https://doi.org/10.4018/978-1-5225-8350-9.ch003

Covell, C. E. (2018). Theoretical Application of Public Sector Planning and Budgeting. In Rodríguez Bolívar, M., & López Subires, M. (Eds.), *Financial Sustainability and Intergenerational Equity in Local Governments* (pp. 248–279). Hershey, PA: IGI Global. DOI: 10.4018/978-1-5225-3713-7.ch011

Cunha, A. M., Ferreira, A. D., & Fernandes, M. J. (2018). The Impact of Accounting Information and Socioeconomic Factors in the Re-Election of Portuguese Mayors. In Azevedo, G., da Silva Oliveira, J., Marques, R., & Ferreira, A. (Eds.), *Handbook of Research on Modernization and Accountability in Public Sector Management* (pp. 406–432). Hershey, PA: IGI Global. DOI: 10.4018/978-1-5225-3731-1.ch019

da Rosa, I., & de Almeida, J. (2017). Digital Transformation in the Public Sector: Electronic Procurement in Portugal. In Shakya, R. (Ed.), *Digital Governance and E-Government Principles Applied to Public Procurement* (pp. 99–125). Hershey, PA: IGI Global. DOI: 10.4018/978-1-5225-2203-4.ch005

Daramola, O. (2018). Revisiting the Legal Framework of Urban Planning in the Global South: An Explanatory Example of Nigeria. In Teshager Alemu, K., & Abebe Alebachew, M. (Eds.), *Handbook of Research on Sustainable Development and Governance Strategies for Economic Growth in Africa* (pp. 258–271). Hershey, PA: IGI Global. DOI: 10.4018/978-1-5225-3247-7.ch014

Dau, L. A., Moore, E. M., Soto, M. A., & LeBlanc, C. R. (2017). How Globalization Sparked Entrepreneurship in the Developing World: The Impact of Formal Economic and Political Linkages. In Christiansen, B., & Kasarcı, F. (Eds.), *Corporate Espionage, Geopolitics, and Diplomacy Issues in International Business* (pp. 72–91). Hershey, PA: IGI Global. DOI: 10.4018/978-1-5225-1031-4.ch005

De Man, P. (2019). In-Situ Resource Utilization: Legal Aspects. In Nakarada Pecujlic, A., & Tugnoli, M. (Eds.), *Promoting Productive Cooperation Between Space Lawyers and Engineers* (pp. 211–224). IGI Global. https://doi.org/10.4018/978-1-5225-7256-5.ch013

Drenner, K. (2017). Introduction to Faith in State Legislatures: Land of the Brave and the Home of the Free – The Star-Spangled Banner. In *Impacts of Faith-Based Decision Making on the Individual-Level Legislative Process: Emerging Research and Opportunities* (pp. 1–25). Hershey, PA: IGI Global. DOI: 10.4018/978-1-5225-2388-8.ch001

Drenner, K. (2017). The Holy Wars of Marriage. In *Impacts of Faith-Based Decision Making on the Individual-Level Legislative Process: Emerging Research and Opportunities* (pp. 92–116). Hershey, PA: IGI Global. DOI: 10.4018/978-1-5225-2388-8.ch004

Drenner, K. (2017). The Implications of Religious Liberty. In *Impacts of Faith-Based Decision Making on the Individual-Level Legislative Process: Emerging Research and Opportunities* (pp. 143–162). Hershey, PA: IGI Global. DOI: 10.4018/978-1-5225-2388-8.ch006

Duncan, S. T., & Geczi, H. (2021). Body-Worn Cameras: Panacea or Distraction for Increased Police Use of Force Accountability? In Pittaro, M. (Ed.), *Global Perspectives on Reforming the Criminal Justice System* (pp. 1–25). IGI Global. https://doi.org/10.4018/978-1-7998-6884-2.ch001

Duran, D. Ş. (2019). Reflections of the Multi-Level Governance Approach on the Turkish Metropolitan Municipality System: Evaluations on the Metropolitan Law No 6360. In Uysal, T., & Aldemir, C. (Eds.), *Multi-Level Governance in Developing Economies* (pp. 52–91). IGI Global. https://doi.org/10.4018/978-1-5225-5547-6.ch003

Durnalı, M., & Eriçok, B. (2019). Legal Challenges on Developing Education Policy for Immigrants in Turkey. In I. Management Association (Ed.), *Immigration and Refugee Policy: Breakthroughs in Research and Practice* (pp. 223-237). IGI Global. https://doi.org/10.4018/978-1-5225-8909-9.ch013

Ehalaiye, D., Redmayne, N. B., & Laswad, F. (2020). The Case of Accounting Information for Infrastructural Assets Reporting: Local Government Borrowings and Investment Choices in the Context of Moral Hazard and Local Government Politics. In Cunha, A., Ferreira, A., Fernandes, M., & Gomes, P. (Eds.), *Financial Determinants in Local Re-Election Rates: Emerging Research and Opportunities* (pp. 176–201). IGI Global. https://doi.org/10.4018/978-1-5225-7820-8.ch007

Elena, S., & van Schalkwyk, F. (2017). Open Data for Open Justice in Seven Latin American Countries. In Jiménez-Gómez, C., & Gascó-Hernández, M. (Eds.), *Achieving Open Justice through Citizen Participation and Transparency* (pp. 210–231). Hershey, PA: IGI Global. DOI: 10.4018/978-1-5225-0717-8.ch011

Eneanya, A. N. (2018). Integrating Ecosystem Management and Environmental Media for Public Policy on Public Health and Safety. In Eneanya, A. (Ed.), *Handbook of Research on Environmental Policies for Emergency Management and Public Safety* (pp. 321–338). Hershey, PA: IGI Global. DOI: 10.4018/978-1-5225-3194-4.ch017

Erickson, G. S. (2019). Sharing Knowledge With the Government: Implications of FOIA Requests. In Albastaki, Y., Al-Alawi, A., & Abdulrahman Al-Bassam, S. (Eds.), *Handbook of Research on Implementing Knowledge Management Strategy in the Public Sector* (pp. 143–158). IGI Global. https://doi.org/10.4018/978-1-5225-9639-4.ch007

Essien, E. D. (2018). Strengthening Performance of Civil Society Through Dialogue and Critical Thinking in Nigeria: Its Ethical Implications. In Chhabra, S. (Ed.), *Handbook of Research on Civic Engagement and Social Change in Contemporary Society* (pp. 82–102). Hershey, PA: IGI Global. DOI: 10.4018/978-1-5225-4197-4.ch005

Eweida, A. M. (2021). Urban Laws in Harmony or at Odds With Knowledge-Based Urban Policies: A Case Study on Egypt. In Galaby, A., & Abdrabo, A. (Eds.), *Handbook of Research on Creative Cities and Advanced Models for Knowledge-Based Urban Development* (pp. 23–40). IGI Global. https://doi.org/10.4018/978-1-7998-4948-3.ch002

Fanaian, T. (2017). The Theocratic Deception Trap: Khomeini's Persuasion Techniques and Communication Patterns in His Books, Guardianship of the Jurist 1979 and Testament 1989. In Lewin, E., Bick, E., & Naor, D. (Eds.), *Comparative Perspectives on Civil Religion, Nationalism, and Political Influence* (pp. 62–105). Hershey, PA: IGI Global. DOI: 10.4018/978-1-5225-0516-7.ch003

Faura-Martínez, U., & Cifuentes-Faura, J. (2020). Does E-Government Promote Transparency and the Fight Against Corruption in the European Union? *International Journal of Electronic Government Research, 16*(4), 42–57. https://doi.org/10.4018/IJEGR.2020100103

Fawsitt, J. (2020). Government Policy and the Disintegration of Village Community Life and Individual Identity in Urbanising Japan. In Merviö, M. (Ed.), *Recent Social, Environmental, and Cultural Issues in East Asian Societies* (pp. 76–94). IGI Global. https://doi.org/10.4018/978-1-7998-1807-6.ch005

Fidanoski, F., Sergi, B. S., Simeonovski, K., Naumovski, V., & Sazdovski, I. (2018). Effects of Foreign Capital Entry on the Macedonian Banking Industry: Two-Edged Sword. In Sergi, B., Fidanoski, F., Ziolo, M., & Naumovski, V. (Eds.), *Regaining Global Stability After the Financial Crisis* (pp. 308–338). Hershey, PA: IGI Global. DOI: 10.4018/978-1-5225-4026-7.ch015

Franconi, A. I. (2018). Economic Variations and Their Impact on Labor Legislation Throughout History in Argentina. In Amine, S. (Ed.), *Employment Protection Legislation in Emerging Economies* (pp. 77–98). Hershey, PA: IGI Global. DOI: 10.4018/978-1-5225-4134-9.ch004

Friedrich, P., & Chebotareva, M. (2017). Options for Applying Functional Overlapping Competing Jurisdictions (FOCJs) for Municipal Cooperation in Russia. In Lewandowski, M., & Kożuch, B. (Eds.), *Public Sector Entrepreneurship and the Integration of Innovative Business Models* (pp. 73–107). Hershey, PA: IGI Global. DOI: 10.4018/978-1-5225-2215-7.ch004

Garad, A., & Qamari, I. N. (2021). Determining Factors Influencing Establishing E-Service Quality in Developing Countries: A Case Study of Yemen E-Government. *International Journal of Electronic Government Research, 17*(1), 15–30. https://doi.org/10.4018/IJEGR.2021010102

Garita, M. (2018). The Negotiation and Effects of Fiscal Privileges in Guatemala. In Garita, M., & Bregni, C. (Eds.), *Economic Growth in Latin America and the Impact of the Global Financial Crisis* (pp. 119–137). Hershey, PA: IGI Global. DOI: 10.4018/978-1-5225-4981-9.ch008

Gascó-Hernández, M. (2017). Digitalizing Police Requirements: Opening up Justice through Collaborative Initiatives. In Jiménez-Gómez, C., & Gascó-Hernández, M. (Eds.), *Achieving Open Justice through Citizen Participation and Transparency* (pp. 157–172). Hershey, PA: IGI Global. DOI: 10.4018/978-1-5225-0717-8.ch008

Gáspár-Szilágyi, S. (2017). Human Rights Conditionality in the EU's Newly Concluded Association Agreements with the Eastern Partners. In Akrivopoulou, C. (Ed.), *Defending Human Rights and Democracy in the Era of Globalization* (pp. 50–79). Hershey, PA: IGI Global. DOI: 10.4018/978-1-5225-0723-9.ch003

Gavrielides, T. (2017). Reconciling Restorative Justice with the Law for Violence Against Women in Europe: A Scheme of Structured and Unstructured Models. In Halder, D., & Jaishankar, K. (Eds.), *Therapeutic Jurisprudence and Overcoming Violence Against Women* (pp. 106–120). Hershey, PA: IGI Global. DOI: 10.4018/978-1-5225-2472-4.ch007

Gechlik, M., Dai, D., & Beck, J. C. (2017). Open Judiciary in a Closed Society: A Paradox in China? In Jiménez-Gómez, C., & Gascó-Hernández, M. (Eds.), *Achieving Open Justice through Citizen Participation and Transparency* (pp. 56–92). Hershey, PA: IGI Global. DOI: 10.4018/978-1-5225-0717-8.ch004

Gerger, A. (2021). Technologies for Connected Government Implementation: Success Factors and Best Practices. In Mahmood, Z. (Ed.), *Web 2.0 and Cloud Technologies for Implementing Connected Government* (pp. 36–66). IGI Global. https://doi.org/10.4018/978-1-7998-4570-6.ch003

Germann, S. K. (2019). The International Space Station: Legal Aspects. In Nakarada Pecujlic, A., & Tugnoli, M. (Eds.), *Promoting Productive Cooperation Between Space Lawyers and Engineers* (pp. 96–113). IGI Global. DOI: 10.4018/978-1-5225-7256-5.ch007

Gillath, N. (2017). Avoiding Conscription in Israel: Were Women Pawns in the Political Game? In Lewin, E., Bick, E., & Naor, D. (Eds.), *Comparative Perspectives on Civil Religion, Nationalism, and Political Influence* (pp. 226–256). Hershey, PA: IGI Global. DOI: 10.4018/978-1-5225-0516-7.ch009

Górski, J. (2019). Northern Sea Route: International Law Perspectives. In Erokhin, V., Gao, T., & Zhang, X. (Eds.), *Handbook of Research on International Collaboration, Economic Development, and Sustainability in the Arctic* (pp. 292–313). IGI Global. https://doi.org/10.4018/978-1-5225-6954-1.ch014

Grant, B., Woods, R., & Tan, S. F. (2017). Subnational Finance in Australia and China: The Case for Municipal Bond Banks. In Schoburgh, E., & Ryan, R. (Eds.), *Handbook of Research on Sub-National Governance and Development* (pp. 150–166). Hershey, PA: IGI Global. DOI: 10.4018/978-1-5225-1645-3.ch007

Gurpinar, B. (2018). Supporter, Activist, Rebel, Terrorist: Children in Syria. In Akrivopoulou, C. (Ed.), *Global Perspectives on Human Migration, Asylum, and Security* (pp. 97–114). Hershey, PA: IGI Global. DOI: 10.4018/978-1-5225-2817-3.ch005

Gussen, B. F. (2018). The United States. In *Ranking Economic Performance and Efficiency in the Global Market: Emerging Research and Opportunities* (pp. 109–136). Hershey, PA: IGI Global. DOI: 10.4018/978-1-5225-2756-5.ch005

Halder, D., & Bhati, D. (2021). Culture, Ethnicity, and Hate Crimes: A Comparative Analysis of Preventive Laws Between India and the USA. In Pittaro, M. (Ed.), *Global Perspectives on Reforming the Criminal Justice System* (pp. 236–245). IGI Global. https://doi.org/10.4018/978-1-7998-6884-2.ch013

Haque, T. (2018). Women-Friendly Working Environment in Bangladesh: Critical Analysis. In Mahtab, N., Haque, T., Khan, I., Islam, M., & Wahid, I. (Eds.), *Handbook of Research on Women's Issues and Rights in the Developing World* (pp. 52–68). Hershey, PA: IGI Global. DOI: 10.4018/978-1-5225-3018-3.ch004

Heuva, W. E. (2017). Deferring Citizens' "Right to Know" in an Information Age: The Information Deficit in Namibia. In Mhiripiri, N., & Chari, T. (Eds.), *Media Law, Ethics, and Policy in the Digital Age* (pp. 245–267). Hershey, PA: IGI Global. DOI: 10.4018/978-1-5225-2095-5.ch014

Hwangbo, Y. (2022). Government Challenges Over Global Electronic Commerce Using FinTech: Design of Consumer Payment Tax (CPT) System. In Anshari, M., Almunawar, M., & Masri, M. (Eds.), *FinTech Development for Financial Inclusiveness* (pp. 197–213). IGI Global. https://doi.org/10.4018/978-1-7998-8447-7.ch011

Ibrahim, F., Suhip, H., Kura, K. M., & Noor, H. M. L. (2022). Exploratory Study on User Satisfaction of E-HRM: Evidence From Brunei Government Employee Management System (GEMS). In P. Ordóñez de Pablos (Eds.), *Handbook of Research on Developing Circular, Digital, and Green Economies in Asia* (pp. 243-271). IGI Global. https://doi.org/10.4018/978-1-7998-8678-5.ch014

Islam, M. R. (2018). Abuse Among Child Domestic Workers in Bangladesh. In Tshabangu, I. (Ed.), *Global Ideologies Surrounding Children's Rights and Social Justice* (pp. 1–21). Hershey, PA: IGI Global. DOI: 10.4018/978-1-5225-2578-3.ch001

Jankovic-Milic, V., & Džunić, M. (2017). Measuring Governance: The Application of Grey Relational Analysis on World Governance Indicators. In Stanković, J., Delias, P., Marinković, S., & Rochhia, S. (Eds.), *Tools and Techniques for Economic Decision Analysis* (pp. 104–128). Hershey, PA: IGI Global. DOI: 10.4018/978-1-5225-0959-2.ch005

Jenkins, B., Semple, T., Quail, J., & Bennell, C. (2021). Optimizing Scenario-Based Training for Law Enforcement. In Arble, E., & Arnetz, B. (Eds.), *Interventions, Training, and Technologies for Improved Police Well-Being and Performance* (pp. 18–37). IGI Global. https://doi.org/10.4018/978-1-7998-6820-0.ch002

Jiménez-Gómez, C. E. (2017). Open Judiciary Worldwide: Best Practices and Lessons Learnt. In Jiménez-Gómez, C., & Gascó-Hernández, M. (Eds.), *Achieving Open Justice through Citizen Participation and Transparency* (pp. 1–15). Hershey, PA: IGI Global. DOI: 10.4018/978-1-5225-0717-8.ch001

Karatzimas, S., & Miquela, C. G. (2018). Two Approaches on Local Governments' Financial Sustainability: Law vs. Practice in Catalan Municipalities. In Rodríguez Bolívar, M., & López Subires, M. (Eds.), *Financial Sustainability and Intergenerational Equity in Local Governments* (pp. 58–81). Hershey, PA: IGI Global. DOI: 10.4018/978-1-5225-3713-7.ch003

Khachaturyan, M., & Klicheva, E. (2021). Risks of Introducing E-Governance Into Strategic Management Systems of Russian Companies in the Context of the Pandemic. *International Journal of Electronic Government Research, 17*(4), 84–102. https://doi.org/10.4018/IJEGR.2021100105

Khan, S. A., & Alag, A. (2020). Arbitration in Patent Disputes: To What Extent Is It Possible? In Dewani, N., & Gurtu, A. (Eds.), *Intellectual Property Rights and the Protection of Traditional Knowledge* (pp. 76–102). IGI Global. https://doi.org/10.4018/978-1-7998-1835-9.ch004

Kirsanov, S., Safonov, E., Tuzcuoglu, F., & Mammadov, Z. (2022). Modern Problems of Staff Training for State and Municipal Services in Russia. In Kulaç, O., Babaoğlu, C., & Akman, E. (Eds.), *Public Affairs Education and Training in the 21st Century* (pp. 325–337). IGI Global. https://doi.org/10.4018/978-1-7998-8243-5.ch021

Kita, Y. (2017). An Analysis of a Lay Adjudication System and Open Judiciary: The New Japanese Lay Adjudication System. In Jiménez-Gómez, C., & Gascó-Hernández, M. (Eds.), *Achieving Open Justice through Citizen Participation and Transparency* (pp. 93–109). Hershey, PA: IGI Global. DOI: 10.4018/978-1-5225-0717-8.ch005

Kuatova, A., Bekbasarova, T., & Abdrashev, R. (2020). Introducing E-Government in Kazakhstan: The Concept of E-Democracy for the State-Public Interaction. In Tazhina, G., & Parker, J. (Eds.), *Toward Sustainability Through Digital Technologies and Practices in the Eurasian Region* (pp. 1–16). IGI Global. https://doi.org/10.4018/978-1-7998-2551-7.ch001

Kumari, S., Patil, Y., & Rao, P. (2017). An Approach to Sustainable Watershed Management: Case Studies on Enhancing Sustainability with Challenges of Water in Western Maharashtra. In Rao, P., & Patil, Y. (Eds.), *Reconsidering the Impact of Climate Change on Global Water Supply, Use, and Management* (pp. 252–271). Hershey, PA: IGI Global. DOI: 10.4018/978-1-5225-1046-8.ch014

Kumburu, N. P., & Pande, V. S. (2018). Decentralization and Local Governance in Tanzania: Theories and Practice on Sustainable Development. In Teshager Alemu, K., & Abebe Alebachew, M. (Eds.), *Handbook of Research on Sustainable Development and Governance Strategies for Economic Growth in Africa* (pp. 131–148). Hershey, PA: IGI Global. DOI: 10.4018/978-1-5225-3247-7.ch007

Kunock, A. I. (2017). Boko Haram Insurgency in Cameroon: Role of Mass Media in Conflict Management. In Mhiripiri, N., & Chari, T. (Eds.), *Media Law, Ethics, and Policy in the Digital Age* (pp. 226–244). Hershey, PA: IGI Global. DOI: 10.4018/978-1-5225-2095-5.ch013

Kurebwa, J. (2019). Young People-Sensitive and Participatory Governance Approaches: Lessons for the Zimbabwean Government. In Kurebwa, J., & Dodo, O. (Eds.), *Participation of Young People in Governance Processes in Africa* (pp. 80–99). IGI Global. https://doi.org/10.4018/978-1-5225-9388-1.ch005

Lawrie, A. (2017). The Subnational Region: A Utopia? The Challenge of Governing Through Soft Power. In Schoburgh, E., & Ryan, R. (Eds.), *Handbook of Research on Sub-National Governance and Development* (pp. 96–115). Hershey, PA: IGI Global. DOI: 10.4018/978-1-5225-1645-3.ch005

Lentzis, D. (2020). Revisiting the Basics of EU Data Protection Law: On the Material and Territorial Scope of the GDPR. In Tzanou, M. (Ed.), *Personal Data Protection and Legal Developments in the European Union* (pp. 19–33). IGI Global. https://doi.org/10.4018/978-1-5225-9489-5.ch002

Leote, F. J., Teixeira, N. M., & Galvão, R. (2021). Entrepreneurship and Unemployment: Government Grants and Challenges in a Pandemic Context. In N. Teixeira, & I. Lisboa (Eds.), *Handbook of Research on Financial Management During Economic Downturn and Recovery* (pp. 20-40). IGI Global. https://doi.org/10.4018/978-1-7998-6643-5.ch002

Lewin, E., & Bick, E. (2017). Introduction: Civil Religion and Nationalism on a Godly-Civil Continuum. In Lewin, E., Bick, E., & Naor, D. (Eds.), *Comparative Perspectives on Civil Religion, Nationalism, and Political Influence* (pp. 1–31). Hershey, PA: IGI Global. DOI: 10.4018/978-1-5225-0516-7.ch001

Luyombya, D. (2018). Management of Records and Archives in Uganda's Public Sector. In Ngulube, P. (Ed.), *Handbook of Research on Heritage Management and Preservation* (pp. 275–297). Hershey, PA: IGI Global. DOI: 10.4018/978-1-5225-3137-1.ch014

Mabe, M., & Ashley, E. A. (2017). The Local Command Structure and How the Library Fits. In *In The Developing Role of Public Libraries in Emergency Management: Emerging Research and Opportunities* (pp. 44–60). Hershey, PA: IGI Global. DOI: 10.4018/978-1-5225-2196-9.ch004

Macilotti, G. (2020). Online Child Pornography: Conceptual Issues and Law Enforcement Challenges. In Balloni, A., & Sette, R. (Eds.), *Handbook of Research on Trends and Issues in Crime Prevention, Rehabilitation, and Victim Support* (pp. 226–247). IGI Global. https://doi.org/10.4018/978-1-7998-1286-9.ch013

Maher, C. (2018). Legal Framework, Funding, and Procurement Polices to Accelerate the Growth of the Social Enterprise Ecosystem. In *Influence of Public Policy on Small Social Enterprises: Emerging Research and Opportunities* (pp. 52–83). Hershey, PA: IGI Global. DOI: 10.4018/978-1-5225-2770-1.ch003

Mahmood, M. (2019). Transformation of Government and Citizen Trust in Government: A Conceptual Model. In Molnar, A. (Ed.), *Strategic Management and Innovative Applications of E-Government* (pp. 107–122). IGI Global. https://doi.org/10.4018/978-1-5225-6204-7.ch005

Mahmood, Z. (2021). Cloud Computing Technologies for Connected Digital Government. In Mahmood, Z. (Ed.), *Web 2.0 and Cloud Technologies for Implementing Connected Government* (pp. 19–35). IGI Global. https://doi.org/10.4018/978-1-7998-4570-6.ch002

Malik, I., Putera, V. S., & Putra, I. E. (2018). Traditional Leaders in the Reconciliation of Muslim-Christian Conflicts in Moluccas. In Campbell, A. (Ed.), *Global Leadership Initiatives for Conflict Resolution and Peacebuilding* (pp. 235–248). Hershey, PA: IGI Global. DOI: 10.4018/978-1-5225-4993-2.ch011

Martin, S. M. (2017). Transnational Crime and the American Policing System. In M. Dawson, D. Kisku, P. Gupta, J. Sing, & W. Li (Eds.), *Developing Next-Generation Countermeasures for Homeland Security Threat Prevention* (pp. 72-92). Hershey, PA: IGI Global. https://doi.org/DOI: 10.4018/978-1-5225-0703-1.ch004

Mekonnen, G. A., & Kassie, W. A. (2020). Fiscal Decentralization at Local Government of Ethiopia: Theory vs Practices. In Chhabra, S., & Kumar, M. (Eds.), *Civic Engagement Frameworks and Strategic Leadership Practices for Organization Development* (pp. 171–197). IGI Global. https://doi.org/10.4018/978-1-7998-2372-8.ch008

Mensah, I. K., Luo, C., & Abu-Shanab, E. (2021). Citizen Use of E-Government Services Websites: A Proposed E-Government Adoption Recommendation Model (EGARM). *International Journal of Electronic Government Research*, *17*(2), 19–42. https://doi.org/10.4018/IJEGR.2021040102

Mhiripiri, N. A., & Chikakano, J. (2017). Criminal Defamation, the Criminalisation of Expression, Media and Information Dissemination in the Digital Age: A Legal and Ethical Perspective. In Mhiripiri, N., & Chari, T. (Eds.), *Media Law, Ethics, and Policy in the Digital Age* (pp. 1–24). Hershey, PA: IGI Global. DOI: 10.4018/978-1-5225-2095-5.ch001

Mishaal, D. A., & Abu-Shanab, E. A. (2017). Utilizing Facebook by the Arab World Governments: The Communication Success Factor. *International Journal of Public Administration in the Digital Age*, *4*(3), 53–78. DOI: 10.4018/IJPADA.2017070105

Morim, A. C., Inácio, H., & Vieira, E. (2018). Internal Control in a Public Hospital: The Case of Financial Services Expenditure Department. In Azevedo, G., da Silva Oliveira, J., Marques, R., & Ferreira, A. (Eds.), *Handbook of Research on Modernization and Accountability in Public Sector Management* (pp. 77–102). Hershey, PA: IGI Global. DOI: 10.4018/978-1-5225-3731-1.ch005

Mupepi, M. G. (2017). Developing Democratic Paradigms to Effectively Manage Business, Government, and Civil Society: The African Spring. In Schoburgh, E., & Ryan, R. (Eds.), *Handbook of Research on Sub-National Governance and Development* (pp. 432–462). Hershey, PA: IGI Global. DOI: 10.4018/978-1-5225-1645-3.ch020

Mwakisisya, H. J., Rugeiyamu, R., & Cyprian, S. (2021). Blending Local Government Authorities and Grassroots for Industrial Economy Through Participatory Development Communication in Tanzania. In Nafukho, F., & Boniface Makulilo, A. (Eds.), *Handbook of Research on Nurturing Industrial Economy for Africa's Development* (pp. 74–98). IGI Global. https://doi.org/10.4018/978-1-7998-6471-4.ch005

Naidoo, V., & Nzimakwe, T. I. (2019). M-Government and Its Application on Public Service Delivery. In Abassi, R., & Ben Chehida Douss, A. (Eds.), *Security Frameworks in Contemporary Electronic Government* (pp. 1–14). IGI Global. https://doi.org/10.4018/978-1-5225-5984-9.ch001

Navaratnam, R., & Lee, I. Y. (2017). Globalization as a New Framework for Human Rights Protection. In Akrivopoulou, C. (Ed.), *Defending Human Rights and Democracy in the Era of Globalization* (pp. 17–49). Hershey, PA: IGI Global. DOI: 10.4018/978-1-5225-0723-9.ch002

Nemec, J., Meričková, B. M., Svidroňová, M. M., & Klimovský, D. (2017). Co-Creation as a Social Innovation in Delivery of Public Services at Local Government Level: The Slovak Experience. In Schoburgh, E., & Ryan, R. (Eds.), *Handbook of Research on Sub-National Governance and Development* (pp. 281–303). Hershey, PA: IGI Global. DOI: 10.4018/978-1-5225-1645-3.ch013

Neupane, A., Soar, J., Vaidya, K., & Aryal, S. (2017). Application of E-Government Principles in Anti-Corruption Framework. In Shakya, R. (Ed.), *Digital Governance and E-Government Principles Applied to Public Procurement* (pp. 56–74). Hershey, PA: IGI Global. DOI: 10.4018/978-1-5225-2203-4.ch003

Njie, S. N., Wogu, I. A., Ogbuehi, U. K., Misra, S., & Udoh, O. D. (2021). Rising Global Challenges in Energy Demand and the Politics of Climate Change in Government Operations: Policy and Economic Development Implications. In Babaoğlu, C., Akman, E., & Kulaç, O. (Eds.), *Handbook of Research on Global Challenges for Improving Public Services and Government Operations* (pp. 242–263). IGI Global. https://doi.org/10.4018/978-1-7998-4978-0.ch013

Ogunde, O. (2017). Democracy and Child Rights Protection: The Problem of the Nigerian Constitution. In Akrivopoulou, C. (Ed.), *Defending Human Rights and Democracy in the Era of Globalization* (pp. 123–144). Hershey, PA: IGI Global. DOI: 10.4018/978-1-5225-0723-9.ch006

Ojedokun, U. A. (2017). Crime Witnesses' Non-Cooperation in Police Investigations: Causes and Consequences in Nigeria. In Egharevba, S. (Ed.), *Police Brutality, Racial Profiling, and Discrimination in the Criminal Justice System* (pp. 89–99). Hershey, PA: IGI Global. DOI: 10.4018/978-1-5225-1088-8.ch005

Okeke, G. S. (2018). The Politics of Environmental Pollution in Nigeria: Emerging Trends, Issues, and Challenges. In Eneanya, A. (Ed.), *Handbook of Research on Environmental Policies for Emergency Management and Public Safety* (pp. 300–320). Hershey, PA: IGI Global. DOI: 10.4018/978-1-5225-3194-4.ch016

Ökten, S., Akman, E., & Akman, Ç. (2018). Modernization and Accountability in Public-Sector Administration: Turkey Example. In Azevedo, G., da Silva Oliveira, J., Marques, R., & Ferreira, A. (Eds.), *Handbook of Research on Modernization and Accountability in Public Sector Management* (pp. 18–39). Hershey, PA: IGI Global. DOI: 10.4018/978-1-5225-3731-1.ch002

Oladapo, O. A., & Ojebuyi, B. R. (2017). Nature and Outcome of Nigeria's #NoToSocialMediaBill Twitter Protest against the Frivolous Petitions Bill 2015. In Nelson, O., Ojebuyi, B., & Salawu, A. (Eds.), *Impacts of the Media on African Socio-Economic Development* (pp. 106–124). Hershey, PA: IGI Global. DOI: 10.4018/978-1-5225-1859-4.ch007

Olmos, S., & Nares, J. J. (2020). Applying Fault Trees to the Analysis at the Minimum Age for Sexual Consent in the Criminal Law of México. In Balloni, A., & Sette, R. (Eds.), *Handbook of Research on Trends and Issues in Crime Prevention, Rehabilitation, and Victim Support* (pp. 60–78). IGI Global. https://doi.org/10.4018/978-1-7998-1286-9.ch005

Olukolu, Y. R. (2017). Harmful Traditional Practices, Laws, and Reproductive Rights of Women in Nigeria: A Therapeutic Jurisprudence Approach. In Halder, D., & Jaishankar, K. (Eds.), *Therapeutic Jurisprudence and Overcoming Violence Against Women* (pp. 1–14). Hershey, PA: IGI Global. DOI: 10.4018/978-1-5225-2472-4.ch001

Onyebadi, U., & Mbunyuza-Memani, L. (2017). Women and South Africa's Anti-Apartheid Struggle: Evaluating the Political Messages in the Music of Miriam Makeba. In Onyebadi, U. (Ed.), *Music as a Platform for Political Communication* (pp. 31–51). Hershey, PA: IGI Global. DOI: 10.4018/978-1-5225-1986-7.ch002

Osmani, A. R. (2017). Tipaimukh Multipurpose Hydroelectric Project: A Policy Perspective – Indo-Bangla Priorities, Indigenous Peoples' Rights, and Environmental Concerns. In Rao, P., & Patil, Y. (Eds.), *Reconsidering the Impact of Climate Change on Global Water Supply, Use, and Management* (pp. 227–251). Hershey, PA: IGI Global. DOI: 10.4018/978-1-5225-1046-8.ch013

Owolabi, T. O. (2018). Free Media and Bank Reforms in West Africa: Implications for Sustainable Development. In Salawu, A., & Owolabi, T. (Eds.), *Exploring Journalism Practice and Perception in Developing Countries* (pp. 18–39). Hershey, PA: IGI Global. DOI: 10.4018/978-1-5225-3376-4.ch002

Öztürk, N. K. (2021). Government Systems and Control of Bureaucracy. In Babaoğlu, C., Akman, E., & Kulaç, O. (Eds.), *Handbook of Research on Global Challenges for Improving Public Services and Government Operations* (pp. 133–150). IGI Global. https://doi.org/10.4018/978-1-7998-4978-0.ch008

Pacheco, F. M., & Alves, D. R. (2019). The New Paths of Fundamental Rights in the 21st Century: Globalization and Knowledge in a Digital Age as a Proposal. In Melro, A., & Oliveira, L. (Eds.), *Constitutional Knowledge and Its Impact on Citizenship Exercise in a Networked Society* (pp. 1–26). IGI Global. https://doi.org/10.4018/978-1-5225-8350-9.ch001

Panda, P., & Sahu, G. P. (2017). Public Procurement Framework in India: An Overview. In Shakya, R. (Ed.), *Digital Governance and E-Government Principles Applied to Public Procurement* (pp. 229–248). Hershey, PA: IGI Global. DOI: 10.4018/978-1-5225-2203-4.ch010

Pande, V. S., & Kumburu, N. P. (2018). An Overview of Population Growth and Sustainable Development in Sub-Saharan Africa. In Teshager Alemu, K., & Abebe Alebachew, M. (Eds.), *Handbook of Research on Sustainable Development and Governance Strategies for Economic Growth in Africa* (pp. 480–499). Hershey, PA: IGI Global. DOI: 10.4018/978-1-5225-3247-7.ch025

Parikh, M., & Krishna, V. S. (2021). Recent Trends and Repercussions in Civil and Criminal Justice Systems: A Comparative Analysis of England, Singapore, and India. In E. Yin, & N. Kofie (Ed.), *Advancing Civil Justice Reform and Conflict Resolution in Africa and Asia: Comparative Analyses and Case Studies* (pp. 230-242). IGI Global. https://doi.org/10.4018/978-1-7998-7898-8.ch013

Pattnaik, P. N., & Shukla, M. K. (2020). Understanding Indian Political Parties Through the Lens of Marketing Management: Towards a Conceptual Political Marketing Model. In Kavoğlu, S., & Salar, M. (Eds.), *Political Propaganda, Advertising, and Public Relations: Emerging Research and Opportunities* (pp. 170–190). IGI Global. https://doi.org/10.4018/978-1-7998-1734-5.ch008

Paulin, A. A. (2017). Informating Public Governance: Towards a Basis for a Digital Ecosystem. *International Journal of Public Administration in the Digital Age, 4*(2), 14–32. DOI: 10.4018/IJPADA.2017040102

Perelló-Sobrepere, M. (2017). Building a New State from Outrage: The Case of Catalonia. In Adria, M., & Mao, Y. (Eds.), *Handbook of Research on Citizen Engagement and Public Participation in the Era of New Media* (pp. 344–359). Hershey, PA: IGI Global. DOI: 10.4018/978-1-5225-1081-9.ch019

Pohl, G. M. (2017). The Role of Social Media in Enforcing Environmental Justice around the World. In Demirhan, K., & Çakır-Demirhan, D. (Eds.), *Political Scandal, Corruption, and Legitimacy in the Age of Social Media* (pp. 123–156). Hershey, PA: IGI Global. DOI: 10.4018/978-1-5225-2019-1.ch006

Popescu, C. R. (2022). Environmental, Social, and Corporate Governance by Avoiding Management Bias and Tax Minimization: Reaching a General Consensus Regarding a Minimum Global Tax Rate. In Popescu, C. (Ed.), *COVID-19 Pandemic Impact on New Economy Development and Societal Change* (pp. 94–132). IGI Global. https://doi.org/10.4018/978-1-6684-3374-4.ch006

Popoola, T. (2017). Ethical and Legal Challenges of Election Reporting in Nigeria: A Study of Four General Elections, 1999-2011. In Mhiripiri, N., & Chari, T. (Eds.), *Media Law, Ethics, and Policy in the Digital Age* (pp. 78–100). Hershey, PA: IGI Global. DOI: 10.4018/978-1-5225-2095-5.ch005

Prakash, O. (2020). History, Policy Making, and Sustainability. In Das, R., & Mandal, N. (Eds.), *Interdisciplinary Approaches to Public Policy and Sustainability* (pp. 1–17). IGI Global. https://doi.org/10.4018/978-1-7998-0315-7.ch001

Provazníková, R., Sobotková, L., & Sobotka, M. (2021). Local Government Development in the Czech Republic: Dilemmas and Challenges. In Babaoğlu, C., Akman, E., & Kulaç, O. (Eds.), *Handbook of Research on Global Challenges for Improving Public Services and Government Operations* (pp. 151–171). IGI Global. https://doi.org/10.4018/978-1-7998-4978-0.ch009

Qawasmeh, F. A. (2022). Understanding the Field of Public Policy in the Context of Public Administration Evolution. In Kulaç, O., Babaoğlu, C., & Akman, E. (Eds.), *Public Affairs Education and Training in the 21st Century* (pp. 22–44). IGI Global. https://doi.org/10.4018/978-1-7998-8243-5.ch002

Rahman, M. S. (2017). Politics-Administration Relations and the Effect on Local Governance and Development: The Case of Bangladesh. In Schoburgh, E., & Ryan, R. (Eds.), *Handbook of Research on Sub-National Governance and Development* (pp. 256–279). Hershey, PA: IGI Global. DOI: 10.4018/978-1-5225-1645-3.ch012

Ramachandran, M., Chelliah, P. R., & Soundarabai, P. B. (2021). Towards Connected Government Services: A Cloud Software Engineering Framework. In Mahmood, Z. (Ed.), *Web 2.0 and Cloud Technologies for Implementing Connected Government* (pp. 113–135). IGI Global. https://doi.org/10.4018/978-1-7998-4570-6.ch006

Ravotti, N. (2020). In the [Source] C\ode of the Conquerors: On the Need for Culturally-Minded Tribal Law Research Databases. In S. Edwards III, & D. Santos (Eds.), *Digital Transformation and Its Role in Progressing the Relationship Between States and Their Citizens* (pp. 124-137). IGI Global. https://doi.org/10.4018/978-1-7998-3152-5.ch006

Razzante, R. (2020). The Fight Against Corruption. In Balloni, A., & Sette, R. (Eds.), *Handbook of Research on Trends and Issues in Crime Prevention, Rehabilitation, and Victim Support* (pp. 167–186). IGI Global. DOI: 10.4018/978-1-7998-1286-9.ch010

Reddy, P. S. (2017). Political-Administrative Interface at the Local Sphere of Government with Particular Reference to South Africa. In Schoburgh, E., & Ryan, R. (Eds.), *Handbook of Research on Sub-National Governance and Development* (pp. 242–255). Hershey, PA: IGI Global. DOI: 10.4018/978-1-5225-1645-3.ch011

Rombo, D. O., & Lutomia, A. N. (2018). Tracing the Rights of Domestic and International Kenyan House Helps: Profiles, Policy, and Consequences. In Mahtab, N., Haque, T., Khan, I., Islam, M., & Wahid, I. (Eds.), *Handbook of Research on Women's Issues and Rights in the Developing World* (pp. 1–18). Hershey, PA: IGI Global. DOI: 10.4018/978-1-5225-3018-3.ch001

Rouzbehani, K. (2017). Health Policy Implementation: Moving Beyond Its Barriers in United States. In Wickramasinghe, N. (Ed.), *Handbook of Research on Healthcare Administration and Management* (pp. 541–552). Hershey, PA: IGI Global. DOI: 10.4018/978-1-5225-0920-2.ch032

Ryan, R., & Woods, R. (2017). Decentralization and Subnational Governance: Theory and Praxis. In Schoburgh, E., & Ryan, R. (Eds.), *Handbook of Research on Sub-National Governance and Development* (pp. 1–33). Hershey, PA: IGI Global. DOI: 10.4018/978-1-5225-1645-3.ch001

Sabao, C., & Chingwaramusee, V. R. (2017). Citizen Journalism on Facebook and the Challenges of Media Regulation in Zimbabwe: Baba Jukwa. In Mhiripiri, N., & Chari, T. (Eds.), *Media Law, Ethics, and Policy in the Digital Age* (pp. 193–206). Hershey, PA: IGI Global. DOI: 10.4018/978-1-5225-2095-5.ch011

Saidane, A., & Al-Sharieh, S. (2019). A Compliance-Driven Framework for Privacy and Security in Highly Regulated Socio-Technical Environments: An E-Government Case Study. In Abassi, R., & Ben Chehida Douss, A. (Eds.), *Security Frameworks in Contemporary Electronic Government* (pp. 15–50). IGI Global. https://doi.org/10.4018/978-1-5225-5984-9.ch002

Sandill, S. (2020). Law, Equality, and Entrepreneurship Through a Gendered Lens: Bridging the Gap Between Academia, Legislature, and Politics. In Moeke-Pickering, T., Cote-Meek, S., & Pegoraro, A. (Eds.), *Critical Reflections and Politics on Advancing Women in the Academy* (pp. 124–149). IGI Global. https://doi.org/10.4018/978-1-7998-3618-6.ch008

Santos, H. R., & Tonelli, D. F. (2019). Smart Government and the Maturity Levels of Sociopolitical Digital Interactions: Analysing Temporal Changes in Brazilian E-Government Portals. In Molnar, A. (Ed.), *Strategic Management and Innovative Applications of E-Government* (pp. 176–199). IGI Global. https://doi.org/10.4018/978-1-5225-6204-7.ch008

Saponaro, A. (2021). "Visible" and "Invisible" Victims in the Criminal Justice System: Victim-Oriented Paradigms and Models. In Blasdell, R., Krieger-Sample, L., & Kilburn, M. (Eds.), *Invisible Victims and the Pursuit of Justice: Analyzing Frequently Victimized Yet Rarely Discussed Populations* (pp. 1–23). IGI Global. DOI: 10.4018/978-1-7998-7348-8.ch001

Shaikh, A. K., Ahmad, N., Khan, I., & Ali, S. (2021). E-Participation Within E-Government: A Bibliometric-Based Systematic Literature Review. *International Journal of Electronic Government Research*, *17*(4), 15–39. https://doi.org/10.4018/IJEGR.2021100102

Shakya, R. K., & Schapper, P. R. (2017). Digital Governance and E-Government Principles: E-Procurement as Transformative. In Shakya, R. (Ed.), *Digital Governance and E-Government Principles Applied to Public Procurement* (pp. 1–28). Hershey, PA: IGI Global. DOI: 10.4018/978-1-5225-2203-4.ch001

Shambare, R. (2019). Facilitating Consumers' Adoption of E-Government in South Africa: Supply Side-Driven Virtuous Cycles. In Gbadamosi, A. (Ed.), *Exploring the Dynamics of Consumerism in Developing Nations* (pp. 243–265). IGI Global. https://doi.org/10.4018/978-1-5225-7906-9.ch011

Siphambe, H., Kolobe, M., & Oageng, I. P. (2018). Employment Protection Legislation and Unemployment in Botswana. In Amine, S. (Ed.), *Employment Protection Legislation in Emerging Economies* (pp. 157–191). Hershey, PA: IGI Global. DOI: 10.4018/978-1-5225-4134-9.ch008

Song, M. Y., & Abelson, J. (2017). Public Engagement and Policy Entrepreneurship on Social Media in the Time of Anti-Vaccination Movements. In Adria, M., & Mao, Y. (Eds.), *Handbook of Research on Citizen Engagement and Public Participation in the Era of New Media* (pp. 38–56). Hershey, PA: IGI Global. DOI: 10.4018/978-1-5225-1081-9.ch003

Sood, P., Malhotra, M., & Nijjer, S. (2021). Government Policies During Lockdown: Indian vs. International Perspective. In Kumar, V., & Malhotra, G. (Eds.), *Stakeholder Strategies for Reducing the Impact of Global Health Crises* (pp. 18–39). IGI Global. https://doi.org/10.4018/978-1-7998-7495-9.ch002

Stacey, E. (2018). Networked Protests: A Review of Social Movement Literature and the Hong Kong Umbrella Movement (2017). In Chhabra, S. (Ed.), *Handbook of Research on Civic Engagement and Social Change in Contemporary Society* (pp. 347–363). Hershey, PA: IGI Global. DOI: 10.4018/978-1-5225-4197-4.ch020

Stamatakis, N. (2017). Authority and Legitimacy: A Quantitative Study of Youth's Perceptions on the Brazilian Police. In Egharevba, S. (Ed.), *Police Brutality, Racial Profiling, and Discrimination in the Criminal Justice System* (pp. 151–213). Hershey, PA: IGI Global. DOI: 10.4018/978-1-5225-1088-8.ch009

Steinert, S. W. (2021). An Interview With Chief Sargent of the Worcester, MA Police Department. In Arble, E., & Arnetz, B. (Eds.), *Interventions, Training, and Technologies for Improved Police Well-Being and Performance* (pp. 185–197). IGI Global. https://doi.org/10.4018/978-1-7998-6820-0.ch011

Sugars, J. M. (2017). Refoulement and Refugees. In Akrivopoulou, C. (Ed.), *Defending Human Rights and Democracy in the Era of Globalization* (pp. 181–197). Hershey, PA: IGI Global. DOI: 10.4018/978-1-5225-0723-9.ch008

Takaya-Umehara, Y. (2019). Suborbital Spaceflight: Legal Aspects. In Nakarada Pecujlic, A., & Tugnoli, M. (Eds.), *Promoting Productive Co-operation Between Space Lawyers and Engineers* (pp. 64–78). IGI Global. https://doi.org/10.4018/978-1-5225-7256-5.ch005

Tan, S. F. (2017). Local Representation in Australia: Preliminary Findings of a National Survey. In Schoburgh, E., & Ryan, R. (Eds.), *Handbook of Research on Sub-National Governance and Development* (pp. 368–384). Hershey, PA: IGI Global. DOI: 10.4018/978-1-5225-1645-3.ch017

Tavares, M. D., & Rodrigues, L. L. (2018). Strategic Responses of Public Sector Entities to GRI Sustainability Reports. In Azevedo, G., da Silva Oliveira, J., Marques, R., & Ferreira, A. (Eds.), *Handbook of Research on Modernization and Accountability in Public Sector Management* (pp. 159–188). Hershey, PA: IGI Global. DOI: 10.4018/978-1-5225-3731-1.ch008

Thakre, A. G. (2017). Sexual Harassment of Women in Workplace in India: An Assessment of Implementation of Preventive Laws and Practicing of Therapeutic Jurisprudence in New Delhi. In Halder, D., & Jaishankar, K. (Eds.), *Therapeutic Jurisprudence and Overcoming Violence Against Women* (pp. 135–146). Hershey, PA: IGI Global. DOI: 10.4018/978-1-5225-2472-4.ch009

Tiwary, A. (2017). Key Elements of CEAF. In *Driving Efficiency in Local Government Using a Collaborative Enterprise Architecture Framework: Emerging Research and Opportunities* (pp. 25–61). Hershey, PA: IGI Global. DOI: 10.4018/978-1-5225-2407-6.ch002

Toscano, J. P. (2017). Social Media and Public Participation: Opportunities, Barriers, and a New Framework. In Adria, M., & Mao, Y. (Eds.), *Handbook of Research on Citizen Engagement and Public Participation in the Era of New Media* (pp. 73–89). Hershey, PA: IGI Global. DOI: 10.4018/978-1-5225-1081-9.ch005

Trompetter, P. S. (2019). A History of Police Psychology. In I. Management Association (Eds.), *Police Science: Breakthroughs in Research and Practice* (pp. 377-402). IGI Global. https://doi.org/10.4018/978-1-5225-7672-3.ch019

Tryma, K., & Salnikova, N. (2021). The Influence of Religion on Political Parties of the European Union. In E. Alaverdov & M. Bari (Eds.), *Global Development of Religious Tourism* (pp. 98-112). IGI Global. https://doi.org/10.4018/978-1-7998-5792-1.ch007

Tsabedze, V. W. (2020). Strategies for Managing E-Records for Good Governance: Reflection on E-Government in the Kingdom of Eswatini. In Rodríguez Bolívar, M., & Cortés Cediel, M. (Eds.), *Digital Government and Achieving E-Public Participation: Emerging Research and Opportunities* (pp. 63–86). IGI Global. https://doi.org/10.4018/978-1-7998-1526-6.ch004

Tshishonga, N. (2017). Operation Sukuma-Sakhe: A New Social Contract for Decentralized Service Delivery and Responsive Governance in KwaZulu-Natal. In Schoburgh, E., & Ryan, R. (Eds.), *Handbook of Research on Sub-National Governance and Development* (pp. 304–323). Hershey, PA: IGI Global. DOI: 10.4018/978-1-5225-1645-3.ch014

Tsygankov, S., & Gasanova, E. (2017). Electronification of the Public Procurement System: A Comparative Analysis of the Experience of the Russian Federation and Ukraine. In Shakya, R. (Ed.), *Digital Governance and E-Government Principles Applied to Public Procurement* (pp. 267–277). Hershey, PA: IGI Global. DOI: 10.4018/978-1-5225-2203-4.ch013

Tüzünkan, D. (2018). The International Migration Movements and Immigrant Policies From the Ottoman Empire 1299 to Republican Turkey 2016. In Erçetin, Ş. (Ed.), *Social Considerations of Migration Movements and Immigration Policies* (pp. 13–45). Hershey, PA: IGI Global. DOI: 10.4018/978-1-5225-3322-1.ch002

Ullah, Z. (2022). Violent Extremism and the Politics of Education in Pakistan: An Analysis of the Links Between Anti-Terror Laws, the Curriculum, and the Islamised Public Sphere. In Kulaç, O., Babaoğlu, C., & Akman, E. (Eds.), *Public Affairs Education and Training in the 21st Century* (pp. 256–275). IGI Global. https://doi.org/10.4018/978-1-7998-8243-5.ch017

Valenzuela, R., & Ochoa, A. (2018). Open Mexico Network in the Implementation of National Open Data Policy. In Kok, A. (Ed.), *Proliferation of Open Government Initiatives and Systems* (pp. 50–67). Hershey, PA: IGI Global. DOI: 10.4018/978-1-5225-4987-1.ch003

Valera-Ordaz, L., & Humanes, M. L. (2022). What Drives Selective Exposure to Political Information in Spain? Comparing Political Interest and Ideology. In Palau-Sampio, D., López García, G., & Iannelli, L. (Eds.), *Contemporary Politics, Communication, and the Impact on Democracy* (pp. 93–112). IGI Global. https://doi.org/10.4018/978-1-7998-8057-8.ch006

van der Vliet-Bakker, J. M. (2019). Environmentally Forced Migration and Human Rights. In I. Management Association (Eds.), *Immigration and Refugee Policy: Breakthroughs in Research and Practice* (pp. 336-362). IGI Global. https://doi.org/10.4018/978-1-5225-8909-9.ch019

Waller, P. (2017). Co-Production and Co-Creation in Public Services: Resolving Confusion and Contradictions. *International Journal of Electronic Government Research, 13*(2), 1–17. DOI: 10.4018/IJEGR.2017040101

Wodecka-Hyjek, A. (2017). Co-Operation between the Public Administration and Non-Profit Organisations as a Condition of the Development of Public Entrepreneurship: On the Example of the Selected World Solutions. In Potocan, V., Üngan, M., & Nedelko, Z. (Eds.), *Handbook of Research on Managerial Solutions in Non-Profit Organizations* (pp. 253–275). Hershey, PA: IGI Global. DOI: 10.4018/978-1-5225-0731-4.ch012

Yang, K. C., & Kang, Y. (2017). Social Media, Political Mobilization, and Citizen Engagement: A Case Study of the March 18, 2014, Sunflower Student Movement in Taiwan. In Adria, M., & Mao, Y. (Eds.), *Handbook of Research on Citizen Engagement and Public Participation in the Era of New Media* (pp. 360–388). Hershey, PA: IGI Global. DOI: 10.4018/978-1-5225-1081-9.ch020

Yang, K. C., & Kang, Y. (2020). Will Microblogs Shape China's Civil Society Under President's Xi's Surveillance State?: The Case of Anti-Extradition Law Protests in Hong Kong. In Kumar, V., & Malhotra, G. (Eds.), *Examining the Roles of IT and Social Media in Democratic Development and Social Change* (pp. 156–184). IGI Global. https://doi.org/10.4018/978-1-7998-1791-8.ch007

Yasmeen, H., Wang, Y., Zameer, H., & Ismail, H. (2020). Modeling the Role of Government, Firm, and Civil Society for Environmental Sustainability. In I. Management Association (Ed.), *Developing Eco-Cities Through Policy, Planning, and Innovation: Can It Really Work?* (pp. 62-83). IGI Global. https://doi.org/10.4018/978-1-7998-0441-3.ch003

Yavuz, N., Karkın, N., & Sevinç Çubuk, E. B. (2020). Explaining Government Crowdsourcing Decisions: A Theoretical Model. In Rodríguez Bolívar, M., & Cortés Cediel, M. (Eds.), *Digital Government and Achieving E-Public Participation: Emerging Research and Opportunities* (pp. 159–183). IGI Global. https://doi.org/10.4018/978-1-7998-1526-6.ch008

Zhaleleva, S., Zhaleleva, R., & Pasternak, A. (2020). Evolution of Business-Government Interaction Models: Their Use and Management. In Tazhina, G., & Parker, J. (Eds.), *Toward Sustainability Through Digital Technologies and Practices in the Eurasian Region* (pp. 17–35). IGI Global. https://doi.org/10.4018/978-1-7998-2551-7.ch002

Zhao, B. (2018). A Privacy Perspective of Open Government: Sex, Wealth, and Transparency in China. In Kok, A. (Ed.), *Proliferation of Open Government Initiatives and Systems* (pp. 29–48). Hershey, PA: IGI Global. DOI: 10.4018/978-1-5225-4987-1.ch002

About the Contributors

George M. Korres holds a doctorate in Economic Sciences (Economics of Innovation) from University of London (QMW) and an M.Sc from Essex University. Currently, he is a Professor at the University of the Aegean, Department of Geography, School of Social Science. He was also a visiting fellow, for the academic period 2010-20111, at the University of Newcastle, Centre from Urban Regional & Development Studies, (CURDS), School of Geography, Sociology and Politics. He was visiting scholar at the University of Leeds during 2006-2007. Over the last 10 years, during both his academic and professional career, he has gained an in depth experience in the fields of economics, business and politics in the area of European Economics and Innovation Systems. His main areas of interest and specialisation include: European Integration, Social Policy and Social Inclusion, Economic and Innovation Policies, EU enlargement and the Euro-Mediterranean partnership. He has collaborated with many European universities, Institutions, NGOs as well as academia. George Korres has also been involved in various trans-European and international projects and he has published widely in this area in many International Journals, such as Applied Econometrics, Regional and Sectoral Economic Studies, Southwestern Economic Review, Pensions, Sage, Management Sciences and Regional Development etc, also he has published a number of books with international publishers, such as MacMillan-Palgrave Press, Springer, Edward and Elgar, Ashgate Publishers and Nova (New York) Publishers.

Maria P. Michailidis Leonardo da Vinci; Socrates/Erasmus Thematic Networks and Grundtvig Multilateral Projects.

Anastasios Sepetis, PhD., MSc and BA, is an Assistant Professor at the Department of Business Administration of the University of West Attica specializing in Policies and Finance of Sustainable Development and Social Protection. He is also a member of the Research Unit of the Laboratory of Social Administration of the University of West Attica. By decision of the Minister of Finance (Government Gazette FEK 1313/B/21.03.2022), he is a member of the Working Group on sustainable finance and green economic transition. The task of the working group is to develop strategic orientations and a roadmap for effective integration of sustainability into economic policy and the financial system. He has undertaken research and teaching since 2003 in various Universities in Greece, in areas related to Sustainable Development and Corporate Environmental and Social Policy Strategies in international, European and comparative management, finance, health, social security, CSR social economy and circular economy. He has also worked as a President and Administrator of Hospitals and Social Organizations, as General Manager of Operations and business consultant, while he is an expert in European and national programs for Sustainable and Environmental Management, Sustainable Capital Market, Sustainable and Social Investment, Corporate Social Responsibility, Total Quality Management, Sustainable Employment, Social Entrepreneurship, Sustainable and Environmental Management in Public Health, Healthcare Management and Finance. He is an IEMA certified auditor for Environmental Management and Total Quality Management (ISO 14001, ISO 9001), as well as a certified auditor by the United Nations for Environmental and Social Risk Assessment (UNEP FI-ESRA). His research interests focus on Sustainable Management and financing of environmental and social responsibility policies for health, capital market, business, sustainable education, social protection, anti-poverty and employment. He has published monographs, books and articles in Greek and international scientific journals, while he has published the books entitled: "Sustainable Finance: The contribution of policies and financial methods to sustainable development and the new social state" and "Environmental and Sustainable Management in Public

Health" Papazisis Publications, which is taught in Greek universities and is a manual of environmental and sustainable management in the financial and social system. Protection.

Spyros Anagnostou is an Assistant Professor at the University of the Aegean-Department of Geography. He has obtained a Ph.D from the Department of Geography at the University of the Aegean, also he has a DEA, Urban and Spatial Management from the Université d'Aix-Marseille III DESS, Law and Urban Planning – Université d'Aix-Marseille III and a B.A. degree (Maîtrise) Regional and Urban Planning – Université d'Aix-Marseille III. His research interests focusing in the fields of City Planning, Regional Development with Emphasis on Island Space, Culture and Local Development, Transport Infrastructures, Geoeconomics, Geopolitics, Urban History, and Historical Geography. He has also collaborated in research projects, has presented her work in a number of international conferences and has published in established international journals.

***

Athanasios Asmenoudis possesses a strong academic background in geopolitical analysis and regional studies, currently pursuing a PhD at the University of the Aegean with a thesis centered on the geopolitical dynamics of the Middle East through the lens of N. Spykman's theory. He holds a Master's degree in Human Geography, Spatial Development, and Planning, where he explored the Kurdish issue as a central geopolitical factor in the region. His undergraduate studies in Turkish and Modern Asian Studies further enriched his understanding of regional politics, culminating in a thesis on the evolving geopolitical role of the Kurdish issue in Turkey. He has also completed specialized training in geopolitics and security within the Turkey–Middle East Islamic context. His academic journey reflects a deep commitment to the study of political geography and regional power structures.

Konstantinos Bogiatzis is a PhD candidate in Geopolitics, focusing on Turkey's strategic sphere of influence, which includes the Middle East, the Balkans, Central Asia, and North Africa. His doctoral research employs both qualitative and quantitative methodologies, incorporating indicators and geographic mapping analysis. In addition, he examines Greece-Turkey trade relations, international sanctions, and the geoeconomic aspects of Turkish foreign policy. He also writes critical, news-based articles aimed at enhancing public understanding of geopolitical developments.

Thanasis Kizos is Professor in "Rural Geography" in the Department of Geography, University of the Aegean since 2005. He is the Director of "PrecFarm: Laboratory of Rural Geography and Precision Agriculture Systems" and does research in the Rural – Urban continuum, Rural Development, Land Management and Precision Framing Systems. His publications are on landscape change, land use planning, sustainable land use systems, biodiversity impacts of agricultural systems among other topics. Some recent projects are soil O-Live, Terra Lemnia, SIPATH (Operationalizing Sustainable Agricultural Intensification Pathways in Europe) and in the past "Sustainable futures for Europe's HERitage in CULtural landscapES: Tools for understanding, managing, and protecting landscape functions and values " (HERCULES).

Charalambos Louca, holds an M.Sc. and a PhD in Economics from the University of Economics – Varna. Dr. Louca is Associate Professor, Head of Business Department and Director of Research at the American College, Nicosia, Cyprus. He has published in the international journals, Journal of Regional & Socio-Economic Issues, the International Journal of Sustainable Agricultural Management and Informatics, the PM World Journal, Pensions, the PM World Today and Tourism Economics. Dr. Louca is the Editor of, The Cyprus Journal of Sciences, the academic journal publication of American College. He has been also serving as guest editor at the Journal of Regional & Socio-Economic Issues and as a reviewer for the Southern Management Association, Sage Open, The International Journal of Tourism Research, The Letters in Spatial and Resource Sciences and the Inderscience Publications. Dr. Charalambos Louca, is a member of the Southern Management Association and the American Economic Association.

Nectarios Oudeniotis is a political analyst with specialization in international policy and public administration. He received his PhD in

Sociology from the Univesrity of the Aegean (2024). His main research interests include social entrepreneurship in the EU and the Euro-Mediterannean countries, social innovation and social finance theory and practice.

Eleni Prassa holds a Ph. D from the Department of Sociology, University of the Aegean. She has published a lot of papers in International Journals and books.

Georgia (Ioli) Topaka holds a Bachelor's degree in Geography from the University of the Aegean (2011–2017), as well as a Master's degree in Human Geography, Spatial Development and Planning from the same institution (2017–2019). Her postgraduate research focused on geopolitical analysis, specifically the representation of Europe in American strategic discourse. Since 2022, she has been a PhD candidate in Geography at the University of the Aegean. Her doctoral research examines the geopolitical role of religious minorities in the Near East, with a focus on Alevis and Alawites. Her academic interests lie within the broader field of geopolitics, with an emphasis on the historical and contemporary dynamics of the Eastern Mediterranean and Middle East.

George O. Tsobanoglou received his PhD in Sociology and Public Policy from Carleton University, Ottawa, Canada. He is Vice-President elect at World Congress of Sociology, 2023, Melbourne, International Sociological Association, Research Committee on Sociotechnics and Sociological Practice (ISA-RC26). Professor Cultural Policy Management, Hellenic Open University and Visiting Professor University of Athens, Athens, Greece on Sociology and Pedagogics. He taught for 25 years at the University of the Aegean, Greece on Sociology of Work Organization and Local Economic Employment Development and Social Innovation. He taught and researched at various Institutes and Universities in Canada and Europe working on issues of working-life, social development, and social cohesion. He worked on comparative development issues between Greece and Norway at the Institute of Social Research, Oslo. He founded and directed for 20 yrs the Sociology of Work and Professions Laboratory at the University of the Aegean, Lesvos, Greece. Among his books are The Debt Crisis in the Eurozone: Social Impacts, 2014, Divisions of Greece:

The Organizational Impact of Labor Policies during 1949-1981, (trans. in German, Dutch, Italian, Spanish, French, and Portuguese), Citizen's Participation and Empowerment: Emerging Policies, Practices and Trends, 2021, Delhi, Mutuality: Sustaining Communities, 2019 Papazisis (in Greek), The Rise of the Anthropocentric Community, 2021, Stamoulis (in Greek) and Sustaining Communities: Prospects and Changes, 2022, NOVA Scientific Publishers, New York.

Panagiota Varela holds a Ph. D from the Department of Geography, University of the Aegean and a Master degree from LSE/UK. Currently she is a post-doctoral researcher in the University of the Aegean, Department of Environment. She has published a lot of papers in International Journals and books.

Ioannis Voudouris holds the position of Assistant Professor and is the academic coordinator of the "LLM in Maritime Law and Shipping Business" programme. His areas of expertise lie in Business & Commercial Law, with a specific focus on subjects such as Maritime Law & Law of the Sea, Private International Law, Carriage of Goods Law, and Dispute Resolution. He earned his LL.B. degree from Athens Law School at the National and Kapodistrian University of Athens. He further pursued his studies by obtaining an LL.M. degree in International Commercial Law from the University of Kent, followed by a Ph.D. from Queen Mary, University of London. Additionally, he conducted Post-Doctoral Research (Post-Doc) on Commercial Mediation at the University of Cyprus. With over 20 years' experience working internationally as both a lawyer and maritime sector professional across various roles, Ioannis brings valuable practical insights to his teaching and research endeavours in commercial and maritime law spanning more than 20 years. Currently, his research primarily focuses on maritime law along with business and contract law matters. Notably bilingual in Greek & English while also fluent in French.

Index

www.ingramcontent.com/pod-product-compliance
Lightning Source LLC
LaVergne TN
LVHW080855300926
849162LV00003B/425